C-4728   CAREER EXAMINATION SERIES

This is your
PASSBOOK for...

Medical Record Coder

Test Preparation Study Guide
Questions & Answers

COPYRIGHT NOTICE

This book is SOLELY intended for, is sold ONLY to, and its use is RESTRICTED to individual, bona fide applicants or candidates who qualify by virtue of having seriously filed applications for appropriate license, certificate, professional and/or promotional advancement, higher school matriculation, scholarship, or other legitimate requirements of education and/or governmental authorities.

This book is NOT intended for use, class instruction, tutoring, training, duplication, copying, reprinting, excerption, or adaptation, etc., by:

1) Other publishers
2) Proprietors and/or Instructors of "Coaching" and/or Preparatory Courses
3) Personnel and/or Training Divisions of commercial, industrial, and governmental organizations
4) Schools, colleges, or universities and/or their departments and staffs, including teachers and other personnel
5) Testing Agencies or Bureaus
6) Study groups which seek by the purchase of a single volume to copy and/or duplicate and/or adapt this material for use by the group as a whole without having purchased individual volumes for each of the members of the group
7) Et al.

Such persons would be in violation of appropriate Federal and State statutes.

PROVISION OF LICENSING AGREEMENTS – Recognized educational, commercial, industrial, and governmental institutions and organizations, and others legitimately engaged in educational pursuits, including training, testing, and measurement activities, may address request for a licensing agreement to the copyright owners, who will determine whether, and under what conditions, including fees and charges, the materials in this book may be used them. In other words, a licensing facility exists for the legitimate use of the material in this book on other than an individual basis. However, it is asseverated and affirmed here that the material in this book CANNOT be used without the receipt of the express permission of such a licensing agreement from the Publishers. Inquiries re licensing should be addressed to the company, attention rights and permissions department.

All rights reserved, including the right of reproduction in whole or in part, in any form or by any means, electronic or mechanical, including photocopying, recording, or by any information storage and retrieval system, without permission in writing from the Publisher.

Copyright © 2025 by
National Learning Corporation

212 Michael Drive, Syosset, NY 11791
(516) 921-8888 • www.passbooks.com
E-mail: info@passbooks.com

PASSBOOK® SERIES

THE *PASSBOOK® SERIES* has been created to prepare applicants and candidates for the ultimate academic battlefield – the examination room.

At some time in our lives, each and every one of us may be required to take an examination – for validation, matriculation, admission, qualification, registration, certification, or licensure.

Based on the assumption that every applicant or candidate has met the basic formal educational standards, has taken the required number of courses, and read the necessary texts, the *PASSBOOK® SERIES* furnishes the one special preparation which may assure passing with confidence, instead of failing with insecurity. Examination questions – together with answers – are furnished as the basic vehicle for study so that the mysteries of the examination and its compounding difficulties may be eliminated or diminished by a sure method.

This book is meant to help you pass your examination provided that you qualify and are serious in your objective.

The entire field is reviewed through the huge store of content information which is succinctly presented through a provocative and challenging approach – the question-and-answer method.

A climate of success is established by furnishing the correct answers at the end of each test.

You soon learn to recognize types of questions, forms of questions, and patterns of questioning. You may even begin to anticipate expected outcomes.

You perceive that many questions are repeated or adapted so that you can gain acute insights, which may enable you to score many sure points.

You learn how to confront new questions, or types of questions, and to attack them confidently and work out the correct answers.

You note objectives and emphases, and recognize pitfalls and dangers, so that you may make positive educational adjustments.

Moreover, you are kept fully informed in relation to new concepts, methods, practices, and directions in the field.

You discover that you are actually taking the examination all the time: you are preparing for the examination by "taking" an examination, not by reading extraneous and/or supererogatory textbooks.

In short, this PASSBOOK®, used directedly, should be an important factor in helping you to pass your test.

MEDICAL RECORD CODER

DUTIES;
   As a **Medical Record Coder I**, you would reviews outpatient ambulatory surgery and emergency room charts, and selects appropriate codes for principal and secondary diagnoses and procedures according to Uniform Hospital Discharge Data Set guidelines; performs related duties as required.
   As a **Medical Record Coder II,** You would reviews inpatient charts and selects appropriate codes for principal and secondary diagnoses and procedures according to Uniform Hospital Discharge Data Set guidelines; performs related duties as required.

SUBJECT OF EXAMINATION:
The written test is designed to test for knowledge, skills, and/or abilities in such areas as:
1. **Coding/decoding information** - These questions test for the ability to follow a set of coding rules. Some questions will require you to code information by converting certain 3information into letters or numbers. Other questions will require you to decode information by determining if the information that has already been converted into letters or numbers is correct. Complete directions will be provided; no previous knowledge of or training in any coding system is required.
2. **Medical terminology** - These questions test for knowledge of words, phrases, and abbreviations used in medical diagnosis and therapy. Questions may cover such topics as diseases, symptoms, pharmaceuticals, medical specialties, anatomy, treatment modalities, medical supplies, and medical equipment. Prefixes and suffixes used in medical terminology may also be included.
3. **Name and number checking** - These questions test for the ability to distinguish between sets of words, letters, and/or numbers that are almost exactly alike. Material is usually presented in two or three columns, and you will have to determine how the entry in the first column compares with the entry in the second column and possibly the third. You will be instructed to mark your answers according to a designated code provided in the directions.
4. **Office record keeping** - These questions test your ability to perform common office record keeping tasks. The test consists of two or more "sets" of questions, each set concerning a different problem. Typical record keeping problems might involve the organization or collation of data from several sources; scheduling; maintaining a record system using running balances; or completion of a table summarizing data using totals, subtotals, averages and percents.
5. **Understanding and interpreting written material** - These questions test how well you comprehend written material. You will be provided with brief reading selections and will be asked questions about the selections. All the information required to answer the questions will be presented in the selections; you will not be required to have any special knowledge relating to the subject areas of the selections.
6. **Supervision** - These questions test for knowledge of the principles and practices employed in planning, organizing, and controlling the activities of a work unit toward predetermined objectives. The concepts covered, usually in a situational question format, include such topics as assigning and reviewing work; evaluating performance; maintaining work standards; motivating and developing subordinates; implementing procedural change; increasing efficiency; and dealing with problems of absenteeism, morale, and discipline.

HOW TO TAKE A TEST

I. YOU MUST PASS AN EXAMINATION

A. WHAT EVERY CANDIDATE SHOULD KNOW

Examination applicants often ask us for help in preparing for the written test. What can I study in advance? What kinds of questions will be asked? How will the test be given? How will the papers be graded?

As an applicant for a civil service examination, you may be wondering about some of these things. Our purpose here is to suggest effective methods of advance study and to describe civil service examinations.

Your chances for success on this examination can be increased if you know how to prepare. Those "pre-examination jitters" can be reduced if you know what to expect. You can even experience an adventure in good citizenship if you know why civil service exams are given.

B. WHY ARE CIVIL SERVICE EXAMINATIONS GIVEN?

Civil service examinations are important to you in two ways. As a citizen, you want public jobs filled by employees who know how to do their work. As a job seeker, you want a fair chance to compete for that job on an equal footing with other candidates. The best-known means of accomplishing this two-fold goal is the competitive examination.

Exams are widely publicized throughout the nation. They may be administered for jobs in federal, state, city, municipal, town or village governments or agencies.

Any citizen may apply, with some limitations, such as the age or residence of applicants. Your experience and education may be reviewed to see whether you meet the requirements for the particular examination. When these requirements exist, they are reasonable and applied consistently to all applicants. Thus, a competitive examination may cause you some uneasiness now, but it is your privilege and safeguard.

C. HOW ARE CIVIL SERVICE EXAMS DEVELOPED?

Examinations are carefully written by trained technicians who are specialists in the field known as "psychological measurement," in consultation with recognized authorities in the field of work that the test will cover. These experts recommend the subject matter areas or skills to be tested; only those knowledges or skills important to your success on the job are included. The most reliable books and source materials available are used as references. Together, the experts and technicians judge the difficulty level of the questions.

Test technicians know how to phrase questions so that the problem is clearly stated. Their ethics do not permit "trick" or "catch" questions. Questions may have been tried out on sample groups, or subjected to statistical analysis, to determine their usefulness.

Written tests are often used in combination with performance tests, ratings of training and experience, and oral interviews. All of these measures combine to form the best-known means of finding the right person for the right job.

II. HOW TO PASS THE WRITTEN TEST

A. NATURE OF THE EXAMINATION

To prepare intelligently for civil service examinations, you should know how they differ from school examinations you have taken. In school you were assigned certain definite pages to read or subjects to cover. The examination questions were quite detailed and usually emphasized memory. Civil service exams, on the other hand, try to discover your present ability to perform the duties of a position, plus your potentiality to learn these duties. In other words, a civil service exam attempts to predict how successful you will be. Questions cover such a broad area that they cannot be as minute and detailed as school exam questions.

In the public service similar kinds of work, or positions, are grouped together in one "class." This process is known as *position-classification*. All the positions in a class are paid according to the salary range for that class. One class title covers all of these positions, and they are all tested by the same examination.

B. FOUR BASIC STEPS

1) Study the announcement

How, then, can you know what subjects to study? Our best answer is: "Learn as much as possible about the class of positions for which you've applied." The exam will test the knowledge, skills and abilities needed to do the work.

Your most valuable source of information about the position you want is the official exam announcement. This announcement lists the training and experience qualifications. Check these standards and apply only if you come reasonably close to meeting them.

The brief description of the position in the examination announcement offers some clues to the subjects which will be tested. Think about the job itself. Review the duties in your mind. Can you perform them, or are there some in which you are rusty? Fill in the blank spots in your preparation.

Many jurisdictions preview the written test in the exam announcement by including a section called "Knowledge and Abilities Required," "Scope of the Examination," or some similar heading. Here you will find out specifically what fields will be tested.

2) Review your own background

Once you learn in general what the position is all about, and what you need to know to do the work, ask yourself which subjects you already know fairly well and which need improvement. You may wonder whether to concentrate on improving your strong areas or on building some background in your fields of weakness. When the announcement has specified "some knowledge" or "considerable knowledge," or has used adjectives like "beginning principles of…" or "advanced … methods," you can get a clue as to the number and difficulty of questions to be asked in any given field. More questions, and hence broader coverage, would be included for those subjects which are more important in the work. Now weigh your strengths and weaknesses against the job requirements and prepare accordingly.

3) Determine the level of the position

Another way to tell how intensively you should prepare is to understand the level of the job for which you are applying. Is it the entering level? In other words, is this the position in which beginners in a field of work are hired? Or is it an intermediate or advanced level? Sometimes this is indicated by such words as "Junior" or "Senior" in the class title. Other jurisdictions use Roman numerals to designate the level – Clerk I, Clerk II, for example. The word "Supervisor" sometimes appears in the title. If the level is not indicated by the title, check the description of duties. Will you be working under very close supervision, or will you have responsibility for independent decisions in this work?

4) Choose appropriate study materials

Now that you know the subjects to be examined and the relative amount of each subject to be covered, you can choose suitable study materials. For beginning level jobs, or even advanced ones, if you have a pronounced weakness in some aspect of your training, read a modern, standard textbook in that field. Be sure it is up to date and has general coverage. Such books are normally available at your library, and the librarian will be glad to help you locate one. For entry-level positions, questions of appropriate difficulty are chosen — neither highly advanced questions, nor those too simple. Such questions require careful thought but not advanced training.

If the position for which you are applying is technical or advanced, you will read more advanced, specialized material. If you are already familiar with the basic principles of your field, elementary textbooks would waste your time. Concentrate on advanced textbooks and technical periodicals. Think through the concepts and review difficult problems in your field.

These are all general sources. You can get more ideas on your own initiative, following these leads. For example, training manuals and publications of the government agency which employs workers in your field can be useful, particularly for technical and professional positions. A letter or visit to the government department involved may result in more specific study suggestions, and certainly will provide you with a more definite idea of the exact nature of the position you are seeking.

III. KINDS OF TESTS

Tests are used for purposes other than measuring knowledge and ability to perform specified duties. For some positions, it is equally important to test ability to make adjustments to new situations or to profit from training. In others, basic mental abilities not dependent on information are essential. Questions which test these things may not appear as pertinent to the duties of the position as those which test for knowledge and information. Yet they are often highly important parts of a fair examination. For very general questions, it is almost impossible to help you direct your study efforts. What we can do is to point out some of the more common of these general abilities needed in public service positions and describe some typical questions.

1) General information

Broad, general information has been found useful for predicting job success in some kinds of work. This is tested in a variety of ways, from vocabulary lists to questions about current events. Basic background in some field of work, such as sociology or economics, may be sampled in a group of questions. Often these are principles which have become familiar to most persons through exposure rather than through formal training. It is difficult to advise you how to study for these questions; being alert to the world around you is our best suggestion.

2) Verbal ability

An example of an ability needed in many positions is verbal or language ability. Verbal ability is, in brief, the ability to use and understand words. Vocabulary and grammar tests are typical measures of this ability. Reading comprehension or paragraph interpretation questions are common in many kinds of civil service tests. You are given a paragraph of written material and asked to find its central meaning.

3) Numerical ability

Number skills can be tested by the familiar arithmetic problem, by checking paired lists of numbers to see which are alike and which are different, or by interpreting charts and graphs. In the latter test, a graph may be printed in the test booklet which you are asked to use as the basis for answering questions.

4) Observation

A popular test for law-enforcement positions is the observation test. A picture is shown to you for several minutes, then taken away. Questions about the picture test your ability to observe both details and larger elements.

5) Following directions

In many positions in the public service, the employee must be able to carry out written instructions dependably and accurately. You may be given a chart with several columns, each column listing a variety of information. The questions require you to carry out directions involving the information given in the chart.

6) Skills and aptitudes

Performance tests effectively measure some manual skills and aptitudes. When the skill is one in which you are trained, such as typing or shorthand, you can practice. These tests are often very much like those given in business school or high school courses. For many of the other skills and aptitudes, however, no short-time preparation can be made. Skills and abilities natural to you or that you have developed throughout your lifetime are being tested.

Many of the general questions just described provide all the data needed to answer the questions and ask you to use your reasoning ability to find the answers. Your best preparation for these tests, as well as for tests of facts and ideas, is to be at your physical and mental best. You, no doubt, have your own methods of getting into an exam-taking mood and keeping "in shape." The next section lists some ideas on this subject.

IV. KINDS OF QUESTIONS

Only rarely is the "essay" question, which you answer in narrative form, used in civil service tests. Civil service tests are usually of the short-answer type. Full instructions for answering these questions will be given to you at the examination. But in case this is your first experience with short-answer questions and separate answer sheets, here is what you need to know:

1) **Multiple-choice Questions**

Most popular of the short-answer questions is the "multiple choice" or "best answer" question. It can be used, for example, to test for factual knowledge, ability to solve problems or judgment in meeting situations found at work.

A multiple-choice question is normally one of three types—
- It can begin with an incomplete statement followed by several possible endings. You are to find the one ending which *best* completes the statement, although some of the others may not be entirely wrong.
- It can also be a complete statement in the form of a question which is answered by choosing one of the statements listed.

- It can be in the form of a problem – again you select the best answer.

Here is an example of a multiple-choice question with a discussion which should give you some clues as to the method for choosing the right answer:

When an employee has a complaint about his assignment, the action which will *best* help him overcome his difficulty is to
  A. discuss his difficulty with his coworkers
  B. take the problem to the head of the organization
  C. take the problem to the person who gave him the assignment
  D. say nothing to anyone about his complaint

In answering this question, you should study each of the choices to find which is best. Consider choice "A" – Certainly an employee may discuss his complaint with fellow employees, but no change or improvement can result, and the complaint remains unresolved. Choice "B" is a poor choice since the head of the organization probably does not know what assignment you have been given, and taking your problem to him is known as "going over the head" of the supervisor. The supervisor, or person who made the assignment, is the person who can clarify it or correct any injustice. Choice "C" is, therefore, correct. To say nothing, as in choice "D," is unwise. Supervisors have and interest in knowing the problems employees are facing, and the employee is seeking a solution to his problem.

2) True/False Questions

The "true/false" or "right/wrong" form of question is sometimes used. Here a complete statement is given. Your job is to decide whether the statement is right or wrong.

SAMPLE: A roaming cell-phone call to a nearby city costs less than a non-roaming call to a distant city.

This statement is wrong, or false, since roaming calls are more expensive.

This is not a complete list of all possible question forms, although most of the others are variations of these common types. You will always get complete directions for answering questions. Be sure you understand *how* to mark your answers – ask questions until you do.

V. RECORDING YOUR ANSWERS

Computer terminals are used more and more today for many different kinds of exams.
For an examination with very few applicants, you may be told to record your answers in the test booklet itself. Separate answer sheets are much more common. If this separate answer sheet is to be scored by machine – and this is often the case – it is highly important that you mark your answers correctly in order to get credit.
An electronic scoring machine is often used in civil service offices because of the speed with which papers can be scored. Machine-scored answer sheets must be marked with a pencil, which will be given to you. This pencil has a high graphite content which responds to the electronic scoring machine. As a matter of fact, stray dots may register as answers, so do not let your pencil rest on the answer sheet while you are pondering the correct answer. Also, if your pencil lead breaks or is otherwise defective, ask for another.

Since the answer sheet will be dropped in a slot in the scoring machine, be careful not to bend the corners or get the paper crumpled.

The answer sheet normally has five vertical columns of numbers, with 30 numbers to a column. These numbers correspond to the question numbers in your test booklet. After each number, going across the page are four or five pairs of dotted lines. These short dotted lines have small letters or numbers above them. The first two pairs may also have a "T" or "F" above the letters. This indicates that the first two pairs only are to be used if the questions are of the true-false type. If the questions are multiple choice, disregard the "T" and "F" and pay attention only to the small letters or numbers.

Answer your questions in the manner of the sample that follows:

32. The largest city in the United States is
   A. Washington, D.C.
   B. New York City
   C. Chicago
   D. Detroit
   E. San Francisco

1) Choose the answer you think is best. (New York City is the largest, so "B" is correct.)
2) Find the row of dotted lines numbered the same as the question you are answering. (Find row number 32)
3) Find the pair of dotted lines corresponding to the answer. (Find the pair of lines under the mark "B.")
4) Make a solid black mark between the dotted lines.

VI. BEFORE THE TEST

Common sense will help you find procedures to follow to get ready for an examination. Too many of us, however, overlook these sensible measures. Indeed, nervousness and fatigue have been found to be the most serious reasons why applicants fail to do their best on civil service tests. Here is a list of reminders:

- Begin your preparation early – Don't wait until the last minute to go scurrying around for books and materials or to find out what the position is all about.
- Prepare continuously – An hour a night for a week is better than an all-night cram session. This has been definitely established. What is more, a night a week for a month will return better dividends than crowding your study into a shorter period of time.
- Locate the place of the exam – You have been sent a notice telling you when and where to report for the examination. If the location is in a different town or otherwise unfamiliar to you, it would be well to inquire the best route and learn something about the building.
- Relax the night before the test – Allow your mind to rest. Do not study at all that night. Plan some mild recreation or diversion; then go to bed early and get a good night's sleep.
- Get up early enough to make a leisurely trip to the place for the test – This way unforeseen events, traffic snarls, unfamiliar buildings, etc. will not upset you.
- Dress comfortably – A written test is not a fashion show. You will be known by number and not by name, so wear something comfortable.

- Leave excess paraphernalia at home – Shopping bags and odd bundles will get in your way. You need bring only the items mentioned in the official notice you received; usually everything you need is provided. Do not bring reference books to the exam. They will only confuse those last minutes and be taken away from you when in the test room.
- Arrive somewhat ahead of time – If because of transportation schedules you must get there very early, bring a newspaper or magazine to take your mind off yourself while waiting.
- Locate the examination room – When you have found the proper room, you will be directed to the seat or part of the room where you will sit. Sometimes you are given a sheet of instructions to read while you are waiting. Do not fill out any forms until you are told to do so; just read them and be prepared.
- Relax and prepare to listen to the instructions
- If you have any physical problem that may keep you from doing your best, be sure to tell the test administrator. If you are sick or in poor health, you really cannot do your best on the exam. You can come back and take the test some other time.

VII. AT THE TEST

The day of the test is here and you have the test booklet in your hand. The temptation to get going is very strong. Caution! There is more to success than knowing the right answers. You must know how to identify your papers and understand variations in the type of short-answer question used in this particular examination. Follow these suggestions for maximum results from your efforts:

1) Cooperate with the monitor

The test administrator has a duty to create a situation in which you can be as much at ease as possible. He will give instructions, tell you when to begin, check to see that you are marking your answer sheet correctly, and so on. He is not there to guard you, although he will see that your competitors do not take unfair advantage. He wants to help you do your best.

2) Listen to all instructions

Don't jump the gun! Wait until you understand all directions. In most civil service tests you get more time than you need to answer the questions. So don't be in a hurry. Read each word of instructions until you clearly understand the meaning. Study the examples, listen to all announcements and follow directions. Ask questions if you do not understand what to do.

3) Identify your papers

Civil service exams are usually identified by number only. You will be assigned a number; you must not put your name on your test papers. Be sure to copy your number correctly. Since more than one exam may be given, copy your exact examination title.

4) Plan your time

Unless you are told that a test is a "speed" or "rate of work" test, speed itself is usually not important. Time enough to answer all the questions will be provided, but this does not mean that you have all day. An overall time limit has been set. Divide the total time (in minutes) by the number of questions to determine the approximate time you have for each question.

5) Do not linger over difficult questions

If you come across a difficult question, mark it with a paper clip (useful to have along) and come back to it when you have been through the booklet. One caution if you do this – be sure to skip a number on your answer sheet as well. Check often to be sure that you have not lost your place and that you are marking in the row numbered the same as the question you are answering.

6) Read the questions

Be sure you know what the question asks! Many capable people are unsuccessful because they failed to *read* the questions correctly.

7) Answer all questions

Unless you have been instructed that a penalty will be deducted for incorrect answers, it is better to guess than to omit a question.

8) Speed tests

It is often better NOT to guess on speed tests. It has been found that on timed tests people are tempted to spend the last few seconds before time is called in marking answers at random – without even reading them – in the hope of picking up a few extra points. To discourage this practice, the instructions may warn you that your score will be "corrected" for guessing. That is, a penalty will be applied. The incorrect answers will be deducted from the correct ones, or some other penalty formula will be used.

9) Review your answers

If you finish before time is called, go back to the questions you guessed or omitted to give them further thought. Review other answers if you have time.

10) Return your test materials

If you are ready to leave before others have finished or time is called, take ALL your materials to the monitor and leave quietly. Never take any test material with you. The monitor can discover whose papers are not complete, and taking a test booklet may be grounds for disqualification.

VIII. EXAMINATION TECHNIQUES

1) Read the general instructions carefully. These are usually printed on the first page of the exam booklet. As a rule, these instructions refer to the timing of the examination; the fact that you should not start work until the signal and must stop work at a signal, etc. If there are any *special* instructions, such as a choice of questions to be answered, make sure that you note this instruction carefully.

2) When you are ready to start work on the examination, that is as soon as the signal has been given, read the instructions to each question booklet, underline any key words or phrases, such as *least, best, outline, describe* and the like. In this way you will tend to answer as requested rather than discover on reviewing your paper that you *listed without describing*, that you selected the *worst* choice rather than the *best* choice, etc.

3) If the examination is of the objective or multiple-choice type – that is, each question will also give a series of possible answers: A, B, C or D, and you are called upon to select the best answer and write the letter next to that answer on your answer paper – it is advisable to start answering each question in turn. There may be anywhere from 50 to 100 such questions in the three or four hours allotted and you can see how much time would be taken if you read through all the questions before beginning to answer any. Furthermore, if you come across a question or group of questions which you know would be difficult to answer, it would undoubtedly affect your handling of all the other questions.

4) If the examination is of the essay type and contains but a few questions, it is a moot point as to whether you should read all the questions before starting to answer any one. Of course, if you are given a choice – say five out of seven and the like – then it is essential to read all the questions so you can eliminate the two that are most difficult. If, however, you are asked to answer all the questions, there may be danger in trying to answer the easiest one first because you may find that you will spend too much time on it. The best technique is to answer the first question, then proceed to the second, etc.

5) Time your answers. Before the exam begins, write down the time it started, then add the time allowed for the examination and write down the time it must be completed, then divide the time available somewhat as follows:
    - If 3-1/2 hours are allowed, that would be 210 minutes. If you have 80 objective-type questions, that would be an average of 2-1/2 minutes per question. Allow yourself no more than 2 minutes per question, or a total of 160 minutes, which will permit about 50 minutes to review.
    - If for the time allotment of 210 minutes there are 7 essay questions to answer, that would average about 30 minutes a question. Give yourself only 25 minutes per question so that you have about 35 minutes to review.

6) The most important instruction is to *read each question* and make sure you know what is wanted. The second most important instruction is to *time yourself properly* so that you answer every question. The third most important instruction is to *answer every question*. Guess if you have to but include something for each question. Remember that you will receive no credit for a blank and will probably receive some credit if you write something in answer to an essay question. If you guess a letter – say "B" for a multiple-choice question – you may have guessed right. If you leave a blank as an answer to a multiple-choice question, the examiners may respect your feelings but it will not add a point to your score. Some exams may penalize you for wrong answers, so in such cases *only*, you may not want to guess unless you have some basis for your answer.

7) Suggestions
    a. Objective-type questions
        1. Examine the question booklet for proper sequence of pages and questions
        2. Read all instructions carefully
        3. Skip any question which seems too difficult; return to it after all other questions have been answered
        4. Apportion your time properly; do not spend too much time on any single question or group of questions

5. Note and underline key words – *all, most, fewest, least, best, worst, same, opposite*, etc.
6. Pay particular attention to negatives
7. Note unusual option, e.g., unduly long, short, complex, different or similar in content to the body of the question
8. Observe the use of "hedging" words – *probably, may, most likely*, etc.
9. Make sure that your answer is put next to the same number as the question
10. Do not second-guess unless you have good reason to believe the second answer is definitely more correct
11. Cross out original answer if you decide another answer is more accurate; do not erase until you are ready to hand your paper in
12. Answer all questions; guess unless instructed otherwise
13. Leave time for review

b. Essay questions
   1. Read each question carefully
   2. Determine exactly what is wanted. Underline key words or phrases.
   3. Decide on outline or paragraph answer
   4. Include many different points and elements unless asked to develop any one or two points or elements
   5. Show impartiality by giving pros and cons unless directed to select one side only
   6. Make and write down any assumptions you find necessary to answer the questions
   7. Watch your English, grammar, punctuation and choice of words
   8. Time your answers; don't crowd material

8) Answering the essay question

Most essay questions can be answered by framing the specific response around several key words or ideas. Here are a few such key words or ideas:

M's: manpower, materials, methods, money, management
P's: purpose, program, policy, plan, procedure, practice, problems, pitfalls, personnel, public relations

   a. Six basic steps in handling problems:
      1. Preliminary plan and background development
      2. Collect information, data and facts
      3. Analyze and interpret information, data and facts
      4. Analyze and develop solutions as well as make recommendations
      5. Prepare report and sell recommendations
      6. Install recommendations and follow up effectiveness

   b. Pitfalls to avoid
      1. *Taking things for granted* – A statement of the situation does not necessarily imply that each of the elements is necessarily true; for example, a complaint may be invalid and biased so that all that can be taken for granted is that a complaint has been registered

2. *Considering only one side of a situation* – Wherever possible, indicate several alternatives and then point out the reasons you selected the best one
3. *Failing to indicate follow up* – Whenever your answer indicates action on your part, make certain that you will take proper follow-up action to see how successful your recommendations, procedures or actions turn out to be
4. *Taking too long in answering any single question* – Remember to time your answers properly

IX. AFTER THE TEST

Scoring procedures differ in detail among civil service jurisdictions although the general principles are the same. Whether the papers are hand-scored or graded by machine we have described, they are nearly always graded by number. That is, the person who marks the paper knows only the number – never the name – of the applicant. Not until all the papers have been graded will they be matched with names. If other tests, such as training and experience or oral interview ratings have been given, scores will be combined. Different parts of the examination usually have different weights. For example, the written test might count 60 percent of the final grade, and a rating of training and experience 40 percent. In many jurisdictions, veterans will have a certain number of points added to their grades.

After the final grade has been determined, the names are placed in grade order and an eligible list is established. There are various methods for resolving ties between those who get the same final grade – probably the most common is to place first the name of the person whose application was received first. Job offers are made from the eligible list in the order the names appear on it. You will be notified of your grade and your rank as soon as all these computations have been made. This will be done as rapidly as possible.

People who are found to meet the requirements in the announcement are called "eligibles." Their names are put on a list of eligible candidates. An eligible's chances of getting a job depend on how high he stands on this list and how fast agencies are filling jobs from the list.

When a job is to be filled from a list of eligibles, the agency asks for the names of people on the list of eligibles for that job. When the civil service commission receives this request, it sends to the agency the names of the three people highest on this list. Or, if the job to be filled has specialized requirements, the office sends the agency the names of the top three persons who meet these requirements from the general list.

The appointing officer makes a choice from among the three people whose names were sent to him. If the selected person accepts the appointment, the names of the others are put back on the list to be considered for future openings.

That is the rule in hiring from all kinds of eligible lists, whether they are for typist, carpenter, chemist, or something else. For every vacancy, the appointing officer has his choice of any one of the top three eligibles on the list. This explains why the person whose name is on top of the list sometimes does not get an appointment when some of the persons lower on the list do. If the appointing officer chooses the second or third eligible, the No. 1 eligible does not get a job at once, but stays on the list until he is appointed or the list is terminated.

X. HOW TO PASS THE INTERVIEW TEST

The examination for which you applied requires an oral interview test. You have already taken the written test and you are now being called for the interview test – the final part of the formal examination.

You may think that it is not possible to prepare for an interview test and that there are no procedures to follow during an interview. Our purpose is to point out some things you can do in advance that will help you and some good rules to follow and pitfalls to avoid while you are being interviewed.

What is an interview supposed to test?

The written examination is designed to test the technical knowledge and competence of the candidate; the oral is designed to evaluate intangible qualities, not readily measured otherwise, and to establish a list showing the relative fitness of each candidate – as measured against his competitors – for the position sought. Scoring is not on the basis of "right" and "wrong," but on a sliding scale of values ranging from "not passable" to "outstanding." As a matter of fact, it is possible to achieve a relatively low score without a single "incorrect" answer because of evident weakness in the qualities being measured.

Occasionally, an examination may consist entirely of an oral test – either an individual or a group oral. In such cases, information is sought concerning the technical knowledges and abilities of the candidate, since there has been no written examination for this purpose. More commonly, however, an oral test is used to supplement a written examination.

Who conducts interviews?

The composition of oral boards varies among different jurisdictions. In nearly all, a representative of the personnel department serves as chairman. One of the members of the board may be a representative of the department in which the candidate would work. In some cases, "outside experts" are used, and, frequently, a businessman or some other representative of the general public is asked to serve. Labor and management or other special groups may be represented. The aim is to secure the services of experts in the appropriate field.

However the board is composed, it is a good idea (and not at all improper or unethical) to ascertain in advance of the interview who the members are and what groups they represent. When you are introduced to them, you will have some idea of their backgrounds and interests, and at least you will not stutter and stammer over their names.

What should be done before the interview?

While knowledge about the board members is useful and takes some of the surprise element out of the interview, there is other preparation which is more substantive. It *is* possible to prepare for an oral interview – in several ways:

1) Keep a copy of your application and review it carefully before the interview

This may be the only document before the oral board, and the starting point of the interview. Know what education and experience you have listed there, and the sequence and dates of all of it. Sometimes the board will ask you to review the highlights of your experience for them; you should not have to hem and haw doing it.

2) Study the class specification and the examination announcement

Usually, the oral board has one or both of these to guide them. The qualities, characteristics or knowledges required by the position sought are stated in these documents. They offer valuable clues as to the nature of the oral interview. For example, if the job involves supervisory responsibilities, the announcement will usually indicate that knowledge of modern supervisory methods and the qualifications of the candidate as a supervisor will be tested. If so, you can expect such questions, frequently in the form of a hypothetical situation which you are expected to solve. NEVER go into an oral without knowledge of the duties and responsibilities of the job you seek.

3) Think through each qualification required

Try to visualize the kind of questions you would ask if you were a board member. How well could you answer them? Try especially to appraise your own knowledge and background in each area, *measured against the job sought*, and identify any areas in which you are weak. Be critical and realistic – do not flatter yourself.

4) Do some general reading in areas in which you feel you may be weak

For example, if the job involves supervision and your past experience has NOT, some general reading in supervisory methods and practices, particularly in the field of human relations, might be useful. Do NOT study agency procedures or detailed manuals. The oral board will be testing your understanding and capacity, not your memory.

5) Get a good night's sleep and watch your general health and mental attitude

You will want a clear head at the interview. Take care of a cold or any other minor ailment, and of course, no hangovers.

What should be done on the day of the interview?

Now comes the day of the interview itself. Give yourself plenty of time to get there. Plan to arrive somewhat ahead of the scheduled time, particularly if your appointment is in the fore part of the day. If a previous candidate fails to appear, the board might be ready for you a bit early. By early afternoon an oral board is almost invariably behind schedule if there are many candidates, and you may have to wait. Take along a book or magazine to read, or your application to review, but leave any extraneous material in the waiting room when you go in for your interview. In any event, relax and compose yourself.

The matter of dress is important. The board is forming impressions about you – from your experience, your manners, your attitude, and your appearance. Give your personal appearance careful attention. Dress your best, but not your flashiest. Choose conservative, appropriate clothing, and be sure it is immaculate. This is a business interview, and your appearance should indicate that you regard it as such. Besides, being well groomed and properly dressed will help boost your confidence.

Sooner or later, someone will call your name and escort you into the interview room. *This is it.* From here on you are on your own. It is too late for any more preparation. But remember, you asked for this opportunity to prove your fitness, and you are here because your request was granted.

What happens when you go in?

The usual sequence of events will be as follows: The clerk (who is often the board stenographer) will introduce you to the chairman of the oral board, who will introduce you to the other members of the board. Acknowledge the introductions before you sit down. Do not be surprised if you find a microphone facing you or a stenotypist sitting by. Oral interviews are usually recorded in the event of an appeal or other review.

Usually the chairman of the board will open the interview by reviewing the highlights of your education and work experience from your application – primarily for the benefit of the other members of the board, as well as to get the material into the record. Do not interrupt or comment unless there is an error or significant misinterpretation; if that is the case, do not hesitate. But do not quibble about insignificant matters. Also, he will usually ask you some question about your education, experience or your present job – partly to get you to start talking and to establish the interviewing "rapport." He may start the actual questioning, or turn it over to one of the other members. Frequently, each member undertakes the questioning on a particular area, one in which he is perhaps most competent, so you can expect each member to participate in the examination. Because time is limited, you may also expect some rather abrupt switches in the direction the questioning takes, so do not be upset by it. Normally, a board member will not pursue a single line of questioning unless he discovers a particular strength or weakness.

After each member has participated, the chairman will usually ask whether any member has any further questions, then will ask you if you have anything you wish to add. Unless you are expecting this question, it may floor you. Worse, it may start you off on an extended, extemporaneous speech. The board is not usually seeking more information. The question is principally to offer you a last opportunity to present further qualifications or to indicate that you have nothing to add. So, if you feel that a significant qualification or characteristic has been overlooked, it is proper to point it out in a sentence or so. Do not compliment the board on the thoroughness of their examination – they have been sketchy, and you know it. If you wish, merely say, "No thank you, I have nothing further to add." This is a point where you can "talk yourself out" of a good impression or fail to present an important bit of information. Remember, *you close the interview yourself.*

The chairman will then say, "That is all, Mr. _____, thank you." Do not be startled; the interview is over, and quicker than you think. Thank him, gather your belongings and take your leave. Save your sigh of relief for the other side of the door.

How to put your best foot forward

Throughout this entire process, you may feel that the board individually and collectively is trying to pierce your defenses, seek out your hidden weaknesses and embarrass and confuse you. Actually, this is not true. They are obliged to make an appraisal of your qualifications for the job you are seeking, and they want to see you in your best light. Remember, they must interview all candidates and a non-cooperative candidate may become a failure in spite of their best efforts to bring out his qualifications. Here are 15 suggestions that will help you:

1) Be natural – Keep your attitude confident, not cocky

If you are not confident that you can do the job, do not expect the board to be. Do not apologize for your weaknesses, try to bring out your strong points. The board is interested in a positive, not negative, presentation. Cockiness will antagonize any board member and make him wonder if you are covering up a weakness by a false show of strength.

2) Get comfortable, but don't lounge or sprawl

Sit erectly but not stiffly. A careless posture may lead the board to conclude that you are careless in other things, or at least that you are not impressed by the importance of the occasion. Either conclusion is natural, even if incorrect. Do not fuss with your clothing, a pencil or an ashtray. Your hands may occasionally be useful to emphasize a point; do not let them become a point of distraction.

3) Do not wisecrack or make small talk

This is a serious situation, and your attitude should show that you consider it as such. Further, the time of the board is limited – they do not want to waste it, and neither should you.

4) Do not exaggerate your experience or abilities

In the first place, from information in the application or other interviews and sources, the board may know more about you than you think. Secondly, you probably will not get away with it. An experienced board is rather adept at spotting such a situation, so do not take the chance.

5) If you know a board member, do not make a point of it, yet do not hide it

Certainly you are not fooling him, and probably not the other members of the board. Do not try to take advantage of your acquaintanceship – it will probably do you little good.

6) Do not dominate the interview

Let the board do that. They will give you the clues – do not assume that you have to do all the talking. Realize that the board has a number of questions to ask you, and do not try to take up all the interview time by showing off your extensive knowledge of the answer to the first one.

7) Be attentive

You only have 20 minutes or so, and you should keep your attention at its sharpest throughout. When a member is addressing a problem or question to you, give him your undivided attention. Address your reply principally to him, but do not exclude the other board members.

8) Do not interrupt

A board member may be stating a problem for you to analyze. He will ask you a question when the time comes. Let him state the problem, and wait for the question.

9) Make sure you understand the question

Do not try to answer until you are sure what the question is. If it is not clear, restate it in your own words or ask the board member to clarify it for you. However, do not haggle about minor elements.

10) Reply promptly but not hastily

A common entry on oral board rating sheets is "candidate responded readily," or "candidate hesitated in replies." Respond as promptly and quickly as you can, but do not jump to a hasty, ill-considered answer.

11) Do not be peremptory in your answers

A brief answer is proper – but do not fire your answer back. That is a losing game from your point of view. The board member can probably ask questions much faster than you can answer them.

12) Do not try to create the answer you think the board member wants

He is interested in what kind of mind you have and how it works – not in playing games. Furthermore, he can usually spot this practice and will actually grade you down on it.

13) Do not switch sides in your reply merely to agree with a board member

Frequently, a member will take a contrary position merely to draw you out and to see if you are willing and able to defend your point of view. Do not start a debate, yet do not surrender a good position. If a position is worth taking, it is worth defending.

14) Do not be afraid to admit an error in judgment if you are shown to be wrong

The board knows that you are forced to reply without any opportunity for careful consideration. Your answer may be demonstrably wrong. If so, admit it and get on with the interview.

15) Do not dwell at length on your present job

The opening question may relate to your present assignment. Answer the question but do not go into an extended discussion. You are being examined for a *new* job, not your present one. As a matter of fact, try to phrase ALL your answers in terms of the job for which you are being examined.

Basis of Rating

Probably you will forget most of these "do's" and "don'ts" when you walk into the oral interview room. Even remembering them all will not ensure you a passing grade. Perhaps you did not have the qualifications in the first place. But remembering them will help you to put your best foot forward, without treading on the toes of the board members.

Rumor and popular opinion to the contrary notwithstanding, an oral board wants you to make the best appearance possible. They know you are under pressure – but they also want to see how you respond to it as a guide to what your reaction would be under the pressures of the job you seek. They will be influenced by the degree of poise you display, the personal traits you show and the manner in which you respond.

ABOUT THIS BOOK

This book contains tests divided into Examination Sections. Go through each test, answering every question in the margin. We have also attached a sample answer sheet at the back of the book that can be removed and used. At the end of each test look at the answer key and check your answers. On the ones you got wrong, look at the right answer choice and learn. Do not fill in the answers first. Do not memorize the questions and answers, but understand the answer and principles involved. On your test, the questions will likely be different from the samples. Questions are changed and new ones added. If you understand these past questions you should have success with any changes that arise. Tests may consist of several types of questions. We have additional books on each subject should more study be advisable or necessary for you. Finally, the more you study, the better prepared you will be. This book is intended to be the last thing you study before you walk into the examination room. Prior study of relevant texts is also recommended. NLC publishes some of these in our Fundamental Series. Knowledge and good sense are important factors in passing your exam. Good luck also helps. So now study this Passbook, absorb the material contained within and take that knowledge into the examination. Then do your best to pass that exam.

EXAMINATION SECTION

EXAMINATION SECTION
TEST 1

DIRECTIONS: Each question or incomplete statement is followed by several suggested answers or completions. Select the one that BEST answers the question or completes the statement. *PRINT THE LETTER OF THE CORRECT ANSWER IN THE SPACE AT THE RIGHT.*

1. According to the Joint Commission on the Accreditation of Health Care Organizations, medical records must meet _____ standard(s) of performance.   1.____

    A. one B. two C. four D. five

2. The MAIN purpose of medical records is to provide a vehicle for   2.____

    A. documenting action taken in patient management
    B. documenting patient progress
    C. providing meaningful medical information to other practitioners
    D. all of the above

3. According to the JCAHO manual, all of the following information must be included in all medical records EXCEPT   3.____

    A. medical history of the patient
    B. events occurring after discharge from the hospital
    C. reports of relevant physical examination
    D. reports of procedures, tests, and their results

4. Medical records of the licensed and certified health care professional MUST contain   4.____

    A. dates of treatment
    B. action taken by non-licensed persons when ordered or authorized by the provider
    C. doctors' orders, nurses' notes and charts, birth certificate worksheets
    D. all of the above

5. According to the JCAHO manual, medical records must be completed within a period of time that does NOT exceed _____ days.   5.____

    A. 10 B. 20 C. 30 D. 40

6. Of the following, the CORRECT statement regarding medical record correction is: 6.____

    A. Errors should be erased or obliterated
    B. Errors should not be lined out
    C. Corrections should be initialed and dated
    D. All of the above

7. Individual health care providers MUST maintain patient records for _____ year(s) from the last date of treatment.   7.____

    A. one B. three C. five D. seven

8. After the patient's death, an individual health care provider must maintain his record for _____ year(s).

   A. one   B. three   C. five   D. seven

9. All of the following are true statements regarding health care providers EXCEPT:

   A. If a health care facility or organization retains medical records for a patient, the provider must maintain a duplicate set
   B. A health care provider must give public and private notice of his retirement to his patients
   C. Pathology slides and EEG and ECG tracings must be kept for seven years
   D. If a claim of malpractice or neglect of a patient is made, all records for that patient must be retained until the matter is resolved

10. To prevent the disclosure of medical records that must be destroyed, each provider should adopt a policy outlining destruction procedures, which should include

    A. the title of the person who may authorize destruction
    B. the data bases that would be affected
    C. the method of shipment of the records
    D. all of the above

11. Of the following, the confidentiality obligation in medical records is based on _____ factors.

    A. ethical   B. legal
    C. therapeutic argument   D. all of the above

12. Certified independent social workers may not disclose communication or records related to evaluation or treatment EXCEPT

    A. to other individuals engaged in diagnosis or treatment
    B. when there is a substantial risk of imminent injury to the person or others
    C. in an evaluation ordered by the court if the person concerned is informed in advance
    D. all of the above

13. All of the following individuals may act as the patient representative who reviews and receives copies of the patient's medical records EXCEPT a

    A. surrogate parent   B. divorced parent
    C. brother   D. patient's attorney

14. Consequences of wrongful disclosure may include

    A. invasion of privacy claim
    B. breach of duty of confidentiality
    C. breach of contract
    D. all of the above

15. When considering a request for disclosure subsequent to receiving the patient's consent, the provider should consider whether the

    A. authorization is specifically addressed to the institution
    B. authorization is signed by the patient

C. authorization is witnessed or notarized
D. all of the above

16. Of the following, the TRUE statement regarding incident reports is:

    A. Reports should be treated as confidential documents
    B. Incident report is not a part of medical records
    C. It is not necessary to address the reports to the institution's attorney
    D. All of the above

17. In medical terminology, the healing arts include the practice of

    A. medicine
    B. osteopathy
    C. chiropractice
    D. all of the above

18. Of the following, medical records contain _____ data about an individual patient.

    A. medical
    B. financial
    C. personal
    D. all of the above

19. A physician's verbal orders should be limited as much as possible to telephone orders and in all cases must be transcribed in the medical records and signed by the physician within

    A. 24 hours
    B. one week
    C. one month
    D. one year

20. Every time a patient visits the emergency department, all of the following information must be entered in the patient's medical record EXCEPT

    A. pertinent history of the illness or injury
    B. emergency care given to the patient prior to the arrival
    C. annual income
    D. patient identification

KEY (CORRECT ANSWERS)

1.	C	11.	D
2.	D	12.	D
3.	B	13.	C
4.	D	14.	D
5.	C	15.	D
6.	C	16.	A
7.	D	17.	D
8.	B	18.	D
9.	A	19.	A
10.	D	20.	C

EXAMINATION SECTION
TEST 1

Questions 1-30.

DIRECTIONS: Questions 1 through 30 consist of statements. You are to decide whether the statement is true or false. Then, in the answer space on the right, PRINT the letter "T" if the statement is true, or PRINT the letter "F" if the statement is false. In order to help you understand the procedure, the following sample items are given:

SAMPLE ITEM: Albany is the capital of New York State.
Since this statement is correct, your answer should be written as follows:
SAMPLE ANSWER: T
SAMPLE ITEM: Buffalo is the largest city in New York State.
Since the statement is wrong, your answer should be written as follows:
SAMPLE ANSWER: F

1. It is worse for the hospital clerk to give a visitor incorrect information than for the clerk to say that he is unable to furnish the information.   1.____

2. If a visitor speaks to a hospital clerk in a loud and impertinent manner, the clerk is justified in then replying in the same manner   2.____

3. If a hospital clerk must deny a visitor's request for information, it is better for him to be firm than to explain tactfully the reason for the denial.   3.____

4. The manner in which a hospital clerk deals with visitors tends to affect the visitors' opinion of the hospital.   4.____

5. A hospital clerk who does not understand his instructions regarding an assignment should ask to have the instructions explained again before he begins to work on the assignment.   5.____

6. A hospital clerk is justified in reporting late for work if his immediate superior also reports late for work.   6.____

7. A hospital clerk should permit visitors to inspect patients' medical records.   7.____

8. The generally approved method of answering a telephone in a hospital is for the hospital clerk to say "Hello."   8.____

9. A proper method of obtaining a telephone number which cannot be located in the telephone directory is to dial 0.   9.____

10. The Classified Telephone Directory is also known as the "Yellow Pages."   10.____

11. Person-to-Person long distance telephone calls are more expensive than station-to-station long distance calls.   11.____

12. A clerk should usually wait until he is out of stock in certain items before reordering these items.   12.____

13. A semi-annual report is one that is issued every six months.   13.____

14. Letters filed in chronological order are those filed according to their dates. 14.____

15. "Out" cards are usually placed in a file when a useless record has been removed from the file and destroyed. 15.____

16. A clerk who notices that a letter has been misfiled should destroy the letter if he believes it is unimportant. 16.____

17. In alphabetic filing, Mary Brown is generally filed before Anna Browne. 17.____

18. In alphabetical filing, John Dewey is generally filed after Joan Dewey. 18.____

19. In alphabetical filing, Frank T. Mill is generally filed after Donald Millard. 19.____

20. If certain records must be attached together before being placed in the files, it is generally better to staple them together than to attach them together by a paper clip. 20.____

21. An exact copy of a letter or record can be made by means of a photostatic machine. 21.____

22. The symbol "c/o" appearing on an envelope as part of the address stands for the phrase "official correspondence." 22.____

23. Before starting to deliver mail addressed to patients in different wards of a hospital, the clerk should first sort the mail according to the wards in which the patients are located. 23.____

24. A copy machine cannot be used if the fax has been removed from the machine. 24.____

25. A clerk who notices that the signature has been omitted from an outgoing letter should ignore the omission and mail the letter. 25.____

26. A hospital clerk should allow patients' visitors to remain after visiting hours are over as long as the other patients in the ward are not disturbed. 26.____

27. The domestic postage rate for ordinary post cards is now fifty cents. 27.____

28. When a mail clerk opens an envelope containing both a letter and an enclosure, it is ordinarily desirable for him to attach the enclosure to the letter. 28.____

29. The postage meter is a machine that stamps and seals envelopes. 29.____

30. Aid to the blind and old age assistance are of no concern to the hospital clerk. 30.____

KEY (CORRECT ANSWERS)

1. T	11. F	21. T
2. F	12. F	22. F
3. F	13. T	23. T
4. T	14. T	24. F
5. T	15. F	25. F
6. F	16. F	26. F
7. F	17. T	27. F
8. F	18. T	28. T
9. T	19. F	29. F
10. T	20. T	30. F

TEST 2

DIRECTIONS: Questions 1 through 13 consist of statements. You are to decide whether the statement is true or false. Then, in the answer space on the right, PRINT the letter "T" if the statement is true, or PRINT the letter "F" if the statement is false. In order to help you understand the procedure, the following sample items are given:

SAMPLE ITEM: Albany is the capital of New York State.
Since this statement is correct, your answer should be written as follows:
SAMPLE ANSWER: T
SAMPLE ITEM: Buffalo is the largest city in New York State.
Since the statement is wrong, your answer should be written as follows:
SAMPLE ANSWER: F

Questions 1-6.

DIRECTIONS: Questions 1 through 6 inclusive are to be answered SOLELY on the basis of the information contained in the following statement and NOT upon any other information you may have.

Blood transfusions are given to patients at the hospital upon recommendation of the physicians attending such cases. The physician fills out a "Request for Blood Transfusion" form in duplicate and sends both copies to the Medical Director's office where a list is maintained of persons called "donors" who desire to sell their blood for transfusions. A suitable donor is selected and the transfusion is given. Donors are in many instances medical students and employees of the hospital. Donors receive twenty-five dollars for each transfusion.

1. According to the above paragraph, a blood donor is paid twenty-five dollars for each transfusion. 1.____

2. According to the above paragraph, only medical students and employees of the hospital are selected as blood donors. 2.____

3. According to the above paragraph, the "Request for Blood Transfusion" form is filled out by the patient and sent to the Medical Director's Office. 3.____

4. According to the above paragraph, a list of blood donors is maintained in the Medical Director's office. 4.____

5. According to the above paragraph, cases for which the attending physicians recommend blood transfusions are usually emergency cases. 5.____

6. According to the above paragraph, one copy of the "Request for Blood Transfusion" form is kept by the patient and one copy is sent to the Medical Director's office. 6.____

Questions 7-13.

DIRECTIONS: Questions numbered 7 to 13 inclusive are to be answered SOLELY on the basis of the information contained in the following statement and NOT upon any other information you may have.

Before being admitted to a hospital ward, a patient is first interviewed by the Admitting Clerk who records the patient's name, age, sex, race, birthplace, and mother's maiden name. This clerk takes all of the money and valuables that the patient has on his person. A list of the valuables is written on the back of the envelope in which the valuables are afterwards placed. Cash is counted and placed in a separate envelope, and the amount of money and the name of the patient are written on the outside of the envelope. Both envelopes are sealed, fastened together, and placed in a compartment of a safe.

An orderly then escorts the patient to a dressing room where the patient's clothes are removed and placed in a bundle. A tag bearing the patient's name is fastened to the bundle. A list of the contents of the bundle is written on property slips which are made out in triplicate. The information contained on the outside of the envelopes containing the cash and valuables belonging to the patient is also copied on the property slips.

7. According to the above paragraph, patients are escorted to the dressing room by the Admitting Clerk. 7.____

8. According to the above paragraph, the patient's cash and valuables are placed together in one envelope. 8.____

9. According to the above paragraph, the number of identical property slips that are made out when a patient is being admitted to a hospital ward is three. 9.____

10. According to the above paragraph, the full names of both parents of a patient are recorded by the Admitting Clerk before a patient is admitted to a hospital ward. 10.____

11. According to the above paragraph, the amount of money that a patient has on his person when admitted to the hospital is entered on the patient's property slips. 11.____

12. According to the above paragraph, an orderly takes all the money and valuables that a patient has on his person. 12.____

13. According to the above paragraph, the patient's name is placed on the tag that is attached to the bundle containing the patient's clothing. 13.____

Questions 14-28.

DIRECTIONS: Each of Questions numbered 14 to 28 inclusive consists of a sentence. Some of these sentences contain errors in grammar or word usage; others are correct as they stand. If a sentence is correct as it stands, you are to print the letter "C" (Correct) in your answer space on the right; if a sentence contains an error in grammar or word usage, you are to print the letter "W" (Wrong).

14. The supervisor learned the new clerks their duties. 14.____

15. This report is the better of the two. 15.____

16. He wants you and me to distribute the mail. 16.____

17. She performs her work very careless. 17.____

18. Each of the four patients is talking to a visitor. 18.____

19. The new clerk don't know where to obtain the supplies. 19.____

20. The clerk would not of made the mistake if he had been trained properly. 20.____

21. Please give the report to either the nurse or I. 21.____

22. He begun to work immediately. 22.____

23. The clerk was asked to lay the charts on the nurse's desk. 23.____

24. The visitor was told whom to see regarding his request. 24.____

25. He suggested a more faster method of preparing the reports. 25.____

26. The clerk seen the charts last week. 26.____

27. He can hardly raise his head. 27.____

28. Most of the patients was eating their breakfast. 28.____

Questions 29-45.

DIRECTIONS: Each of Questions numbered 29 to 45 inclusive consists of a single word which is spelled either correctly or incorrectly. If the word is spelled correctly, you are to print the letter "C" (Correct) in your answer space on the right; if the word is spelled incorrectly, you are to print the letter "W "(Wrong).

29. pospone 29.____
30. diffrent 30.____
31. height 31.____
32. carefully 32.____
33. ability 33.____
34. temper 34.____
35. deslike 35.____
36. seldem 36.____
37. alcohol 37.____
38. expense 38.____
39. vegatable 39.____
40. dispensary 40.____
41. specemin 41.____
42. allowance 42.____
43. exersise 43.____
44. artifical 44.____
45. disagreeable 45.____

Questions 46-50.

DIRECTIONS: Each of Questions numbered 46 to 50 inclusive consists of a problem in arithmetic and the answer to the problem. If the answer given is correct, you are to print the letter "C" for Correct in the answer space at the right; if the answer given is incorrect, you are to print the letter "W" for Wrong.

46. If a temperature of 98.6 degrees is normal, then a temperature of 103.2 degrees is 4.6 degrees above normal. 46._____

47. If a hospital with a bed capacity of 2100 beds reports that 87% of its beds are occupied, then the number of beds not occupied is 373. 47._____

48. It takes a hospital clerk 8 minutes to prepare an admission report on one patient. At this rate, it will take the hospital clerk 5 hours and 36 minutes to prepare the admission reports on 42 patients. 48._____

49. Three-fifths of the patients in Hospital X are males. If the total number of patients in Hospital X is 1550, then the number of male patients is 930. 49._____

50. In a certain hospital, requests for laboratory examinations are made out in duplicate on a special laboratory request form. The laboratory request forms are bound in pads, each pad containing 80 forms. If 480 laboratory examinations were requested during the month of November, the number of pads used in November was 6 pads. 50._____

KEY (CORRECT ANSWERS)

1. T	11. T	21. W	31. C	41. W
2. F	12. F	22. W	32. W	42. C
3. F	13. T	23. C	33. C	43. W
4. T	14. W	24. C	34. C	44. W
5. T	15. C	25. W	35. W	45. C
6. F	16. C	26. W	36. W	46. C
7. F	17. W	27. C	37. C	47. W
8. F	18. C	28. W	38. C	48. C
9. T	19. W	29. W	39. W	49. C
0. F	20. W	30. W	40. C	50. W

TEST 3

Questions 1-12.

DIRECTIONS: Questions numbered 1 to 12 inclusive are to be answered *SOLELY* on the basis of the information which is given on the Weekly Patient Action Record shown on the following pages.

This record lists the names of fifty (50) patients who were newly admitted to, transferred into, transferred out of, discharged from, or who died, in four hospital wards during the week of May 4-10.

A key to the abbreviations for these types of actions is shown below the list of patients.

Each of Questions 1 through 12 consists of a statement relating to the information given on the Weekly Patient Action Record shown on the following pages.

You are to decide whether the statement is true or false. Then, in the answer space to the right of the question, you are to print the letter "T" if the statement is true or corect; or print the letter "F" if the statement is false or wrong.

WEEKLY PATIENT ACTION RECORD

Week of: May 4-10

Wards: Gyneoology (Gyn.)
Medical (Med.)
Obstetrical (Obs.)
Surgical (Sur.)

DATE	WARD	PATIENT	ACTION *
May 4	Gyn.	Niles, J.	D
4	Med.	Lewis, N.	N
4	Med.	Wiley, C.	N
4	Med.	Crump, D.	N
4	Sur.	Klein, B.	T I
4	Sur.	Okun, N.	D
May 5	Med.	Braun, M.	TO
5	Med.	Speer, S.	TO
5	Med.	Anson, R.	D
5	Med.	Darby, J.	D
5	Obs.	Pack, W.	N
5	Obs.	Heide, K.	N
5	Sur.	Wills, H.	N
5	Sur.	Amato, D.	N
May 6	Gyn.	Marks, H.	N
6	Med.	Hall, A.	N
6	Med.	Tracy, W.	N
6	Med.	Michel, F.	T I
6	Sur.	Crone, P.	D
May 7	Gyn.	Reid, W.	D
7	Med.	Usher, S.	T I
7	Med.	Dion, C.	T I
7	Med.	Kidd, O.	TO
7	Med.	Bryan, W.	E
7	Sur.	Vance, P.	D

*KEY TO ABBREVIATION OF ACTIONS
  N - Newly admitted
  T I - Transferred into the ward (from another ward)

2 (#3)

TO - Transferred out of ward (to another ward)
D - Discharged from ward (to go home)
E - Died

	7	Sur.	Elder, K.	D
May	8	Gyn.	Lyons, B.	N
	8	Gyn.	Gong, S.	D
	8	Gyn.	Kahn, J.	D
	8	Med.	Pearl, E.	N
	8	Obs.	Bandor, N.	TO
	8	Sur.	Jason, A.	N
	8	Sur.	Sawyer, V.	N
	8	Sur.	Perez, G.	TO
May	9	Gyn.	Gutman, R.	T I
	9	Gyn.	Klein, I.	TO
	9	Med.	Welsh, H.	D
	9	Med.	Cole, F.	D
	9	Med.	Jacobs, K.	E
	9	Obs.	Madden, W.	N
	9	Sur.	Endler, L.	N
	9	Sur.	Lieber, R.	N
	9	Sur.	Ross, T.	D
May	10	Gyn.	Zayas, I.	N
	10	Med.	Smith, A.	N
	10	Med.	Pagan, C.	TO
	10	Obs.	Casey, M.	D
	10	Obs.	Taylor, R.	D
	10	Sur.	Knopf, F.	T I
	10	Sur.	Olsen, O.	E

*KEY TO ABBREVIATION OF ACTIONS
N - Newly admitted
T I - Transferred into the ward (from another ward)
TO - Transferred out of ward (to another ward)
D - Discharged from ward (to go home)
E - Died

1. On May 5, M. Braun was transferred out of the Medical ward. 1.____

2. On May 7, K. Elder was discharged from the Surgical ward. 2.____

3. Three patients were newly admitted to the Medical ward on May 4. 3.____

4. R. Lieber was transferred into the Surgical ward on May 9. 4.____

5. The number of patients who died during this seven-day period was two. 5.____

6. No patients were transferred into the Obstetrical ward during this seven-day period. 6.____

7. There are five (5) patients whose last names begin with the letter K. 7.____

8. More patients were transferred into these four wards than were transferred out of these wards during this week. 8.____

9. During this week, more patients were newly admitted to the Gynecology ward than were discharged from this ward. 9.____

10. More patients were discharged from the four wards on May 5 than were discharged on May 7. 10.____

11. The total number of patients newly admitted to the four wards during this week was nineteen. 11.____

12. During this week, the number of patients transferred out of the Medical ward was the same as the number discharged from this ward. 12.____

Questions 13-30.

DIRECTIONS: Each of questions numbered 13 to 30 inclusive consists of a pair of words which are either the same or opposite in meaning. If the two words of a pair are the same or nearly the same in meaning, you are to print the letter "S" (Same) in the answer space alongside the number of the question; if he words of a pair are opposite or nearly opposite in meaning, you are to print the letter "O" (Opposite).

13. stimulant–sedative 13.____
14. flexible–rigid 14.____
15. detrimental–harmful 15.____
16. incision–cut 16.____
17. antidote–poison 17.____
18. dilute–strengthen 18.____
19. immune–susceptible 19.____
20. expensive–costly 20.____
21. probe–search 21.____
22. retard–delay 22.____
23. relapse–recovery 23.____
24. stagger–totter 24.____
25. exaggerate–minimize 25.____
26. induce–persuade 26.____
27. remuneration–compensation 27.____

28. ominous—favorable	28.____
29. adept—skillful	29.____
30. dissipate—waste	30.____

KEY (CORRECT ANSWERS)

1.	T	11.	T	21.	S
2.	T	12.	T	22.	S
3.	T	13.	O	23.	O
4.	F	14.	O	24.	S
5.	F	15.	S	25.	O
6.	T	16.	S	26.	S
7.	T	17.	O	27.	S
8.	F	18.	O	28.	O
9.	F	19.	O	29.	S
10.	F	20.	S	30.	S

EXAMINATION SECTION
TEST 1

DIRECTIONS: Each question or incomplete statement is followed by several suggested answers or completions. Select the one that BEST answers the question or completes the statement. *PRINT THE LETTER OF THE CORRECT ANSWER IN THE SPACE AT THE RIGHT.*

QUESTIONS 1-25.

Questions 1-25 contain often used medical terms. Choose the lettered choice that is CLOSEST in meaning to the numbered items.

1. BIOPSY:

    A. routine physical
    B. exploratory surgery
    C. examination of living tissues
    D. excision of a tumor

2. CARDIOVASCULAR: relating to

    A. heart and blood vessels
    B. stress tests
    C. circulation in one's extremities
    D. blood supply to the muscles

3. CHOLECYSTECTOMY: excision of the

    A. kidneys   B. gall bladder
    C. pancreas   D. spleen

4. COAGULATION:

    A. thickening   B. dispersion
    C. separation into categories   D. suffocation

5. CONGENITAL:

    A. relating to the reproductive organs
    B. sexually reproductive
    C. normal
    D. from birth

6. DORSAL: relating to

    A. the sides   B. aquatic animals
    C. the back   D. sharks only

7. EDEMA:

    A. cleansing of the digestive tract
    B. fluid in the joints
    C. a skin condition
    D. a food-borne disease

8. EMBOLISM:

   A. shortage of breath
   B. reddening of the skin
   C. deficiency of vitamin E
   D. sudden blockage of a vessel

9. FETUS:

   A. relating to foot disease
   B. physiological reaction to hunger
   C. unborn offspring
   D. infant

10. HEMATURIA:

    A. subdural blood clot
    B. red blood cell count
    C. blood cells in the urine
    D. platelet count

11. HEPATIC: relating to the

    A. liver
    B. blood
    C. skin
    D. leg muscles

12. INCIPIENT:

    A. in the final stages
    B. beginning to become apparent
    C. fatal
    D. intermediary

13. INFRACOSTAL:

    A. behind the lungs
    B. near the spine
    C. above the ribs
    D. below the ribs

14. LAPAROTOMY: surgical section of the

    A. lung
    B. liver
    C. abdominal wall
    D. heart

15. NECROSIS:

    A. obsession with corpses
    B. localized death of living tissue
    C. kidney disease
    D. state of deep depression

16. NEONATAL: relating to

    A. period before birth
    B. gestation
    C. infancy
    D. childhood

17. POSTPARTUM:

    A. after birth
    B. after death
    C. isolated during childhood
    D. quarantined

    17.____

18. RENAL: relating to the

    A. kidneys
    B. colon
    C. adrenal gland
    D. throat

    18.____

19. SARCOID: disease characterized by

    A. a sore throat
    B. a red, itchy rash
    C. growths on the heart
    D. nodules under the skin

    19.____

20. SEPTIC: relating to

    A. poison
    B. sewage
    C. infection
    D. contamination

    20.____

21. SEQUELA:

    A. aftereffect of a disease
    B. follow-up examination
    C. repeat of a surgical procedure
    D. medication after surgery

    21.____

22. TACHYCARDIA:

    A. irregular pulse
    B. infection of the heart
    C. heart attack
    D. rapid heartbeat

    22.____

23. TOXEMIA: a condition associated with

    A. lack of nutrients
    B. toxins in the blood
    C. loss of appetite
    D. ingestion of human wastes

    23.____

24. TRAUMATIC:

    A. fatal
    B. contagions
    C. causing injury to tissue
    D. chronic

    24.____

25. VENTRAL: relating to the

    A. respiratory system
    B. circulatory system
    C. belly
    D. palms of the hands

    25.____

QUESTIONS 26-35.

In questions 26-35, choose the word that is spelled INCORRECTLY.

26. A. angioma B. cereberum 26.___
    C. dorsal D. embolism

27. A. urethra B. peritoneum 27.___
    C. deficiency D. duodinum

28. A. deltoid B. cardiac 28.___
    C. histerectomy D. colon

29. A. syringe B. ovarian 29.___
    C. vitamin D. legament

30. A. mussle B. transfusion 30.___
    C. rickets D. ulna

31. A. tendon B. subcutaneous 31.___
    C. ocipital D. fracture

32. A. metacarpal B. podiatry 32.___
    C. patela D. sprain

33. A. clavicle B. fallopian 33.___
    C. calcium D. pancreis

34. A. hematocrit B. surgicle 34.___
    C. tumor D. paroxysm

35. A. vertebri B. uterus 35.___
    C. hemoglobin D. toxicity

QUESTIONS 36-55.

Questions 36-55 refer to the lists below. List I contains the names of 20 diseases or conditions. List II gives the 17 major subdivisions of the International Statistical Classification of Diseases, Injuries, and Causes of Death. For each of the diseases or conditions given in List I, write in the space provided at the right for the corresponding number, the letter preceding the major subdivision into which the disease or condition properly falls. (The same letter may be used more than once.)

EXAMPLE: x. acute appendicitis. Since this is a disease of the digestive system, the answer should be "i."

LIST I	LIST II	
36. abscess of scalp	A. infective and parasitic diseases	36._____
37. acute poliomyelitis	B. neoplasms	37._____
38. adhesive peritonitis	C. allergic, endocrine system, metabolic and nutritional diseases	38._____
39. aortic stenosis	D. diseases of the blood and blood-forming organs	39._____
40. arteriosclerosis	E. mental, psychoneurotic and personality disorders	40._____
41. burns and trauma due to explosion of stove	F. diseases of the nervous system and sense organs	41._____
42. cerebral hemorrhage	G. diseases of the circulatory system	42._____
43. chronic glomerular nephritis	H. diseases of the respiratory system	43._____
44. hypothyroidism	I. diseases of the digestive system	44._____
45. influenza	J. diseases of the genitourinary system	45._____
46. muscular dystrophy	K. deliveries and complications of pregnancy, childbirth and the puerperium	46._____
47. multiple sclerosis	L. diseases of the skin and cellular tissue	47._____
48. osteomyelitis	M. diseases of the bones and organs of movement	48._____
49. pernicious anemia	N. congenital malformations	49._____
50. postnatal asphyxia	O. certain diseases of early infancy	50._____
51. prolapse of umbilical cord	P. symptoms, senility and ill-defined conditions	51._____
52. pulmonary congestion	Q. accidents, poisonings and violence	52._____
53. rectal cancer		53._____
54. syphilis		54._____
55. ulcerative colitis		55._____

KEY (CORRECT ANSWERS)

1.	C	16.	C	31.	C	46.	N
2.	A	17.	A	32.	C	47.	F
3.	B	18.	A	33.	D	48.	M
4.	A	19.	D	34.	B	49.	D
5.	D	20.	C	35.	A	50.	O
6.	C	21.	A	36.	L	51.	K
7.	B	22.	D	37.	F	52.	H
8.	D	23.	B	38.	L	53.	I
9.	C	24.	C	39.	G	54.	J
10.	C	25.	C	40.	G	55.	I
11.	A	26.	B	41.	G		
12.	B	27.	D	42.	F		
13.	D	28.	C	43.	J		
14.	C	29.	D	44.	C		
15.	B	30.	A	45.	A		

TEST 2

DIRECTIONS: Each question or incomplete statement is followed by several suggested answers or completions. Select the one that BEST answers the question or completes the statement. *PRINT THE LETTER OF THE CORRECT ANSWER IN THE SPACE AT THE RIGHT.*

QUESTIONS 1-5.

Questions 1-5 are to be answered *solely* on the basis of the following paragraphs.

"No person shall disinter a coffin or casket containing human remains unless a disinterment permit has been issued by the Department of Health, except when the disinterment is ordered by the Office of the Chief Medical Examiner. Application for a disinterment permit shall be submitted at the office of the Department of Health in the borough in which the remains are buried. The application shall be accompanied by an affidavit from the next of kin or other authorized person."

No person shall remove human remains from the place of death unless a removal permit has been issued by the Department of Health or authorization to remove has been granted by telephone. A removal permit or telephone authorization to remove does not authorize burial or cremation. Human remains shall not be brought into the City unless a permit for their transportation or burial has been issued by the authorized agency of the municipality or -county within the United States within whose jurisdiction death occurred. A burial permit issued by such agency which specifies the cemetery in which burial is to take place shall be accepted for burial in New York City. If, however, such permit specifies no cemetery or a cemetery other than the one intended for burial then application for a permit must be made to the Department of Health. No permit to cremate shall be issued unless the application is accompanied by an affidavit from the next of kin or other authorized person, and unless the application is approved by the Office of the Chief Medical Examiner.

On the basis of the information given above, determine which of the following statements are TRUE and which are FALSE. Indicate your answer by using (T) for TRUE and (F) for FALSE.

1. A body now buried in Brooklyn is to be reburied in Queens. A permit to disinter must be obtained from the Queens office of the Department of Health.   1.____

2. The Office of the Chief Medical Examiner must approve an application to disinter a body.   2.____

3. A person who has died in Manhattan is to be buried in Staten Island. The Department of Health may give permission by telephone to have the body taken to Staten Island and buried there.   3.____

4. A permit is sought to cremate a dead body. Even though the Office of the Chief Medical Examiner agrees to the cremation, the next of kin or other authorized person must submit an affidavit.   4.____

5. A woman calls and tells the medical clerk that her cousin just died in Columbus, Ohio. She wants the body buried in Brooklyn, New York. The medical clerk should tell her that a burial permit must be obtained from the Brooklyn office of the Department of Health.   5.____

QUESTIONS 6-12.

Questions 6-12 refer to the following code tables which are to be used for classifying cases of death.

TABLE I	
Code	Sex
X	Male
Y	Female

TABLE II	
Code	Age
01	Under 1 year
02	1-10 years
03	11-20 years
04	21-30 years
05	31-40 years
06	41-50 years
07	51-60 years
08	Over 60 years

TABLE III	
Code	Cause of Death
10	Heart Disease
20	Poliomyelitis
30	Cancer
40	Meningitis
50	Accident
60	Other

TABLE IV	
Code	Borough Where Person Died
1	Manhattan
2	Brooklyn
3	Bronx
4	Queens
5	Richmond

TABLE V	
Code	Present Occupation
101	Professional
102	Office Worker
103	Skilled Worker
104	Unskilled Worker
105	Housewife
106	Student
107	Other

TABLE VI	
Code	Marital Status
a	Single
b	Married
c	Divorced
d	Widowed

Below are 7 cases of death which are to be classified. In accordance with the code tables given above, assign the proper code number to each case. The codes are to be arranged from left to right, in the order indicated by the numbers of the six code tables. <u>EXAMPLE</u>: A 3-year-old girl died in Richmond of meningitis. Her code number is: Y-02-40-5-107-a.

6. A 12-year-old high school boy died in the Bronx of injuries sustained in a traffic collision. 6.____

7. A 53-year-old clerk, divorced, died of a heart attack while shoveling snow in front of his home in Queens. 7.____

8. A 70-year-old widow, a housewife, died of cancer in a Queens hospital after a short stay. 8.____

9. A 37-year-old married porter died of pneumonia in his home in Brooklyn. 9.____

10. A 24-year-old lawyer, divorced from her husband, died in Manhattan of poliomyelitis. 10.____

11. A 4-month-old infant girl died in a Richmond hospital of a malformed kidney. 11.____

12. A 47-year-old machinist, married, died in the Bronx of injuries resulting from a fall at his place of employment. 12.____

QUESTIONS 13-22.

Questions 13-22 are to be answered based on the rules of filing. Column I containing the numbers 13-22, lists the names of 10 death certificates which are to be filed. Column II contains the heading of file drawers into which you are to file the certificates. For each number 13-22, choose the correct lettered file drawer and indicate said letter in the space at the right.

EXAMPLE: Eileen Sacks. The certificate of Eileen Sacks shouldbe filed in drawer headed Sa - Scl. The answer, therefore, would be A.

Column I

13. Donald Spiller
14. Stuart Simon
15. Sidney Schofield
16. Mark Stetner
17. Nelson Sklar
18. Daisy Saunders
19. Peter Sharpman
20. Arnold Snyder
21. Nathan Sentner
22. Marion Stoup

Column II

A. Drawer 1. Sa - Scl
B. Drawer 2. Sco - Ses
C. Drawer 3. Set - Sik
D. Drawer 4. Sil - Sni
E. Drawer 5. Sno - Suc

QUESTIONS 23-30.

In questions 23-30, choose the letter that corresponds to the correct answer.

23. Assume that total deaths in one year amounted to 80,000. If heart disease accounted for 44% of these deaths, how many people died of all other causes?

 A. 35,200   B. 79,000   C. 44,800   D. 80,000

24. Assume that, of 885 people who died of hepatitis during a given year, 1/3 died between January 1 and May 31. What was the average number of deaths per month between January and May?

 A. 59   B. 295   C. 147   D. 49

25. Of 1200 deaths from diabetes in one year, 1/4 were in Manhattan and 1/6 in the Bronx. Of the remaining number, 2/5 were in Brooklyn. How many deaths from diabetes occurred in Brooklyn?

 A. 200   B. 300   C. 280   D. 500

26. Assume that in one year there were 840 deaths from all causes among a given age group. If 247 people died as a result of accidents and 73 died as a result of homicides, what percentage of people in this group died as a result of accidents and homicides (taken together)?

    A. 29 B. 38 C. 73 D. 84

27. Assume that in 2000, deaths from tuberculosis were 1400 and deaths from diabetes were 1260. If in 2001 deaths from tuberculosis declined to 1120, and deaths from diabetes declined at the same rate, how many deaths from diabetes occurred in 2001?

    A. 1008 B. 1120 C. 1260 D. 1400

28. In a given year, the number of deaths from enteritis, duodenitis and colitis totalled 280. The following year, deaths from enteritis remained the same and deaths from duodenitis increased; total deaths from the 3 causes was 250. Did deaths from colitis increase, decrease, or remain the same?

    A. Increased
    B. Decreased
    C. Remained the same
    D. Cannot be determined

29. Assume that 200 men and 100 women died of influenza in one year. If the next year the total number of such deaths remained the same, but 25% fewer died of influenza, how many women died of influenza?

    A. 100 B. 110 C. 125 D. 150

30. Assume that in one year, in the 45 to 64 year age group, 17,000 men and 10,000 women died. Of this number, 23% of the men and 35% of the women died of malignant neoplasms. In the 65 year and over age group, 25,000 men and 23,000 women died. Of this number, 19% of the men and 16% of the women died of malignant neoplasms.
    Of these 4 groups of people, which had the largest number of deaths from malignant neoplasms?

    A. Men, 45-64 years
    B. Women, 45-64 years
    C. Men, 65 and over
    D. Women, 65 and over

5 (#2)

KEY (CORRECT ANSWERS)

1. F
2. F
3. T
4. T
5. F

6. X-03-50-3-106-a
7. X-07-10-4-102-c
8. Y-08-30-4-105-d
9. X-05-60-2-104-b
10. Y-04-20-1-101-c

11. Y-01-60-5-107-a
12. X-06-50-3-103-b
13. E
14. D
15. A

16. E
17. D
18. A
19. C
20. E

21. B
22. E
23. C
24. A
25. C

26. B
27. A
28. B
29. D
30. C

EXAMINATION SECTION
TEST 1

DIRECTIONS: Each question or incomplete statement is followed by several suggested answers or completions. Select the one that BEST answers the question or completes the statement. *PRINT THE LETTER OF THE CORRECT ANSWER IN THE SPACE AT THE RIGHT.*

1. Assume that you are working in an admitting office near the main entrance of a hospital. Visitors often come into your office to ask questions about hospital procedures and your supervisor has told you to be as helpful as possible in these situations.
   If a visitor comes in and asks you some questions about hospital procedures in a loud and emotional voice, the BEST course of action for you to take would be to

   A. ask him to leave the hospital and come back when he can control himself
   B. ask him to write the questions on a sheet of paper
   C. remain calm and try to answer his questions
   D. tell him to calm down or you will not answer any questions

   1.____

2. A certain hospital office administers a community health program in which members of the public are enrolled. There has been a recent change of procedure in the program and the office expects to receive a large number of letters from those enrolled asking about the change.
   Of the following, the MOST appropriate method of answering these letters is to

   A. invite each person who sends in a letter to come to the office so that the change can be explained in a personal interview
   B. prepare a form letter which explains the change of procedure and send a copy to each person who sends in a letter
   C. stamp the notation *Procedure Changed/Please Comply* on each letter and mail it back to the sender together with a description of the change of procedure
   D. telephone each person who sends in a letter and explain the change of procedure

   2.____

3. Assume that you work in a business office of a hospital and your supervisor gives you an assignment to be completed in one week. Part of the assignment requires you to obtain information from the various departments of the hospital. All departments have cooperated in giving you the required information, except one. Despite your repeated attempts to secure the information, it is still missing the day before your assignment is scheduled for completion. Even if you received the missing information immediately, you could not complete the assignment on time.
   Of the following, the FIRST action you should take in this situation is to

   A. advise your supervisor that you were not given enough time to complete the assignment
   B. contact the department which has the information you need and tell them that their failure to cooperate has made it impossible for you to complete your assignment on time
   C. explain to your supervisor why you cannot complete the assignment on time and ask him if he wishes to receive what you will be able to finish
   D. tell your supervisor that you will try to finish the assignment whenever the information is forthcoming

   3.____

4. Suppose that you work in a hospital office and you are speaking on the telephone with another employee on hospital business. While you are speaking on the telephone, a co-worker enters the office and indicates that she would like to speak with you.
   Of the following, the BEST course of action for you to take in this situation is to

   A. excuse yourself on the telephone and ask your co-worker to wait until you are finished with the call
   B. ignore your co-worker and continue your telephone conversation
   C. immediately end your telephone conversation and tell your co-worker not to interrupt you again when you are speaking on the telephone
   D. tell the employee on the telephone that you have to speak with someone else and will call back as soon as you are finished

5. Assume that you are in charge of the petty cash fund for your office. When an individual wants to be paid back for an expense, he must complete a receipt explaining the expense and sign the receipt when you give him the money. One day, a clerk in your office tells you that she has just returned after delivering a package and wants to be paid back immediately for the carfare she spent. The clerk says that she has a lot of work to do in the next few hours and will complete the receipt later in the day. The BEST course of action for you to take in this situation is to

   A. explain to her that in order to receive the money she must complete and sign the receipt
   B. give her the money and leave a note on her desk reminding her to complete and sign the receipt
   C. give her the money and leave a note for yourself to make sure that she completes and signs the receipt
   D. tell her that you will give her the money and that you will complete the receipt yourself

6. Suppose that you have recently been assigned to an office and that one of your tasks is to keep files in proper order. You observe that some of your co-workers remove folders from the files, with no indication of removal. These actions have made it difficult for you to locate the folders when you need them.
   Of the following, the MOST desirable method of correcting this situation is to

   A. make photocopies of the materials in all the folders and organize a duplicate set of files so that you will always have the folders readily available
   B. make sure that there are enough out-guides available and that everyone in the office is instructed to use them whenever a folder is removed
   C. tell your co-workers that they can use the files only after they tell you what folders they are going to remove
   D. ask your co-workers to leave a note on your desk whenever anyone removes a folder from the files

7. Of the following, the LEAST desirable action to take when writing out a check to a person is to

   A. fill out the check in pencil
   B. date the check
   C. number the check
   D. write the person's full name

Questions 8-17.

DIRECTIONS: Questions 8 through 17 each show in Column I names written on four cards (lettered w, x, y, z) which have to be filed. You are to choose the option (lettered A, B, C, or D) in Column II which BEST represents the proper order of filing according to the rules and sample question given below. The cards are to be filed according to the following Rules for Alphabetical Filing.

RULES FOR ALPHABETICAL FILING

1. The names of individuals are filed in strict alphabetical order, first according to the last name, then according to first name or initial, and finally according to middle name or initial. For example: George Allen precedes Edward Bell; Leonard Reston precedes Lucille Reston.

2. When last names are the same, for example, A. Green and Agnes Green, the one with the initial comes before the one with the name written out when the first initials are identical.

3. When first and last names are the same, a name without a middle initial comes before one with a middle initial. For example: Ralph Simon comes before both Ralph A. Simon and Ralph Adam Simon.

4. When first and last names are the same, a name with a middle initial comes before one with a middle name beginning with the same initial. For example: Sam P. Rogers comes before Sam Paul Rogers.

5. Prefixes such as De, O', Mac, Mc, and Van are filed as written and are treated as part of the names to which they are connected. For example: Gladys McTeaque is filed before Frances Meadows.

6. Titles and designations such as Dr., Mr., and Prof, are ignored in filing.

SAMPLE QUESTION

COLUMN I

w. Jane Earl
x. James A. Earle
y. James Earl
z. J. Earle

COLUMN II

A. w, y, z, x
B. y, w, z, x
C. x, y, w, z
D. x, w, y, z

The correct way to file the cards is:

y. James Earl
w. Jane Earl
z. J. Earle
x. James A. Earle

The correct filing order is shown by the letters y, w, z, x (in that order). Since, in Column II, B appears in front of the letters y, w, z, x (in that order), B is the correct answer to the sample question.

Now answer Questions 8 through 17 using the same procedure.

4 (#1)

		COLUMN I		COLUMN II	
8.	w.	John Smith	A.	w, x, y, z	8.____
	x.	Joan Smythe	B.	y, z, x, w	
	y.	Gerald Schmidt	C.	y, z, w, x	
	z.	Gary Schmitt	D.	z, y, w, x	
9.	w.	A. Black	A.	w, x, y, z	9.____
	x.	Alan S. Black	B.	w, y, x, z	
	y.	Allan Black	C.	w, y, z, x	
	z.	Allen A. Black	D.	x, w, y, z	
10.	w.	Samuel Haynes	A.	w, x, y, z	10.____
	x.	Sam C. Haynes	B.	x, w, z, y	
	y.	David Haynes	C.	y, z, w, x	
	z.	Dave L. Haynes	D.	z, y, x, w	
11.	w.	Lisa B. McNeil	A.	x, y, w, z	11.____
	x.	Tom MacNeal	B.	x, z, y, w	
	y.	Lisa McNeil	C.	y, w, z, x	
	z.	Lorainne McNeal	D.	z, x, y, w	
12.	w.	Larry Richardson	A.	w, y, x, z	12.____
	x.	Leroy Richards	B.	y, x, z, w	
	y.	Larry S. Richards	C.	y, z, x, w	
	z.	Leroy C. Richards	D.	x, w, z, y	
13.	w.	Arlene Lane	A.	w, z, y, x	13.____
	x.	Arlene Cora Lane	B.	w, z, x, y	
	y.	Arlene Clair Lane	C.	y, x, z, w	
	z.	Arlene C. Lane	D.	z, y, w, x	
14.	w.	Betty Fish	A.	w, x, z, y	14.____
	x.	Prof. Ann Fish	B.	x, w, y, z	
	y.	Norma Fisch	C.	y, z, x, w	
	z.	Dr. Richard Fisch	D.	z, y, w, x	
15.	w.	Dr. Anthony David Lukak	A.	w, y, z, x	15.____
	x.	Mr. Steven Charles Lucas	B.	x, z, w, y	
	y.	Mr. Anthony J. Lukak	C.	z, x, y, w	
	z.	Prof. Steven C. Lucas	D.	z, x, w, y	
16.	w.	Martha Y. Lind	A.	w, y, z, x	16.____
	x.	Mary Beth Linden	B.	w, y, x, z	
	y.	Martha W. Lind	C.	y, w, z, x	
	z.	Mary Bertha Linden	D.	y, w, x, z	
17.	w.	Prof. Harry Michael MacPhelps	A.	w, z, x, y	17.____
	x.	Mr. Horace M. MacPherson	B.	w, y, z, x	
	y.	Mr. Harold M. McPhelps	C.	z, x, w, y	
	z.	Prof. Henry Martin MacPherson	D.	x, z, y, w	

18. Assume that one of your duties is to make sure that the office supply cabinet contains sufficient quantities of the forms used in your office.
    Of the following, the BEST course of action for you to adopt in order to be able to perform this duty is to

    A. ask your supervisor each day whether the office is low on any form and plan to order only those forms which are mentioned
    B. decide what kind of duplicating equipment will be needed to produce copies of the forms when the current supply is exhausted
    C. plan for your office's needs and order copies of the forms before the number of copies in the cabinet falls below a minimum amount
    D. wait until one of your co-workers tells you that the office is running short of a form and then obtain copies of it as quickly as possible

19. The type of file in which reports are found under the heading *New York State-Queens* is MOST likely to be a _____ file.

    A. chronological   B. geographic
    C. numeric   D. tickler

20. Assume that you are working in the personnel office of a hospital. One day, you answer a telephone call and the caller asks to speak to one of your co-workers, Ms. Wilson, who is on sick leave. You explain this to the caller who then tells you that she is a friend of Ms. Wilson's and would like to invite her to a party but has lost Ms. Wilson's home address and telephone number. The caller then asks you if you can give her this information.
    Of the following, the BEST course of action for you to take then is to

    A. give the caller the information and then leave Ms. Wilson a message about the telephone call
    B. decline to give the caller the information and ask the caller if she wants to leave a message for Ms. Wilson
    C. tell the caller that all information about hospital employees is confidential and that you cannot spend any more time on a personal telephone call
    D. tell the caller that you need some time to look up the information and ask her to call back later in the day

KEY (CORRECT ANSWERS)

1.	C	11.	B
2.	B	12.	B
3.	C	13.	A
4.	A	14.	C
5.	A	15.	D
6.	B	16.	C
7.	A	17.	A
8.	C	18.	C
9.	A	19.	B
10.	D	20.	B

TEST 2

DIRECTIONS: Each question or incomplete statement is followed by several suggested answers or completions. Select the one that BEST answers the question or completes the statement. *PRINT THE LETTER OF THE CORRECT ANSWER IN THE SPACE AT THE RIGHT.*

1. Suppose that you answer a telephone call and a woman asks to speak with your supervisor. Your supervisor, however, is speaking with someone on another telephone line. Of the following, the BEST course of action for you to take in this situation is to

    A. ask the caller for her name and telephone number and tell her that your supervisor will return the call as soon as possible
    B. ask the caller to call again later in the day because your supervisor is busy right now
    C. explain to the caller why your supervisor cannot answer the call and ask her to wait until your supervisor can speak with her
    D. tell the caller that your supervisor is speaking on another line and ask her if she wants to wait until that call is finished or wants to leave a message

    1.____

2. One morning, you receive a telephone call and the caller requests an appointment with your supervisor. Your supervisor is out of the office for the day. You tell the caller that she can meet with your supervisor at 10 A.M. the next day and she agrees. After ending this telephone conversation, you discover that your supervisor already has scheduled an appointment with someone else for that time.
   Of the following, the BEST course of action for you to take in this situation is to

    A. contact your supervisor and find out which appointment he would rather keep
    B. decide which appointment is less important and cancel it
    C. try to change the appointment you made for the caller to another time
    D. wait until the next day and then tell your supervisor that he has a choice of two appointments scheduled at 10 A.M.

    2.____

3. Assume that your supervisor has asked you to go to the stockroom to pick up supplies that your office has ordered. Of the following, the FIRST action you should take when you are given the supplies is to

    A. bring the supplies back to your office immediately
    B. call your supervisor to find out whether any other supplies are needed
    C. check to see whether you have received everything that was ordered
    D. sign a receipt for the supplies

    3.____

Questions 4-8.

DIRECTIONS: In each of Questions 4 through 8, there is a sentence containing one underlined word. Choose the word (lettered A, B, C, or D) which means MOST NEARLY the same as the underlined word as it is used in the sentence.

4. The number of applicants exceeded the anticipated figure.

    A. expected   B. required   C. revised   D. necessary

    4.____

5. The clerk was told to collate the pages of the report.

    A. destroy   B. edit   C. correct   D. assemble

    5.____

35

6. Mr. Wells is not authorized to release the information.

   A. inclined   B. pleased   C. permitted   D. trained

7. The secretary chose an appropriate office for the meeting.

   A. empty   B. decorated   C. nearby   D. suitable

8. The employee performs a complex set of tasks each day.

   A. difficult   B. important   C. pleasant   D. large

9. Of the following, the MOST important purpose of a filing system generally is to

   A. reduce the number of records which must be readily available
   B. make it possible to locate information quickly
   C. organize material under the fewest number of headings
   D. provide a secure storage place if an unexpected emergency occurs

10. Assume that you answer a telephone call and the caller wishes to speak to one of your co-workers, who is out of the office.
    Of the following, the LEAST appropriate information for you to indicate on a message which you leave for your co-worker is

    A. the caller's telephone number and extension
    B. the date and time the call was received
    C. the office telephone on which the call was received
    D. your name or initials

11. The notation *cc: Mr. Rogers* appearing at the bottom of a letter is MOST likely to indicate that Mr. Rogers

    A. typed the letter
    B. is the subject of the letter
    C. wrote the rough draft of the letter for his supervisor
    D. is to receive a copy of the letter

Questions 12-16.

DIRECTIONS: Questions 12 through 16 are to be answered ONLY on the basis of the information provided in the following passage.

For some office workers, it is useful to be familiar with the four main classes of domestic mail; for others, it is essential. Each class has a different rate of postage and some have requirements concerning wrapping, sealing or special information to be placed on the package. First class mail, the class which may not be opened for postal inspection, includes letters, postcards, business reply cards, and other kinds of written matter. There are different rates for some of the kinds of cards which can be sent by first class mail. The maximum weight for an item sent by first class mail is 70 pounds. An item which is not letter size should be marked *First Class* on all sides.

Although office workers most often come into contact with first class mail, they may find it helpful to know something about the other classes. Second class mail is generally used for mailing newspapers and magazines. Publishers of these articles must meet certain U.S. Postal Service requirements in order to obtain a permit to use second class mailing rates. Third class mail, which must weigh less than 1 pound, includes printed materials and merchandise parcels. There are two rate structures for this class, a single piece rate and a bulk rate. Fourth class mail, also known as parcel post, includes packages weighing from one to 40 pounds. For more information about these classes of mail and the actual mailing rates, contact your local post office.

12. According to this passage, first class mail is the only class which

    A. has a limit on the maximum weight of an item
    B. has different rates for items within the class
    C. may not be opened for postal inspection
    D. should be used by office workers

13. According to this passage, the one of the following items which may correctly be sent by fourth class mail is a

    A. magazine weighing one-half pound
    B. package weighing one-half pound
    C. package weighing two pounds
    D. postcard

14. According to this passage, there are different postage rates for

    A. a newspaper sent by second class mail and a magazine sent by second class mail
    B. each of the classes of mail
    C. each pound of fourth class mail
    D. printed material sent by third class mail and merchandise parcels sent by third class mail

15. In order to send a newspaper by second class mail, a publisher must

    A. have met certain postal requirements and obtained a permit
    B. indicate whether he wants to use the single piece or the bulk rate
    C. make certain that the newspaper weighs less than one pound
    D. mark the newspaper *Second Class* on the top and bottom of the wrapper

16. Of the following types of information, the one which is NOT mentioned in the passage is the

    A. class of mail to which parcel post belongs
    B. kinds of items which can be sent by each class of mail
    C. maximum weight for an item sent by fourth class mail
    D. postage rate for each of the four classes of mail

17. Assume that one of your tasks is to complete a form indicating which laboratory test a doctor is ordering.
A doctor has written an order for a laboratory test, but his writing is illegible, and you cannot tell which of two tests he is ordering.
Of the following, the BEST course of action for you to take in this situation is to

A. show the doctor his written order, ask the doctor which test he meant to order, and then fill out the form
B. indicate both tests on the form so that you will be certain that the correct test is performed
C. send the doctor's written order to the laboratory without indicating on the form which test is to be done, since the laboratory technician will know from experience which test the doctor meant to order
D. wait for the doctor to reorder the test when he finds out that it has not been done

18. Suppose that one of your tasks is to mail an application form and covering letter to each applicant for a program administered by your office.
Of the following, the MOST appropriate notation to use at the bottom of the letter to indicate that the form is included in the envelope is

    A. Enc.   B. etc.   C. P.S.   D. R.S.V.P.

18.____

19. Of the following, the LEAST appropriate practice involved in the proper use of a file cabinet and its contents is to

    A. close a cabinet drawer immediately after using it
    B. place active files in top drawers and less active files in bottom drawers
    C. remove a file folder by holding the side of the folder, not the tab
    D. store office supplies behind files in unfilled cabinet drawers

19.____

20. Assume that you are sending out a business letter and have to write *Attention: Mrs. Williams* on the envelope. Of the following, the PROPER place on the envelope for you to write this notation is the _____ of the envelope.

    A. upper right corner of the back
    B. upper right corner on the front
    C. lower left corner of the back
    D. lower left corner on the front

20.____

KEY (CORRECT ANSWERS)

1.	D	11.	D
2.	C	12.	C
3.	C	13.	C
4.	A	14.	B
5.	D	15.	A
6.	C	16.	D
7.	D	17.	A
8.	A	18.	A
9.	B	19.	D
10.	C	20.	D

TEST 3

DIRECTIONS: Each question or incomplete statement is followed by several suggested answers or completions. Select the one that BEST answers the question or completes the statement. *PRINT THE LETTER OF THE CORRECT ANSWER IN THE SPACE AT THE RIGHT.*

1. Which of the following is the MOST efficient method of reproducing 50 copies of a single-page form letter?   1.____

    A. Carbon copying
    B. Scanning and re-editing
    C. Word processing
    D. Photocopying

2. Removing inactive documents from the active files and transferring them to a records storage center is important for which of the following reasons?   2.____

    A. The active records can be filed and retrieved more quickly.
    B. The inactive files will no longer be needed.
    C. No control is necessary with respect to the inactive files.
    D. It allows you to know which documents must be filed and which need not be filed.

3. You are trying to obtain information from someone who is to be admitted to a hospital. The person tells you in an angry tone of voice that he will not give you a certain item of information. You need this information to complete the admission form.   3.____
Of the following, the FIRST action which you should take in this situation is to

    A. tell him that he will not be admitted unless he gives you the information
    B. tell him to wait while you go asks your supervisor to get the information from the person
    C. leave out that item of information but clearly show your anger so he will not act that way again
    D. tell him the reason why you need that item of information

4. Assume that you work in a hospital office which often receives telephone calls from people requesting information about patients in the hospital. One day, you receive a telephone call from a person who says that he is the brother of a patient. The caller asks you what is wrong with the patient and how long he will remain in the hospital.   4.____
Of the following, the BEST course of action for you to take in this situation is to

    A. check the patient's hospital records to make sure the patient has a brother and then give the caller the information he requested
    B. contact the patient's doctor to get the information and then give it to the caller
    C. inform the caller that you are not permitted to give out that information and refer him to the patient's doctor
    D. tell the caller that you will have to check the hospital records to get the information and ask the caller for his telephone number so that you can call him back

Questions 5-14.

DIRECTIONS: Questions 5 through 14 are based on the following table, which shows the number of persons admitted to and discharged from each of five hospitals for each of the first six months of 2005. Admissions are shown under the columns labeled *ADM* and discharges under the columns labeled *DIS*.

ADMISSIONS AND DISCHARGES
January-June, 2005

MONTH	HOSPITAL L		HOSPITAL M		HOSPITAL N		HOSPITAL O		HOSPITAL P	
	ADM	DIS	ADM	DIS	ADM	DIS	ADM	DIS	ADM	DIS
JAN.	367	291	389	372	738	694	1101	942	1567	1373
FEB.	447	473	411	376	874	841	1353	1296	1754	1687
MAR.	426	437	403	436	831	813	1297	1358	1690	1740
APR.	403	390	370	385	794	850	1057	1190	1389	1650
MAY	370	411	361	390	680	692	984	1039	1195	1210
JUNE	334	355	377	384	630	619	1121	1043	1125	1065

5. The TOTAL number of admissions to the five hospitals for the month of April was

   A. 3,833	B. 3,952	C. 3,983	D. 4,013

6. The TOTAL number of discharges from Hospital N for the months of April, May, and June was

   A. 1,159	B. 2,104	C. 2,161	D. 2,251

7. The TOTAL number of admissions to Hospitals L, M, and O for the month of February was

   A. 1,732	B. 2,101	C. 2,145	D. 2,211

8. The TOTAL number of discharges from the five hospitals for the month of January was

   A. 3,542	B. 3,672	C. 3,832	D. 4,162

9. For which month were there MORE discharges at each of the five hospitals than there were admissions?

   A. January	B. March	C. May	D. June

10. The average number of admissions each month at Hospital O for the first six months of 2005 was MOST NEARLY

    A. 1,097	B. 1,152	C. 1,163	D. 1,196

11. Of the total number of admissions at the five hospitals for the month of March, what percentage, to the nearest whole percent, was admitted to Hospital P?

    A. 29%	B. 32%	C. 34%	D. 36%

12. The average number of discharges from each of the five hospitals for the month of May was MOST NEARLY

    A. 748	B. 754	C. 762	D. 764

13. Of the total number of admissions to the five hospitals for the month of June, what percentage, to the nearest whole percent, was admitted to Hospital M?

    A. 7%	B. 9%	C. 11%	D. 13%

14. On the basis of the information given in the table, which one of the following statements is CORRECT?
    The number of

    A. admissions to each hospital for the month of April was less than the number of admissions for the month of March
    B. admissions to Hospital L increased each month from January through April and decreased each month from May through June
    C. discharges from each hospital for the month of June was less than the number of discharges for the month of May
    D. discharges from Hospital O increased each month from January through March and decreased each month from April through June

14._____

Questions 15-20.

DIRECTIONS: Questions 15 through 20 consist of three lines of code letters and numbers. The numbers on each line should correspond with the code letters on the same line in accordance with the table below.

Code Letter	F	X	L	M	R	W	T	S	B	H
Corresponding Number	0	1	2	3	4	5	6	7	8	9

On some of the lines, an error exists in the coding. Compare the letters and numbers in each question carefully. If you find an error or errors on
  only one of the lines in the question, mark your answer A;
  any two lines in the question, mark your answer B;
  all three lines in the question, mark your answer C;
  none of the lines in the question, mark your answer D.

SAMPLE QUESTION: LTSXHMF   2671930
                   TBRWHLM   6845913
                   SXLBFMR   5128034

In the above sample, the first line is correct since each code letter listed has the correct corresponding number. On the second line, an error exists because code letter L should have the number 2 instead of the number 1. On the third line, an error exists because the code letter S should have the number 7 instead of the number 5. Since there are errors on two of the three lines, the correct answer is B.

15. XMWBHLR   1358924
    FWSLRHX   0572491
    MTXBLTS   3618267

15._____

16. XTLSMRF   1627340
    BMHRFLT   8394026
    HLTSWRX   9267451

16._____

17. LMBSFXS   2387016   17. ____
    RWLHBSX   4532871
    SMFXBHW   7301894

18. RSTWTSML   47657632   18. ____
    LXRMHFBS   21439087
    FTLBMRWX   06273451

19. XSRSBWFM   17478603   19. ____
    BRMXRMXT   84314216
    XSTFBWRL   17609542

20. TMSBXHLS   63781927   20. ____
    RBSFLFWM   48702053
    MHFXWTRS   39015647

KEY (CORRECT ANSWERS)

1. D   11. D
2. A   12. A
3. D   13. C
4. C   14. A
5. D   15. D

6. C   16. A
7. D   17. C
8. B   18. B
9. C   19. C
10. B   20. D

EXAMINATION SECTION
TEST 1

DIRECTIONS: Each question or incomplete statement is followed by several suggested answers or completions. Select the one that BEST answers the question or completes the statement. *PRINT THE LETTER OF THE CORRECT ANSWER IN THE SPACE AT THE RIGHT.*

1. According to one suggested filing system, no more than 12 folders should be filed behind any one file guide and from 10 to 20 file guides should be used in each file drawer. Based on this filing system, the MAXIMUM number of folders that a four-drawer file cabinet can hold is

    A. 240	B. 480	C. 960	D. 1200

    1.____

2. A certain office uses three different forms. Last year it used 3500 copies of Form L, 6700 copies of Form M, and 10,500 copies of Form P. This year, the office expects to decrease the use of each of these forms by 5%.
    The TOTAL number of these three forms which the office expects to use this year is

    A. 10,350	B. 16,560	C. 19,665	D. 21,735

    2.____

3. The hourly rate of pay for a certain part-time employee is computed by dividing his yearly salary rate by the number of hours in the work year. The employee's yearly salary rate is $18,928, and there are 1,820 hours in the work year.
    If this employee works 18 hours during one week, his TOTAL earnings for these 18 hours are

    A. $180.00	B. $183.60	C. $187.20	D. $190.80

    3.____

4. Assume that the regular work week of an employee is 35 hours and that the employee is paid for any extra hours worked according to the following schedule. For hours worked in excess of 35 hours, up to and including 40 hours, the employee receives his regular hourly rate of pay. For hours worked in excess of 40 hours, the employee receives 1 1/2 times his hourly rate of pay.
    If the employee's hourly rate of pay is $11.20 and he works 43 hours during a certain week, his TOTAL pay for the week would be

    A. $481.60	B. $498.40	C. $556.00	D. $722.40

    4.____

5. The following table shows the total amount of money owed on the bills sent to each of four different accounts and the total amount of money which has been received from each of these accounts.

Name of Account	Amount Owed	Amount Received
Arnold	$55,989	$37,898
Barry	$97,276	$79,457
Carter	$62,736	$47,769
Daley	$77,463	$59,534

    The balance of an account is determined by subtracting the amount received from the amount owed. Based on this method of determining a balance, the account with the LARGEST balance is

    A. Arnold	B. Barry	C. Carter	D. Daley

    5.____

6. Suppose that you are transferring the charges of a number of hospital patients from each patient's individual records to one form.
   To make sure that the amounts are transferred accurately, it would be BEST for you to

   A. check each amount copies against the appropriate patient's records after completing the transfers
   B. have someone read the amounts from the patient records while you write them on the form
   C. copy the amounts slowly and carefully so that you will not make a mistake
   D. write each amount lightly in pencil and then go over each number heavily with a pen

6.____

7. Assume that your office ordered supplies from a vendor on December 1. These supplies are to be used starting on February 2 of the following year, and it is essential that they arrive by that date.
   Of the following, which is the BEST way to assure that the supplies arrive on time?

   A. Contact the post office before February 2 and inquire about the vendor's record in shipping supplies
   B. Keep in contact with the vendor until the supplies arrive, and follow up on any problems which arise
   C. Mail a duplicate copy of the order to the vendor sometime in January to serve as a reminder
   D. Telephone the vendor a week before February 2, and ask whether the supplies were shipped

7.____

8. Assume that you are working in an admissions area of a hospital and you are completing an admissions form for a new patient. In order to complete the form, you have to obtain certain information from the patient, such as his name, address, and age, and write it on the form.
   Of the following, the FIRST action you should take after the patient tells you his name is to

   A. ask the patient for a copy of his birth certificate in order to verify his name
   B. ask the patient whether he has been a patient in your hospital before
   C. tell the patient to write his name on the form
   D. write his name in the appropriate place on the admissions form

8.____

9. Of the following, the BEST reason for a clerical division to have its own photocopying machine is that the division

   A. frequently needs copies of incoming correspondence
   B. frequently receives photographic negatives in the mail
   C. must enter the receipt date on all incoming mail
   D. uses 5,000 copies of a form each month

9.____

10. In your assignment to a hospital admitting office, you will be required to personally fill out an admissions form for each person before he is admitted to the hospital. Of the following, the MOST accurate way for you to obtain the information you need from a person is to

    A. ask him one question at a time based on the information you need
    B. ask him only those questions which can be answered by the words *yes* or *no*

10.____

C. give him the form and tell him to fill it out correctly
D. have him complete the entire form and then sign it yourself

Questions 11-20.

DIRECTIONS: Each of Questions 11 through 20 gives the identification number and name of aperson who has received treatment at a certain hospital. You are to choose the option (A, B, C, or D) which has EXACTLY the same identification number and name as those given in the question.

SAMPLE QUESTION

123765 Frank Y. Jones
- A. 123675 Frank Y. Jones
- B. 123765 Frank T. Jones
- C. 123765 Frank Y. Johns
- D. 123765 Frank Y. Jones

The correct answer is D. Only option D shows the identification number and name exactly as they are in the sample question. Option A has a mistake in the identification number. Option B has a mistake in the middle initial of the name. Option C has a mistake in the last name.

Now answer Questions 11 through 20 in the same manner.

11. 754898   Diane Malloy   11.____

    A. 745898   Diane Malloy
    B. 754898   Dion Malloy
    C. 754898   Diane Malloy
    D. 754898   Diane Maloy

12. 661018   Ferdinand Figueroa   12.____

    A. 661818   Ferdinand Figeuroa
    B. 661618   Ferdinand Figueroa
    C. 661818   Ferdnand Figueroa
    D. 661818   Ferdinand Figueroa

13. 100101   Norman D. Braustein   13.____

    A. 100101   Norman D. Braustein
    B. 101001   Norman D. Braustein
    C. 100101   Norman P. Braustien
    D. 100101   Norman D. Bruastein

14. 838696   Robert Kittredge   14.____

    A. 838969   Robert Kittredge
    B. 838696   Robert Kittredge
    C. 388696   Robert Kittredge
    D. 838696   Robert Kittridge

15. 243716   Abraham Soletsky   15._____

    A. 243716   Abrahm Soletsky
    B. 243716   Abraham Solestky
    C. 243176   Abraham Soletsky
    D. 243716   Abraham Soletsky

16. 981121   Phillip M. Maas   16._____

    A. 981121   Phillip M. Mass
    B. 981211   Phillip M. Maas
    C. 981121   Phillip M. Maas
    D. 981121   Phillip N. Maas

17. 786556   George Macalusso   17._____

    A. 785656   George Macalusso
    B. 786556   George Macalusso
    C. 786556   George Maculasso
    D. 786556   George Macluasso

18. 639472   Eugene Weber   18._____

    A. 639472   Eugene Weber
    B. 639472   Eugene Webre
    C. 693472   Eugene Weber
    D. 639742   Eugene Weber

19. 724936   John J. Lomonaco   19._____

    A. 724936   John J. Lomanoco
    B. 724396   John J. Lomonaco
    C. 724936   John J. Lomonaco
    D. 724936   John J. Lamonaco

20. 899868   Michael Schnitzer   20._____

    A. 899868   Micheal Schnitzer
    B. 898968   Michael Schnizter
    C. 899688   Michael Schnitzer
    D. 899868   Michael Schnitzer

KEY (CORRECT ANSWERS)

1.	C	11.	C
2.	C	12.	D
3.	C	13.	A
4.	B	14.	B
5.	A	15.	D
6.	A	16.	C
7.	A	17.	B
8.	D	18.	A
9.	A	19.	C
10.	A	20.	D

TEST 2

DIRECTIONS: Each question or incomplete statement is followed by several suggested answers or completions. Select the one that BEST answers the question or completes the statement. *PRINT THE LETTER OF TEE CORRECT ANSWER IN THE SPACE AT THE RIGHT.*

Questions 1-10.

DIRECTIONS: Questions 1 through 10 are to be answered on the basis of the information and the form given below.

The form below is a Daily Summary of Clinic Visits and lists ten persons who used a clinic in Washington Hospital on September 4.

The form includes the following information about each patient: Name, identification number, date of birth, case number, fee, and bill number.

Name of Patient Last, First	Identification Number	Date of Birth Mo.	Day	Yr.	Case Number	Fee	Bill Number
\multicolumn{8}{	c	}{SEPTEMBER 4 — WASHINGTON HOSPITAL - DAILY SUMMARY OF CLINIC VISITS}
Enders, John	89-4143-67	08	01	71	434317	$ 90.00	129631
Dawes, Mary	71-6142-69	11	17	66	187963	$ 47.50	129632
Lang, Donald	54-1213-73	10	07	75	897436	$180.00	129633
Eiger, Alan	18-7649-63	06	19	51	134003	$110.00	129634
Ramirez, Jose	61-4319-69	03	30	96	379030	$130.00	129635
Ilono, Frank	13-9161-57	08	19	83	565645	$ 66.00	129636
Sloan, Irene	55-8643-66	05	13	57	799732	$112.50	129637
Long , Thomas	41-3963-74	12	03	76	009784	$ 37.50	129638
McKay, Cathy	14-9633-44	05	09	66	000162	$ 96.00	129639
Dale, Sarah	86-1113-69	11	13	59	543211	$138.00	129640

1. The fee for Cathy McKay is LESS than the fee for   1.___

    A. John Enders   B. Alan Eiger
    C. Frank Ilono   D. Thomas Long

2. The two patients who were born in the same year are   2.___

    A. John Enders and Frank Ilono
    B. Mary Dawes and Sarah Dale
    C. Donald Lang and Thomas Long
    D. Cathy McKay and Mary Dawes

3. The case number of Irene Sloan is   3.___

    A. 979732   B. 799372   C. 799732   D. 797732

4. Cathy McKay's identification number is   4.___

    A. 44-9633-14   B. 14-9633-44
    C. 000162   D. 129639

48

5. Frank Ilono's case number is

   A. 556645　　B. 565465　　C. 565645　　D. 565654

6. The bill numbers for Jose Ramirez and Thomas Long are

   A. 129635 and 129638
   B. 129635 and 129683
   C. 129634 and 129638
   D. 129634 and 129637

7. The fees for Donald Lang, Sarah Dale, and Mary Dawes are

   A. $47.50, $180.00, and $96.00
   B. $110.00, $138.00, and $90.00
   C. $180.00, $130.00, and $47.50
   D. $180.00, $138.00, and $47.50

8. The case numbers for Thomas Long and Mary Dawes are

   A. 009784 and 187963
   B. 090784 and 187963
   C. 009784 and 187693
   D. 009874 and 187963

9. The identification numbers for Frank Ilono and Donald Lang are

   A. 13-9161-57 and 54-1312-73
   B. 54-1213-73 and 13-6191-57
   C. 13-9161-57 and 54-1213-73
   D. 54-1213-37 and 13-9161-57

10. The birth dates of Irene Sloan, John Enders, and Sarah Dale are

    A. 05/31/57, 01/08/71, and 11/13/69
    B. 05/13/67, 08/01/71, and 11/13/69
    C. 05/31/57, 01/08/71, and 11/13/59
    D. 05/13/57, 08/01/71, and 11/13/59

Questions 11-15.

DIRECTIONS: Questions 11 through 15 consist of sets of names and addresses. In each question, the name and address in Column II should be an EXACT copy of the name and address in Column I. Compare the name and address in Column II with the name and address in Column I.

　　If there is an error in the name only, mark your answer A;
　　If there is an error in the address only, mark your answer B;
　　If there is an error in both the name and address, mark your answer C;
　　If there is NO error in either the name or address, mark your answer D.

SAMPLE QUESTION

COLUMN I	COLUMN II
Mildred Bonilla	Mildred Bonila
511 West 186 Street	511 West 186 Street
New York, N.Y. 10033	New York, N.Y. 10032

Compare the name and address in Column II with the name and address in Column I. The name <u>Bonila</u> in Column II is spelled <u>Bonilla</u> in Column I. The zip code <u>10032</u> in Column II is given as <u>10033</u> in Column I. Since there is an error in both the name and address, the answer to the sample question is C.

Now answer Questions 11 through 15 in the same manner.

<u>COLUMN I</u>   <u>COLUMN II</u>

11. Mr. & Mrs. George Petersson
    87-11 91st Avenue
    Woodhaven, New York 11421

    Mr. & Mrs. George Peterson
    87-11 91st Avenue
    Woodhaven, New York 11421

    11.____

12. Mr. Ivan Klebnikov
    1848 Newkirk Avenue
    Brooklyn, New York 11226

    Mr. Ivan Klebikov
    1848 Newkirk Avenue
    Brooklyn, New York 11622

    12.____

13. Samuel Rothfleisch
    71 Pine Street
    New York, New York 10005

    Samuel Rothfleisch
    71 Pine Street
    New York, New York 10005

    13.____

14. Mrs. Isabel Tonnessen
    198 East 185th Street
    Bronx, New York 10458

    Mrs. Isabel Tonnessen
    189 East 185th Street
    Bronx, New York 10458

    14.____

15. Esteban Perez
    173 Eighth Street
    Staten Island, N.Y. 10306

    Estaban Perez
    173 Eighth Street
    Staten Island, N.Y. 10306

    15.____

16. The MAIN purpose of an invoice is to

    A. confirm receipt of an order
    B. list items being sent to a buyer
    C. order items from a company
    D. provide written proof that a shipment has been received

    16.____

17. You have been told to add various amounts listed on a billing form by operating a calculating machine. The machine prints on a roll of paper tape all amounts added and the answer to the computation.
    Of the following, the LEAST appropriate use for this tape is to

    A. check that no amounts were left out during the computation
    B. check that the amounts were entered correctly into the machine
    C. keep a record of the computation
    D. prove that the amounts on the original document are correct

    17.____

18. Assume that you are working in a storehouse of a hospital system. One of your tasks is to fill requisitions from hospitals for office supplies. When a requisition is received, you much check inventory cards to determine whether an item is available. One day, you receive a requisition for office supplies; and upon checking the inventory cards, you find that one of the items ordered, a particular kind of paper, is not available. However, the other items are ready for shipment to the hospital. Of the following, the BEST course of action for you to take in this situation is to

    18.____

A. have those items which are available sent to the hospital with an indication of which items were sent
B. purchase the missing paper yourself and then have the complete order sent to the hospital
C. substitute any other paper which is available and then have the order sent to the hospital
D. wait until the missing paper is available and then have the complete order sent to the hospital

19. One of your duties is to get certain information from people who are being treated at a hospital clinic. One day, you are trying to get this information from a person who begins to talk about matters unrelated to the information you are trying to obtain.
Of the following, the BEST course of action for you to take in this situation is to

   A. allow the individual to continue talking about the unrelated matters since he will probably return to the information you need in a short time
   B. ask the individual a question that may lead him back to the information you need
   C. end the interview and obtain the information from other sources
   D. tell the individual to give you the information you need and not discuss the unrelated matters

19.____

20. You have just asked a patient a question about the kind of hospitalization insurance he has.
The BEST way for you to make sure that you understand his answer to the question is to

   A. ask the question again in a slightly different way and see if you get approximately the same answer
   B. ask the same question again and listen carefully to see if the answer is the same
   C. repeat the answer in your own words and ask the patient if that is what he meant
   D. write the answer down on a piece of paper and read it back to the patient

20.____

KEY (CORRECT ANSWERS)

1.	B	11.	A
2.	D	12.	C
3.	C	13.	D
4.	B	14.	B
5.	C	15.	A
6.	A	16.	B
7.	D	17.	D
8.	A	18.	A
9.	C	19.	B
10.	D	20.	C

EXAMINATION SECTION
TEST 1

DIRECTIONS: Each question or incomplete statement is followed by several suggested answers or completions. Select the one that BEST answers the question or completes the statement. *PRINT THE LETTER OF THE CORRECT ANSWER IN THE SPACE AT THE RIGHT.*

1. Given the standard methods of forms analysis in health information departments, it is usually sufficient to order a supply of forms that will last _____ months.

    A. 1-3 B. 3-6 C. 6-12 D. 12-18

2. According to the rules of the FLSA (Fair Labor and Standards Act), which of the following positions in the health care department is an *exempt* position?

    A. Coding
    B. Abstracting
    C. Administration
    D. Transcription

3. Which of the following would be considered to be a DISADVANTAGE associated with the use of source-oriented medical records?

    A. Format usually requires additional training of records personnel
    B. Complexity of arrangement makes the record difficult for non-physicians to follow
    C. Format does not facilitate use in acute care facilities
    D. Data from various departments are not integrated in the time sequence

4. The definition of objectives is a MAJOR purpose of the _____ function of management.

    A. controlling
    B. directing
    C. planning
    D. organizing

5. In the _____ HMO, physicians maintain their own medical records yet feed practice data into the HMO for monitoring purposes.

    A. staff model
    B. independent practice
    C. preferred provider
    D. group model or closed

6. Which of the following problems would be considered the MOST serious offense committed by an employee in the department?

    A. Attendance problems
    B. Insubordination
    C. Falsification of employment application
    D. Violation of smoking regulations

7. Of the following methods for measuring work to define a performance standard, _____ is used to establish a standard for new work.

    A. benchmarking
    B. scientific method
    C. work sampling
    D. simulation

8. A disease or operation index would be used administratively to

   A. evaluate the quality of care in the facility
   B. procure data on the utilization of facilities and to establish needs for new equipment, beds, etc. in various departments
   C. determine whether treatment and procedures provided were necessary and appropriate for the diagnosis
   D. accumulate risk management data

9. In a hospital's medical record, the medical history of a patient must be completed within _____ hours of the patient's admission.

   A. 6   B. 12   C. 24   D. 48

10. Which of the following situations would be defined as a *professional contact* according to standard ambulatory health care data practices?
    A(n)

    A. patient receiving services from a supplier
    B. outpatient visiting both a physician's office and a clinic as parts of an individual treatment plan
    C. patient's imaging reports being interpreted when the patient is not physically present by someone other than the referring physician
    D. patient receiving services from a pharmacist

11. In hospitals, computerized R-ADT systems are USUALLY under the control of the _____ department.

    A. admissions   B. nursing
    C. radiology   D. health information

12. Which of the following is a component of managerial decision-making?

    A. Developing alternative solutions to the problem to meet the objective
    B. Collecting complete data about all factors surrounding a problem
    C. Identifying objectives in which change is causing a deviation
    D. Analyzing data fully to understand a problem and how it occurs

13. Which of the following items would appear in the follow-up file of a cancer registry?

    A. Histology
    B. Biopsies
    C. Diagnosis
    D. Radiation/chemotherapy treatments

14. In an inpatient acute care psychiatric facility, a patient's records should be reviewed

    A. daily   B. weekly
    C. monthly   D. annually

15. In the utilization review process, the _____ review would MOST likely be performed by a PRO physician.

    A. preadmission   B. continued stay
    C. discharge   D. retrospective

16. The MAIN advantage in using a straight numeric filing system is

    A. increased production of the clerical staff
    B. easy retrieval of an entire record
    C. accessibility to providers
    D. ease in personnel training

17. A key letter used as a category in the phonetic filing system for a Master Patient Index is

    A. k   B. b   C. s   D. n

18. A final progress note may NOT take the place of a discharge summary in the medical record of

    A. patients with minor problems who are hospitalized less than 48 hours
    B. surgical deliveries
    C. normal newborns
    D. uncomplicated obstetrical deliveries

19. In any research study, which of the following steps would occur LAST?

    A. Research report is prepared
    B. Pilot study is conducted
    C. Data gathering and analysis plans are implemented
    D. Frame of reference is developed

20. A _____ is used by health information management for direct observation of work performed when quality is difficult to quantify?

    A. questionnaire   B. checklist
    C. report   D. audit

21. When interviewing an applicant for a position in the department, _____ questions USUALLY should be avoided.

    A. probing   B. yes/no
    C. situational   D. leading

22. Procedures in the ICD-9-CM classification system are coded as a

    A. series of three-letter units
    B. letter followed by a three-digit number
    C. two-digit number, with one or two decimal digit subcategories
    D. four-digit number, without decimal digits

23. The plan of treatment for home care patients is reviewed by the attending physician and agency personnel at least once every

    A. month   B. 60 days
    C. six months   D. year

24. Which method for measuring work to define a performance standard involves comparing one department to another?

    A. Benchmarking   B. Scientific method
    C. Work sampling   D. Simulation

25. Included in the transfer/referral form for patients in long-term care facilities is the   25._____
    A. treatment plan
    B. estimate of rehabilitative potential
    C. recommended treatment
    D. medical history

KEY (CORRECT ANSWERS)

1. C
2. C
3. D
4. C
5. D

6. C
7. D
8. C
9. C
10. C

11. A
12. A
13. C
14. B
15. D

16. D
17. B
18. B
19. A
20. B

21. D
22. C
23. B
24. A
25. B

TEST 2

DIRECTIONS: Each question or incomplete statement is followed by several suggested answers or completions. Select the one that BEST answers the question or completes the statement. *PRINT THE LETTER OF THE CORRECT ANSWER IN THE SPACE AT THE RIGHT.*

1. Of the following basic methods for the release of authorized information from medical records, _____ should be used as a last resort by health information departments.

    A. direct access
    B. abstracting information
    C. facsimile transmission
    D. verbal release

    1._____

2. Which of the following functions and responsibilities would be LEAST likely to be assigned to the committee responsible for medical record review?

    A. Determination of the record format
    B. Review of records for usefulness in quality assessment activities
    C. Review of records for accuracy in describing patient progress
    D. Imposing disciplinary action on medical staff who submit substandard records

    2._____

3. A hospital had a total of 21 deaths during September. A total of 650 patients were discharged during the month. What was the hospital's GROSS death rate for September?

    A. .03%   B. 3%   C. 7%   D. 32%

    3._____

4. Each of the following is a potential use for the accession file of a cancer registry EXCEPT

    A. monitoring case identification
    B. auditing the registry file for lost abstracts
    C. abstracting nonanalytical cases
    D. assessing registry workload

    4._____

5. In the analysis of computerized data systems, systems analysis tools are MOST often used during the _____ phase.

    A. feasibility
    B. research
    C. implementation
    D. initial investigation

    5._____

6. To determine the total number of file guides needed for record storage, _____ the total number of records _____.

    A. multiply; between each guide by the total number of records
    B. divide; by the number of records between each guide
    C. subtract; between each guide from the total number of records, and multiply by the number of shelves
    D. divide; by the number of records between each guide, and multiply by the number of shelves

    6._____

7. To calculate the delinquency rate of a facility's medical record submissions, divide the total number of _____ by the average number of _____ during a completion period.

    A. delinquent records, minus the death rate; admissions
    B. delinquent records; admissions

    7._____

57

C. required records, minus the number of delinquent records; discharges
D. delinquent records; discharges

8. Which of the following is a *vertical* component of work allocation?

   A. Line-staff responsibility
   B. Departmentalization
   C. Delegation
   D. Coordination

9. According to the alphabetical filing guidelines for entering data into the Master Patient Index, which of the following names would appear FIRST in the Index?

   A. D'Elba
   B. Di Luca
   C. de Armand
   D. De Smet

10. All of the following would describe techniques used by the APG classification system for grouping different services EXCEPT

    A. normally scheduled, significant procedures which dominate time and resources expended during a patient visit
    B. multiple significant procedures and ancillary discounting, for multiple unrelated significant procedures, or multiple performance of the same ancillary procedure
    C. ancillary discounting for multiple performance of different ancillary procedures that contribute to the diagnoses and treatments of different primary physicians
    D. ancillary tests ordered by primary physician to assist in diagnosis and treatment, that do not dominate time and resources

11. The final decision concerning the elimination of an inactive medical record ALWAYS rests with

    A. the health information manager
    B. medical personnel
    C. the facility's legal counsel
    D. clerical personnel

12. The MOST widely used work quantity monitoring technique in health information departments is

    A. stopwatch time study
    B. work sampling
    C. direct inspection
    D. employee-reported volume log

13. The GREATEST source of difficulty in the utilization review of a mental health care institution would be

    A. lack of qualified mental-health personnel to evaluate care for payers
    B. inherent difficulties in evaluating benefit values from claims data
    C. concerns about confidentiality
    D. poor documentation

14. Which of the following risk control techniques is used as a tool to eliminate or reduce future adverse occurrences?

    A. Medical staff minutes
    B. Incident reporting
    C. Occurrence screening
    D. Hazard surveillance

15. The Family Medical Leave Act of 1993 allowing 12 weeks of unpaid leave per year, for specified purposes, applies to all organizations with _____ or more employees.

    A. 10   B. 25   C. 50   D. 100

16. If a court can be assured that a medical record is reliable and trustworthy, the record may be entered into evidence subject to rules relating to all of the following EXCEPT

    A. privilege
    B. adhesion
    C. relevancy
    D. materiality

17. If file cabinets used for storage in a health information department are arranged facing each other, the aisle between cabinets should be _____ wide.

    A. 24 inches
    B. 36 inches
    C. 4 feet
    D. 5 feet

18. The purpose of V codes in the Tabular List of the ICD-9-CM classification system is to code circumstances

    A. particular to obstetric patients and newborns
    B. other than a disease or injury classifiable in the main part of the Tabular List
    C. related to the morphologies and behaviors that are particular to neoplasms
    D. and environmental events as the cause of injury

19. Which of the following data would NOT be a subdivision of clinical data?

    A. Administrative
    B. Ancillary
    C. Medical
    D. Nursing

20. When interviewing an applicant for a position in the department, a _____ question is asked to pose a hypothetical problem.

    A. probing
    B. situational
    C. reflection
    D. clarification

21. When designing a form where data would be entered with a typewriter, how many lines of type should be figured for each vertical inch of space?

    A. 2   B. 4   C. 6   D. 8

22. The GREATEST threat to the confidentiality of health care data is through

    A. re-disclosure by authorized third party
    B. unauthorized disclosure by patients
    C. verbal disclosure of data elements
    D. computerized systems

23. The LEAST productive subject for discussion in a meeting of the health information department would be

    A. deciding which members of the department should take responsibility for specific functions
    B. brainstorming ways to ensure the prompt return of medical records
    C. ensuring the even distribution of filing tasks among clerical personnel
    D. resolution of questions regarding the coding procedure of medical records

24. A _____ would NOT be an effective way to present a frequency distribution.

    A. bar graph   B. histogram
    C. pie graph   D. pictogram

25. Which of the following would be considered an ADVANTAGE of using a problem-oriented medical record?

    A. It requires consideration of the context of a patient's complaint.
    B. Its relative simplicity
    C. The maintenance of a chronological sequence
    D. It allows physicians to rely more on records personnel

KEY (CORRECT ANSWERS)

1. D   11. C
2. D   12. D
3. B   13. C
4. C   14. B
5. D   15. C

6. B   16. B
7. D   17. D
8. C   18. B
9. C   19. A
10. C   20. B

21. C
22. A
23. D
24. A
25. A

TEST 3

DIRECTIONS: Each question or incomplete statement is followed by several suggested answers or completions. Select the one that BEST answers the question or completes the statement. *PRINT THE LETTER OF THE CORRECT ANSWER IN THE SPACE AT THE RIGHT.*

1. Which of the following problems would be considered the LEAST serious offense committed by an employee in the department? 1.____

    A. Discourtesy
    B. Absence without notice for three consecutive days
    C. Negligence
    D. Violation of emergency regulations

2. The *work standard* for transcription staff is 20 units per hour with no more than 2 errors per unit. During a given period, employees completed 144 out of 160 expected units, for a backlog of 16 units. Work sampled from one hour of completed work revealed that 16 of 18 units completed did not meet the error standard.
What is the activity level of the transcription staff? 2.____

    A. 75%   B. 80%   C. 90%   D. 95%

3. What is the productivity level of the transcription staff described in the previous question? 3.____

    A. 75%   B. 80%   C. 90%   D. 95%

4. Which of the following duplicating methods would MOST effectively and economically reproduce the greatest number of forms? 4.____

    A. Photocopying   B. Spirit duplicating
    C. Offset duplicating   D. Stencil duplicating

5. Abstracted case-mix data are used to 5.____

    A. evaluate the quality of care in the facility
    B. accumulate risk management data
    C. determine whether treatment and procedures provided were necessary and appropriate for diagnosis
    D. predict the health care facility's income

6. In determining whether a worker would be defined as *exempt* under the rules of the FLSA (Fair Labor and Standards Act), each of the following factors about the employee should be considered EXCEPT the 6.____

    A. percentage of time spent performing routine, manual, or clerical work
    B. discretionary authority for independent action
    C. earnings level of the employee
    D. overall benefit to the department according to established indexes

7. The 1985 Uniform Health Care Information Act (UHIA) encompasses each of the following principal rules regarding medical information EXCEPT the 7.____

61

A. provision for patient access to any record
B. provision for the patient to request revision or correction of the record
C. provision for the patient to withhold the content of a medical record even if it is subpoenaed
D. prohibition of provider from disseminating information to a third party without the patient's consent

8. Which of the following incentive pay schemes is currently used by the management in health information departments to guarantee a minimum pay to the employees of a transcription department?

   A. Strict unit-of-measure
   B. Calculated average over a specified time period as the basis for determining an hourly rate
   C. Fixed hourly rate
   D. Premium for units of measure over a minimum

9. In devising a plan for disposing inactive records in a department, one must consider each of the following EXCEPT the

   A. readmission rate for inpatients and outpatients
   B. rate at which potentially compensable events occur in the facility
   C. volume of research
   D. applicable statutes of limitations

10. A statistical analysis of medical record documentation is used PRIMARILY to

    A. identify areas of the record that are incomplete
    B. abstract data to aid clinical or administrative decision-making
    C. identify obvious and routine omissions in the record
    D. identify inconsistent or inaccurate documentation

11. At midnight on April 29, there were 455 patients in a hospital. On April 30, 21 more patients were admitted, and 18 patients either died or were discharged. Three patients were both admitted and discharged on April 30. What was the total number of inpatient service days on April 30?

    A. 458   B. 461   C. 473   D. 476

12. Consultations are *usually* required for treatment for each of the following types of patients EXCEPT patients

    A. whose diagnoses are obscure
    B. who may have been involved in criminal activity
    C. who require cytoscopic procedures
    D. who are not good surgical risks

13. In order to generate current listings, a hospital's computerized R-ADT system links the nursing patient database with the

    A. patient acuity database
    B. personnel database
    C. report generator
    D. automated staff scheduling system

14. A 200-bed community hospital has an average occupancy of 82%. The transcription personnel of the health information department are each assigned a minimum daily product of 1000 words, and the average lines of work produced each month is 160,000. There are 20 workdays in each month.
    Factoring in a 15% adjustment requirement, how many full-time equivalents (FTE's) would be considered a MINIMUM staffing requirement for transcription personnel?

    A. 8 B. 8.8 C. 9.2 D. 10

15. Which of the following is NOT a risk financing fund that would be commonly associated with a facility's risk management program?

    A. Commercial insurance
    B. Insurance pools
    C. Insurance hierarchies
    D. Self-insurance

16. According to the American Health Information Management Association, disease indexes should be retained for AT LEAST

    A. 5 years
    B. 10 years
    C. until the age of the majority, plus the operative statute of limitations
    D. permanently

17. Which of the following risk control techniques is used to identify areas of potential environmental risk prior to an adverse occurrence?

    A. Medical staff minutes
    B. Incident reporting
    C. Occurrence screening
    D. Hazard surveillance

18. Which of the following items would be classified as *ordinal* data for the purpose of research studies?

    A. Low/medium/high values
    B. IQ results
    C. True/false responses
    D. 0-100 scale

19. Which of the following items is NOT currently being released by hospitals as a component of the HCFA Mortality Data?

    A. Percentage of Medicare beneficiaries who die within 30 days of admission
    B. Expected percentage of deaths, calculated on the basis of overall national experience
    C. Percentage of Medicare beneficiaries who die during surgical procedures
    D. Number of Medicare beneficiaries treated

20. According to the GLOSSARY OF HEALTH CARE TERMS, the number of inpatients/residents present at census-taking time each day, plus any inpatients/residents who were both admitted and discharged after the census-taking time the previous day, is known as the

    A. daily census
    B. inpatient/resident service day
    C. census
    D. average daily census

21. Most public health laws require health care institutions to report each of the following diseases or occurrences EXCEPT

    A. births
    B. all tumorous growths
    C. deaths
    D. gunshot wounds

22. NOT a commonly used method of analyzing computerized data systems is

    A. structured analysis
    B. HIPO
    C. network analysis
    D. traditional

23. In a given time period, the distribution of fifteen hospital inpatient stays was as follows: 5, 1, 2, 3, 4, 5, 3, 1, 2, 1, 5, 1, 18, 8, 1. The total of these stays is 60. What would the MEDIAN length of stay for this period be?

    A. 4   B. 3   C. 2   D. 1

24. The Joint Commission's legal standards for the medical record state that the medical record must contain sufficient information for each of the following EXCEPT

    A. requisition for data for research purposes
    B. justification of the treatment
    C. accurate documentation of the course and results
    D. facilitation of continuity of care among providers

25. Which of the following is NOT commonly used to control data misuse in the health information department?

    A. Algorithmic scrambling of all data stored in computer systems
    B. Detailed accounting of computer use
    C. Adoption of log-in procedures
    D. Random monitoring of computer use

KEY (CORRECT ANSWERS)

1. A
2. C
3. B
4. C
5. D

6. D
7. C
8. D
9. B
10. B

11. B
12. C
13. A
14. C
15. C

16. B
17. D
18. A
19. C
20. A

21. B
22. C
23. B
24. A
25. A

EXAMINATION SECTION
TEST 1

DIRECTIONS: Each question or incomplete statement is followed by several suggested answers or completions. Select the one that BEST answers the question or completes the statement. *PRINT THE LETTER OF THE CORRECT ANSWER IN THE SPACE AT THE RIGHT.*

1. All of the following data should be collected for case mix management in a physician's office EXCEPT the

    A. patient's sex
    B. payer mix
    C. patient's race/ethnicity
    D. employment status of patients

    1.____

2. In any edition of the Current Procedural Terminology (CPT) nomenclature system, deleted terms are denoted by

    A. a 0 symbol
    B. parentheses
    C. a ^ symbol
    D. quotation marks

    2.____

3. Information concerning _____ would NOT be included in the *therapy* plans section of a problem-oriented medical record.

    A. drugs
    B. medical procedures
    C. patient education
    D. treatment goals

    3.____

4. If a hospital uses a decentralized filing system, *only* the _____ records are stored in a central file.

    A. inpatient
    B. outpatient
    C. emergency
    D. ancillary

    4.____

5. According to the GLOSSARY OF HEALTH CARE TERMS, which of the following is NOT a commonly used meaning for the word *service*?
    A

    A. group of inpatient beds
    B. division or unit of medical staff responsibility
    C. categorical procedure performed on patients with related diseases
    D. group of discharged patients with related diseases or treatments

    5.____

6. Which of the following is NOT one of the main purposes of a subject/title file in a *paper forms control* program?
    To

    A. record all directives authorizing the use of every form
    B. detect those forms that might be eliminated or consolidated with other forms
    C. avoid the creation of a new form when an existing form could be revised to serve the need
    D. generate studies of forms in relation to the systems and procedures used

    6.____

7. Which of the following is a rule for using the phonetic filing system for a Master Patient Index?

   A. When a repeated key letter or its equivalent is separated by a vowel, treat the two letters as a single unit.
   B. If a name contains more than three key letters, add zeros to arrive at the code number.
   C. If two of the same key letters or a key letter and its equivalent are separated by an *h* or *w*, code two key letters.
   D. When two or more key letters or their equivalents occur together, each letter should be considered separately.

8. Of the following components of a managerial planning function, _____ USUALLY takes the form of annual descriptions of departmental activity.

   A. strategic planning
   B. tactical planning
   C. operational planning
   D. mission

9. Of the following, the MOST serious disadvantage associated with a straight numeric filing system would be the

   A. relatively high probability of misfiling
   B. difficulty of quality control
   C. unequal distribution of filing activity throughout a single department
   D. frequent transposition of numbers

10. The employee privacy rights that are defined in various state laws include each of the following subcategories EXCEPT

    A. rights in workplace investigation
    B. substance abuse and drug testing
    C. polygraph and honesty testing
    D. rights to records

11. The implementation of quality assurance in a mental health care facility requires special adaptations.
    Of the following, which adaptive procedure is MOST characteristic of the review of quality assurance in mental health care facilities?

    A. Involvement of professional staff peer review
    B. Income, outcome indicators being measured incrementally over long periods of time
    C. Clinical performance of individuals without clinical privileges being monitored and evaluated
    D. Relevant findings from the review being used to renew or revise individual clinical privileges

12. A hospital rendered 3,650 inpatient service days in April, a month which has 30 days. What was the average daily inpatient census during Apr

    A. 12   B. 42   C. 122   D. 1,216

13. In nomenclature system categories, the cause of a disease or injury is denoted by the term

    A. etiology
    B. immunology
    C. insertion
    D. origin

14. Of the following management systems, which would be considered the MOST successful model for directing the work of others?

    A. Exploitive-authoritative
    B. Representative
    C. Benevolent-authoritative
    D. Consultative

15. Of the following types of information, _____ is LEAST likely to be included on a graphic sheet.

    A. temperature
    B. fluid output
    C. pulse
    D. respiration

16. Which of the following is NOT an advantage associated with the use of self-contained media (such as endless loop or tanks) for the recording of transcription data?

    A. Strict control of input priorities
    B. Elimination of re-recording necessity
    C. Minimization of lost dictation
    D. Elimination of the physical handling of media

17. Health information data indexes direct the process of locating health information for use by

    A. administration in management and financial decisions
    B. funding agencies or third-party payers for reviewing the necessity for care and its appropriateness
    C. licensing bodies for reviewing the quality of care
    D. physicians in patient care and research

18. Which of the following is considered to be a benefit of a management-by-objective program?

    A. Economic time use
    B. Easily quantifiable results
    C. Reduction of role ambiguity
    D. Reduction in paperwork

19. Of the following, which type of patient death would be included in a hospital's calculation of its mortality rate?

    A. Patients who are dead on arrival
    B. Patients who die while receiving lifesaving services in any unit other than the emergency unit
    C. Patients who die in emergency rooms when no decision has been made about room, board, or nursing service
    D. Fetal deaths

4 (#1)

20. A COMMON failure of a management-by-objective program is 20.____

    A. the inadequate use of human resources
    B. the inhibitions of the planning function
    C. overemphasis on short-term results
    D. a reduction in managerial motivation

21. Of the following, which incentive pay scheme is MOST often used by health information department management for employees of a transcription department? 21.____

    A. Strict unit-of-measure
    B. Calculated average over a specified time period as the basis for determining an hourly rate
    C. Fixed hourly rate
    D. Premium for units of measure over a minimum

22. LEAST likely to be monitored by the utilization review of a hospice record is (are) 22.____

    A. appropriateness of admission
    B. stays of fewer than six months
    C. delays in providing team service
    D. appropriateness of the level of service

23. Which of the following is NOT used to measure the central tendency of a grouped set of data? 23.____

    A. Mean   B. Median   C. Range   D. Mode

24. The follow-up generation of computerized tumor registries keep track of the status of all registered cancer patients through letters that are generated at intervals of 24.____

    A. 6 months   B. 15 months   C. 2 years   D. 30 months

25. Which of the following is NOT one of the main item headings in the Uniform Hospital Discharge Data Set (UHDDS)? 25.____

    A. Admission and discharge dates
    B. Diagnoses
    C. Residence
    D. Medical history

KEY (CORRECT ANSWERS)

1. C
2. B
3. C
4. A
5. C

6. A
7. B
8. B
9. C
10. A

11. B
12. C
13. A
14. B
15. B

16. B
17. D
18. C
19. B
20. C

21. B
22. B
23. C
24. B
25. D

TEST 2

DIRECTIONS: Each question or incomplete statement is followed by several suggested answers or completions. Select the one that BEST answers the question or completes the statement. *PRINT THE LETTER OF THE CORRECT ANSWER IN THE SPACE AT THE RIGHT.*

1. Which of the following notations would be considered acceptable, upon being reviewed during a qualitative analysis?

    A. Patient given instructions
    B. Test results normal
    C. Patient doing well
    D. Watch condition of toes

    1._____

2. Open-shelf storage units are recommended instead of cabinets for the storage of medical record files for each of the following reasons EXCEPT

    A. lower cost
    B. faster pulling and filing by personnel
    C. more records can be accommodated in a given floor area
    D. relative neatness

    2._____

3. To be eligible for FMLA (Family Medical Leave Act) leave, an employee must have worked for an organization for AT LEAST _____ months, not necessarily consecutively.

    A. 3   B. 9   C. 12   D. 18

    3._____

4. In nomenclature system categories, the term *function* refers to

    A. a structural change in tissue
    B. physiological or chemical disorders and alterations resulting from a disease or injury
    C. the part of the body affected by disease or injury
    D. the cause of disease or injury

    4._____

5. According to the generally accepted legal principle regarding medical records, the physical record is the property of the

    A. patient   B. payer
    C. provider   D. health care institution

    5._____

6. The health information practitioner should be concerned about each of the following aspects of data loss EXCEPT

    A. a contract with a commercial service that spells out terms of protection and remuneration
    B. back-up systems
    C. financial insurance for off-line storage facility damage
    D. monitoring maintenance procedures

    6._____

7. Which type of HMO is considered to be a discrete organization, possessing its own self-contained records department?

    A. Staff model
    B. Independent practice association
    C. Preferred provider
    D. Group model or closed

8. If a health information department were to switch from serial numbering to unit numbering, which of the following procedures would no longer be performed?

    A. Assigning readmitted patients a new unit number
    B. Cross-referencing empty folders of previous records
    C. Assigning unit numbers to files of patients that have not been readmitted
    D. Leaving empty folders of previous records in their original places in the file

9. In a typical color-coded filing system, two-digit primary numbers from 70-79 would be represented by a band of

    A. purple   B. brown
    C. red   D. light green

10. Of the following, _____ is NOT a basic element of a department's revenue and expense budget.

    A. revenues   B. materials
    C. expenses   D. personnel

11. Currently, the most advanced administrative computer applications include each of the following areas or departments of health care EXCEPT

    A. laboratory   B. pharmacy
    C. surgery   D. dietary

12. When a hospital's medical staff is NOT organized into units, the determining factor for data categorization should be whether

    A. a prescription was ordered by the physician
    B. a surgical operation was performed
    C. ancillary procedures were performed
    D. the patient was an inpatient or outpatient

13. Which of the following types of forms will USUALLY take the longest to reproduce, and therefore require the greatest *lead time* in ordering?

    A. Tags and envelopes
    B. Continuous forms
    C. Carbon-interleaved snapout forms
    D. Single-part forms (larger than 11" x 17")

14. Which element of the paper forms control procedure has been replaced by the *programming logic* element of a computerized environment?

    A. Forms inventory   B. Forms identification
    C. Ongoing review   D. Purchasing

15. When medical records are to be microfilmed for storage, the MOST commonly used size of film is _____ mm.

    A. 16   B. 35   C. 70   D. 105

16. In a terminal digit file, the record number 00-00-97 would be followed by the number

    A. 01-00-97   B. 00-01-97   C. 00-00-98   D. 01-01-97

17. The patient summary of a home care patient must be documented and forwarded to the patient's attending physician, and the referral source, AT LEAST once every

    A. 31 days   B. 61 days   C. 6 months   D. year

18. A health information department's work year, minus vacation, sick leave, and holidays, is equal to 47 weeks per year, or 1,880 hours. The department employs two full-time abstracting personnel, who combine to abstract a total of 20,500 records in one year. The time standard for abstracting one record is 10 minutes.
    What is the productivity of the abstracting personnel?

    A. 76%   B. 88%   C. 91%   D. 98%

19. If the personnel described in the previous question improve their production, how many additional records (maximum) could they be expected to abstract in one year, without increasing the required number of full-time employees (FTEs)?

    A. 540   B. 1230   C. 5400   D. 21,730

20. Which of the following would be included in the database section of a problem-oriented medical record?

    A. Social problems   B. Systemic review
    C. Specific diagnosis   D. Abnormal findings

21. _____ top management plans cover approximately 3-5 years.

    A. Strategic   B. Tactical
    C. Operational   D. Mission

22. The Privacy Act of 1974 was enacted to protect the privacy of individuals identified in information systems, and gives these individuals access to records concerning themselves, in these systems.
    In the area of health care, this act applies to the medical records of patients

    A. at federal government hospitals *only*
    B. at federal government hospitals and all long-term care facilities
    C. at federal government hospitals and all private inpatient facilities
    D. served by any licensed health care professional

23. If a hospital currently has 50 delinquent records in total, and it averages 75 discharges per completion period, what is the hospital's delinquent record rate?

    A. 25%   B. 33%   C. 50%   D. 67%

24. During insurance audits, which part of the medical record is compared to the services rendered by matching the record item-for-item against the itemized bill?

    A. Physician's orders
    B. Physical examination
    C. Attestation statement
    D. Discharge record

25. In the standard formula for approximating the size of a research sample, a certainty factor of 97% would be expressed as the number

    A. 1.281   B. 1.645   C. 1.960   D. 2.170

KEY (CORRECT ANSWERS)

1. D
2. D
3. C
4. B
5. D

6. C
7. A
8. C
9. D
10. B

11. C
12. B
13. B
14. B
15. A

16. A
17. B
18. C
19. B
20. B

21. A
22. A
23. D
24. A
25. D

EXAMINATION SECTION
TEST 1

DIRECTIONS: Each question or incomplete statement is followed by several suggested answers or completions. Select the one that BEST answers the question or completes the statement. *PRINT THE LETTER OF THE CORRECT ANSWER IN THE SPACE AT THE RIGHT.*

1. In residential care facilities, a discharge plan is begun

    A. when news of an impending transfer or referral is received
    B. at the time of admission
    C. when it is clear that the patient will survive treatment
    D. no later than 30 days prior to discharge

2. In hospitals, more statistical data is collected on _____ patients than on any type of patient.

    A. ancillary   B. in-
    C. emergency   D. out-

3. When a phonetic filing system is used for entering data into a Master Patient Index, all names are coded as a

    A. discrete three-letter block
    B. one-syllable surname substitute that excludes vowel sounds
    C. three-digit number
    D. two-digit number preceded by the key consonant in the patient's surname

4. In planning the layout of a health information department, how many square feet of working space should be allowed for each member of the clerical staff?

    A. 10   B. 30   C. 60   D. 120

5. Patient care supplies typically account for about _____ % of a hospital's operating budget.

    A. 10   B. 20   C. 35   D. 50

6. Of the following, an example of a department's risk identification techniques would be

    A. preventive maintenance   B. hazard surveillance
    C. medical staff minutes   D. insurance pools

7. Each of the following is an item in home care records that is *usually* monitored EXCEPT

    A. initial assessments and care plans
    B. documentation of care plan reviews
    C. documentation of all visits
    D. physician's progress notes

8. In a _____ numbering/filing system, the number that the patient receives upon his FIRST visit to a facility is retained for all subsequent visits and treatments.

    A. serial   B. family
    C. unit   D. terminal digit

9. Of the following items, the _____ would NOT be a concern of a PRO physician reviewing a hospital's DRG concerns.

   A. selection of principal diagnosis
   B. quality of patient care
   C. substantiation of diagnosis and procedures by the medical record
   D. correct coding of decision tree procedures

10. The edition date of any form should appear next to the

    A. instructions   B. introduction
    C. form number   D. page number

11. When a patient is discharged from a hospital, the source-oriented record is rearranged according to

    A. date, in reverse chronological order in each section
    B. date, from admission to discharge in each section
    C. section, from admission to discharge in each section
    D. section, according to prominence in treatment

12. Which of the following is NOT a filing option used for keeping an incomplete medical record in a health information department?

    A. Permanent file
    B. Separate incomplete file, by provider name
    C. Separate incomplete file, by medical record number
    D. Separate incomplete file, by patient name

13. Coding employees in a health information department are expected to accurately code 7 records of discharged patients in an hour. 20,500 discharges are expected in a year at the hospital. It is assumed that an employee's regular productive time per year is 47 weeks, or 1,880 hours.
    How many full-time equivalents (FTE's) will be required to staff the coding department?

    A. 1.1   B. 1.56   C. 6.4   D. 10.9

14. A quantitative analysis of medical record documentation is used PRIMARILY to

    A. identify areas of the record that are incomplete
    B. abstract data to aid in clinical or administrative decision-making
    C. identify potentially compensible events to be reported to the facility's risk management
    D. identify inconsistent or inaccurate documentation

15. The term used to describe a condition that exists on admission and may increase the length of a patient's stay by at least one day is

    A. accession   B. comorbidity
    C. recurrence   D. complication

16. The MOST frequently used value to express or measure the variation of a set of data is

    A. variance   B. standard deviation
    C. rate   D. range

17. Of the following components of a managerial planning function, _____ plans are considered to be the MOST specific and verifiable.

    A. strategic B. tactical
    C. operational D. mission

18. According to federal regulations, an Annual Reporting Form must be filed with the EEOC by all employers with _____ or more employees.

    A. 50 B. 100 C. 200 D. 500

19. Which of the following is a binary data representation of the number 13?

    A. 0111 B. 1101 C. 0001 D. 101

20. A health information department's annual budget for supply expenditures is $7,000. Nine months into the year, the department has spent a total of $5,400 on supplies.
    The projection calculation for the department's year-end total expenditures should be _____ budget.

    A. $150 under B. $100 under C. $150 over D. $200 over

21. Of the following commonly recognized management functions, which function would be considered to be the *feedback* mechanism?

    A. Controlling B. Directing
    C. Planning D. Organizing

22. Typically, the fine imposed on a health insurance facility which violates regulations concerning the privacy of medical records more than once would not exceed

    A. $500 B. $1500 C. $5000 D. $25,000

23. Which of the following is considered to be an ADVANTAGE associated with the use of a source-oriented medical record?

    A. Ease in determining the assessments and treatments of particular departments
    B. The clear indication of goals and methods in patient treatment
    C. That it requires consideration of the context of a patient's complaint
    D. That it allows physicians to rely more on records personnel

24. Problems with the use of integrated medical records are MOST frequently associated with

    A. medical histories B. physician's orders
    C. progress notes D. consultation reports

25. In any research study, which of the following steps would occur FIRST?

    A. Pilot study is conducted
    B. Research design is selected
    C. Research hypothesis is stated
    D. Data gathering instruments and procedures are developed

KEY (CORRECT ANSWERS)

1.	B		11.	B
2.	B		12.	D
3.	C		13.	B
4.	C		14.	A
5.	B		15.	B
6.	C		16.	B
7.	D		17.	C
8.	C		18.	B
9.	B		19.	B
10.	C		20.	D

21. A
22. C
23. A
24. C
25. B

TEST 2

DIRECTIONS: Each question or incomplete statement is followed by several suggested answers or completions. Select the one that BEST answers the question or completes the statement. *PRINT THE LETTER OF THE CORRECT ANSWER IN THE SPACE AT THE RIGHT.*

1. In a residential or long-term care psychiatric facility, a patient's records should be reviewed

    A. daily B. weekly C. monthly D. annually

    1._____

2. Which of the following functions in the management of a health care information department is LEAST likely to be facilitated by commercial software packages?

    A. Budgeting
    B. Utilization review
    C. Staff scheduling
    D. Statistical calculations

    2._____

3. Each of the following is a basic element of a nursing department's computerized administrative information system EXCEPT the

    A. report generator
    B. automated scheduling system
    C. automated acuity system
    D. medication administration system

    3._____

4. In order to plan an operating expense budget, each of the following must be known EXCEPT the

    A. unit of service activity
    B. unit cost
    C. work distribution
    D. expense type

    4._____

5. A health information department currently using 1,435 linear filing inches to store records intends to replace its open-shelf filing units. Each of the shelves in a new five-shelf unit measures 33 linear filing inches.
It is estimated that an additional 300 filing inches should be added to allow for five-year expansion capabilities. How many shelving units should be purchased?

    A. 7 B. 10 C. 11 D. 13

    5._____

6. In the *Reason for Encounter* classification system, each item is coded as a

    A. letter followed by two digits
    B. digit followed by two letters
    C. two-digit number with one decimal digit subcategory
    D. three-digit number

    6._____

7. According to the World Health Organization's definitions for reporting reproductive health statistics, any neonate whose birth occurs from the first day (267th day) of the 39th week, through the end of the last day of the 42nd week (294th day) following the onset of the last menstrual period, would be termed _____ neonate.

    A. low birthweight
    B. preterm
    C. term
    D. post-term

    7._____

8. Medicare's UB-92 form for billing data includes space for _____ procedure code(s).
   A. 1 B. 3 C. 6 D. 9

9. Of the following devices, the _____ is commonly used in health information departments to graphically display a specific project's time line and progress.
   A. bar graph
   B. Gantt chart
   C. line graph
   D. histogram

10. Which component of the cancer registry contains the abstracts of cancer patients who received all or part of their FIRST course of treatment at the reporting facility?
    A. Case files
    B. Master index file
    C. Accession register
    D. Follow-up file

11. The _____ technique used by health information management to monitor the *quality* of work is patterned after the production industry.
    A. questionnaire
    B. checklist
    C. report
    D. audit

12. The health information practitioner is *usually* responsible for working with the chair of the record committee to prepare the agenda for committee meetings which must be held AT LEAST
    A. monthly
    B. quarterly
    C. biannually
    D. annually

13. When a patient is admitted to a hospital, a medical history will NOT be required if a previous, unaltered history has been performed no more than _____ prior to the patient's admission.
    A. two weeks
    B. thirty days
    C. six months
    D. one year

14. Of the following types of medical record delinquencies, a missing _____ would be considered LEAST serious.
    A. discharge summary
    B. medical history report
    C. signature on attestation
    D. operative report

15. If a home care patient were to require eight or more hours of daily nursing care, which of the Medicare reimbursement categories would be imposed?
    A. Continuous home care
    B. Routine home care
    C. General inpatient care
    D. Inpatient respite care

16. A quantitative analysis of medical record documentation includes, as a basic requirement, a review of the record for
    A. a recording of all necessary instances of informed consent
    B. a consistent recording of diagnostic statements
    C. the required authentication on all entries
    D. the description and justification of the course of a patient's hospitalization

17. The ideal number of digits in a record number is

    A. 4   B. 5   C. 6   D. 7

18. Which type of HMO follows the same type of record-keeping practices as the independent practice association?

    A. Group model or closed
    B. Staff model
    C. Multi-specialty
    D. Preferred provider

19. Of the following, _____ plans would be considered to be the driving force behind management's planning function.

    A. strategic
    B. tactical
    C. operational
    D. mission

20. When reviewing a medical record for entry consistency, health information professionals should seek entries that could result in the miscommunication of patient care information.
    Each of the following is a common source of this type of miscommunication EXCEPT

    A. progress notes written by different members of a health care team
    B. admission record data recorded by more than one member of a health care team
    C. mismatched orders and medication records
    D. admission and discharge information recorded by different health care personnel

21. A quantitative analysis of medical record documentation is LEAST likely to be useful in solving problems associated with

    A. dating of entries
    B. illegibility or incomplete content
    C. inappropriate correction of errors
    D. spaces that should be lined through to prevent tampering

22. When a health care institution is required by public health laws to report certain diseases or occurrences, the responsibility for reporting USUALLY rests with the

    A. provider
    B. health information department
    C. admissions department
    D. payer

23. An *encounter*, according to standard ambulatory health care data practices, is defined as a

    A. patient receiving laboratory services through a separate provider after the original encounter
    B. outpatient visiting both a physician's office and a clinic as parts of an individual treatment plan
    C. patient's imaging reports being interpreted, when the patient is not physically present, by someone other than the referring physician
    D. patient receiving services from a pharmacist

24. When an applicant is being interviewed for a position in the department, the rules of the EEOC would permit questions about the applicant's

   A. spouse's occupation
   B. convictions for criminal activity
   C. military record
   D. plans for beginning a family

25. The _____ would typically be included in the admitting evaluation or assessment of a patient in a long-term care facility.

   A. stop orders for medications
   B. after-care recommendations
   C. social history
   D. name of the transferring or referring institution

KEY (CORRECT ANSWERS)

1. C	11. D
2. B	12. B
3. D	13. B
4. C	14. A
5. C	15. A
6. A	16. C
7. C	17. C
8. C	18. A
9. B	19. D
10. A	20. B

21. B
22. A
23. A
24. B
25. C

RECORD KEEPING
EXAMINATION SECTION
TEST 1

DIRECTIONS: Each question or incomplete statement is followed by several suggested answers or completions. Select the one that BEST answers the question or completes the statement. *PRINT THE LETTER OF THE CORRECT ANSWER IN THE SPACE AT THE RIGHT.*

Questions 1-7.

DIRECTIONS: In answering Questions 1 through 7, use the following master list. For each question, determine where the name would fit on the master list. Each answer choice indicates right before or after the name in the answer choice.

    Aaron, Jane
    Armstead, Brendan
    Bailey, Charles
    Dent, Ricardo
    Grant, Mark
    Mars, Justin
    Methieu, Justine
    Parker, Cathy
    Sampson, Suzy
    Thomas, Heather

1. Schmidt, William
   A. Right before Cathy Parker
   B. Right after Heather Thomas
   C. Right after Suzy Sampson
   D. Right before Ricardo Dent

2. Asanti, Kendall
   A. Right before Jane Aaron
   B. Right after Charles Bailey
   C. Right before Justine Methieu
   D. Right after Brendan Armstead

3. O'Brien, Daniel
   A. Right after Justine Methieu
   B. Right before Jane Aaron
   C. Right after Mark Grant
   D. Right before Suzy Sampson

4. Marrow, Alison
   A. Right before Cathy Parker
   B. Right before Justin Mars
   C. Right before Mark Grant
   D. Right after Heather Thomas

5. Grantt, Marissa
   A. Right before Mark Grant
   B. Right after Mark Grant
   C. Right after Justin Mars
   D. Right before Suzy Sampson

6. Thompson, Heath   6.____
   A. Right after Justin Mars   B. Right before Suzy Sampson
   C. Right after Heather Thomas   D. Right before Cathy Parker

DIRECTIONS: Before answering Question 7, add in all of the names from Questions 1 through 6. Then fit the name in alphabetical order based on the new list.

7. Francisco, Mildred   7.____
   A. Right before Mark Grant   B. Right after Marissa Grantt
   C. Right before Alison Marrow   D. Right after Kendall Asanti

Questions 8-10.

DIRECTIONS: In answering Questions 8 through 10, compare each pair of names and addresses. Indicate whether they are the same or different in any way.

8. William H. Pratt, J.D.   William H. Pratt, J.D.   8.____
   Attourney at Law   Attorney at Law
   A. No differences   B. 1 difference
   C. 2 differences   D. 3 differences

9. 1303 Theater Drive,; Apt. 3-B   1330 Theatre Drive,; Apt. 3-B   9.____
   A. No differences   B. 1 difference
   C. 2 differences   D. 3 differences

10. Petersdorff, Briana and Mary   Petersdorff, Briana and Mary   10.____
    A. No differences   B. 1 difference
    C. 2 differences   D. 3 differences

11. Which of the following words, if any, are misspelled?   11.____
    A. Affordable   B. Circumstansial
    C. Legalese   D. None of the above

Questions 12-13.

DIRECTIONS: Questions 12 and 13 are to be answered on the basis of the following table.

Standardized Test Results for High School Students in District #1230

	English	Math	Science	Reading
High School 1	21	22	15	18
High School 2	12	16	13	15
High School 3	16	18	21	17
High School 4	19	14	15	16

The scores for each high school in the district were averaged out and listed for each subject tested. Scores of 0-10 are significantly below College Readiness Standards. 11-15 are below College Readiness, 16-20 meet College Readiness, and 21-25 are above College Readiness.

12. If the high schools need to meet or exceed in at least half the categories in order to NOT be considered "at risk," which schools are considered "at risk"?
    A. High School 2
    B. High School 3
    C. High School 4
    D. Both A and C

    12.____

13. What percentage of subjects did the district as a whole meet or exceed College Readiness standards?
    A. 25%	B. 50%	C. 75%	D. 100%

    13.____

Questions 14-15.

DIRECTIONS: Questions 14 and 15 are to be answered on the basis of the following information.

You have seven employees working as a part of your team: Austin, Emily, Jeremy, Christina, Martin, Harriet, and Steve. You have just sent an e-mail informing them that there will be a mandatory training session next week. To ensure that work still gets done, you are offering the training twice during the week: once on Tuesday and also on Thursday. This way half the employees will still be working while the other half attend the training. The only other issue is that Jeremy doesn't work on Tuesdays and Harriet doesn't work on Thursdays due to compressed work schedules.

14. Which of the following is a possible attendance roster for the first training session?
    A. Emily, Jeremy, Steve
    B. Steve, Christina, Harriet
    C. Harriet, Jeremy, Austin
    D. Steve, Martin, Jeremy

    14.____

15. If Harriet, Christina, and Steve attend the training session on Tuesday, which of the following is a possible roster for Thursday's training session?
    A. Jeremy, Emily, and Austin
    B. Emily, Martin, and Harriet
    C. Austin, Christina, and Emily
    D. Jeremy, Emily, and Steve

    15.____

Questions 16-20.

DIRECTIONS: In answering Questions 16 through 20, you will be given a word and will need to choose the answer choice that is MOST similar or different to the word.

16. Which word means the SAME as *annual*?
    A. Monthly	B. Usually	C. Yearly	D. Constantly

    16.____

17. Which word means the SAME as *effort*?
    A. Energy	B. Equate	C. Cherish	D. Commence

    17.____

18. Which word means the OPPOSITE of *forlorn*?
    A. Neglected	B. Lethargy	C. Optimistic	D. Astonished

    18.____

19. Which word means the SAME as *risk*?
    A. Admire	B. Hazard	C. Limit	D. Hesitant

    19.____

20. Which word means the OPPOSITE of *translucent*? 20.____
    A. Opaque   B. Transparent   C. Luminous   D. Introverted

21. Last year, Jamie's annual salary was $50,000. Her boss called her today 21.____
    to inform her that she would receive a 20% raise for the upcoming year. How
    much more money will Jamie receive next year?
    A. $60,000   B. $10,000   C. $1,000   D. $51,000

22. You and a co-worker work for a temp hiring agency as part of their office 22.____
    staff. You both are given 6 days off per month. How many days off are you
    and your co-worker given in a year?
    A. 24   B. 72   C. 144   D. 48

23. If Margot makes $34,000 per year and she works 40 hours per week for 23.____
    all 52 weeks, what is her hourly rate?
    A. $16.34/hour   B. $17.00/hour   C. $15.54/hour   D. $13.23/hour

24. How many dimes are there in $175.00? 24.____
    A. 175   B. 1,750   C. 3,500   D. 17,500

25. If Janey is three times as old as Emily, and Emily is 3, how old is Janey? 25.____
    A. 6   B. 9   C. 12   D. 15

KEY (CORRECT ANSWERS)

1.	C		11.	B
2.	D		12.	A
3.	A		13.	D
4.	B		14.	B
5.	B		15.	A
6.	C		16.	C
7.	A		17.	A
8.	B		18.	C
9.	C		19.	B
10.	A		20.	A

21. B
22. C
23. A
24. B
25. B

TEST 2

DIRECTIONS: Each question or incomplete statement is followed by several suggested answers or completions. Select the one that BEST answers the question or completes the statement. *PRINT THE LETTER OF THE CORRECT ANSWER IN THE SPACE AT THE RIGHT.*

Questions 1-6.

DIRECTIONS: Questions 1 through 6 are to be answered on the basis of the following information.

item	name of item to be ordered
quantity	minimum number that can be ordered
beginning amount	amount in stock at start of month
amount received	amount receiving during month
ending amount	amount in stock at end of month
amount used	amount used during month
amount to order	will need at least as much of each item as used in the previous month
unit price	cost of each unit of an item
total price	total price for the order

Item	Quantity	Beginning	Received	Ending	Amount Used	Amount to Order	Unit Price	Total Price
Pens	10	22	10	8	24	20	$0.11	$2.20
Spiral notebooks	8	30	13	12			$0.25	
Binder clips	2 boxes	3 boxes	1 box	1 box			$1.79	
Sticky notes	3 packs	12 packs	4 packs	2 packs			$1.29	
Dry erase markers	1 pack (dozen)	34 markers	8 markers	40 markers			$16.49	
Ink cartridges (printer)	1 cartridge	3 cartridges	1 cartridge	2 cartridges			$79.99	
Folders	10 folders	25 folders	15 folders	10 folders			$1.08	

1. How many packs of sticky notes were used during the month?   1._____
   A. 16   B. 10   C. 12   D. 14

2. How many folders need to be ordered for next month?   2._____
   A. 15   B. 20   C. 30   D. 40

3. What is the total price of notebooks that you will need to order?   3._____
   A. $6.00   B. $0.25   C. $4.50   D. $2.75

4. Which of the following will you spend the second most money on?   4._____
   A. Ink cartridges   B. Dry erase markers
   C. Sticky notes   D. Binder clips

5. How many packs of dry erase markers should you order?   5._____
   A. 1   B. 8   C. 12   D. 0

6. What will be the total price of the file folders you order? 6.____
   A. $20.16   B. $21.60   C. $10.80   D. $4.32

Questions 7-11.

DIRECTIONS: Questions 7 through 11 are to be answered on the basis of the following table.

Number of Car Accidents, By Location and Cause, for 2014						
	Location 1		Location 2		Location 3	
Cause	Number	Percent	Number	Percent	Number	Percent
Severe Weather	10		25		30	
Excessive Speeding	20	40	5		10	
Impaired Driving	15		15	25	8	
Miscellaneous	5		15		2	4
TOTALS	50	100	60	100	50	100

7. Which of the following is the third highest cause of accidents for all three locations? 7.____
   A. Severe Weather   B. Impaired Driving
   C. Miscellaneous   D. Excessive Speeding

8. The average number of Severe Weather accidents per week at Location 3 for the year (52 weeks) was MOST NEARLY 8.____
   A. 0.57   B. 30   C. 1   D. 1.25

9. Which location had the LARGEST percentage of accidents caused by Impaired Driving? 9.____
   A. 1   B. 2   C. 3   D. Both A and B

10. If one-third of the accidents at all three locations resulted in at least one fatality, what is the LEAST amount of deaths caused by accidents last year? 10.____
    A. 60   B. 106   C. 66   D. 53

11. What is the percentage of accidents caused by miscellaneous means from all three locations in 2014? 11.____
    A. 5%   B. 10%   C. 13%   D. 25%

12. How many pairs of the following groups of letters are exactly alike? 12.____
    ACDOBJ   ACDBOJ
    HEWBWR   HEWRWB
    DEERVS   DEERVS
    BRFQSX   BRFQSX
    WEYRVB   WEYRVB
    SPQRZA   SQRPZA

    A. 2   B. 3   C. 4   D. 5

3 (#2)

Questions 13-19.

DIRECTIONS: Questions 13 through 19 are to be answered on the basis of the following information.

In 2012, the most current information on the American population was finished. The information was compiled by 200 volunteers in each of the 50 states. The territory of Puerto Rico, a sovereign of the United States, had 25 people assigned to compile data. In February of 2010, volunteers in each state and sovereign began collecting information. In Puerto Rico, data collection finished by January 31st, 2011, while work in the United States was completed on June 30, 2012. Each volunteer gathered data on the population of their state or sovereign. When the information was compiled, volunteers sent reports to the nation's capital, Washington, D.C. Each volunteer worked 20 hours per month and put together 10 reports per month. After the data was compiled in total, 50 people reviewed the data and worked from January 2012 to December 2012.

13. How many reports were generated from February 2010 to April 2010 in Illinois and Ohio?
    A. 3,000   B. 6,000   C. 12,000   D. 15,000

14. How many volunteers in total collected population data in January 2012?
    A. 10,000   B. 2,000   C. 225   D. 200

15. How many reports were put together in May 2012?
    A. 2,000   B. 50,000   C. 100,000   D. 100,250

16. How many hours did the Puerto Rican volunteers work in the fall (September-November)?
    A. 60   B. 500   C. 1,500   D. 0

17. How many workers were compiling or reviewing data in July 2012?
    A. 25   B. 50   C. 200   D. 250

18. What was the total amount of hours worked by Nevada volunteers in July 2010?
    A. 500   B. 4,000   C. 4,500   D. 5,000

19. How many reviewers worked in January 2013?
    A. 75   B. 50   C. 0   D. 25

20. John has to file 10 documents per shelf. How many documents would it take for John to fill 40 shelves?
    A. 40   B. 400   C. 4,500   D. 5,000

21. Jill wants to travel from New York City to Los Angeles by bike, which is approximately 2,772 miles. How many miles per day would Jill need to average if she wanted to complete the trip in 4 weeks?
    A. 100   B. 89   C. 99   D. 94

22. If there are 24 CPU's and only 7 monitors, how many more monitors do you need to have the same amount of monitors as CPU's?
    A. Not enough information B. 17
    C. 31 D. 0

    22.____

23. If Gerry works 5 days a week and 8 hours each day, and John works 3 days a week and 10 hours each day, how many more hours per year will Gerry work than John?
    A. They work the same amount of hours.
    B. 450
    C. 520
    D. 832

    23.____

24. Jimmy gets transferred to a new office. The new office has 25 employees, but only 16 are there due to a blizzard. How many coworkers was Jimmy able to meet on his first day?
    A. 16 B. 25 C. 9 D. 7

    24.____

25. If you do a fundraiser for charities in your area and raise $500 total, how much would you give to each charity if you were donating equal amounts to 3 of them?
    A. $250.00 B. $167.77 C. $50.00 D. $111.11

    25.____

KEY (CORRECT ANSWERS)

1. D
2. B
3. A
4. C
5. D

6. B
7. D
8. A
9. A
10. D

11. C
12. B
13. C
14. A
15. C

16. C
17. B
18. B
19. C
20. B

21. C
22. B
23. C
24. A
25. B

TEST 3

DIRECTIONS: Each question or incomplete statement is followed by several suggested answers or completions. Select the one that BEST answers the question or completes the statement. *PRINT THE LETTER OF THE CORRECT ANSWER IN THE SPACE AT THE RIGHT.*

Questions 1-3.

DIRECTIONS: In answering Questions 1 through 3, choose the correctly spelled word.

1. A. allusion B. alusion C. allusien D. allution 1.____

2. A. altitude B. alltitude C. atlitude D. altlitude 2.____

3. A. althogh B. allthough C. althrough D. although 3.____

Questions 4-9.

DIRECTIONS: In answering Questions 4 through 9, choose the answer that BEST completes the analogy.

4. Odometer is to mileage as compass is to 4.____
 A. speed B. needle C. hiking D. direction

5. Marathon is to race as hibernation is to 5.____
 A. winter B. dream C. sleep D. bear

6. Cup is to coffee as bowl is to 6.____
 A. dish B. spoon C. food D. soup

7. Flow is to river as stagnant is to 7.____
 A. pool B. rain C. stream D. canal

8. Paw is to cat as hoof is to 8.____
 A. lamb B. horse C. lion D. elephant

9. Architect is to building as sculptor is to 9.____
 A. museum B. chisel C. stone D. statue

Questions 10-14.

DIRECTIONS: Questions 10 through 14 are to be answered on the basis of the following graph.

Population of Carroll City Broken Down by Age and Gender (in Thousands)			
Age	Female	Male	Total
Under 15	60	60	120
15-23		22	
24-33		20	44
34-43	13	18	31
44-53	20		67
64 and Over	65	65	130
TOTAL	230	232	462

10. How many people in the city are between the ages of 15-23?
    A. 70 B. 46,000 C. 70,000 D. 225,000

11. Approximately what percentage of the total population of the city was female aged 24-33?
    A. 10% B. 5% C. 15% D. 25%

12. If 33% of the males have a job and 55% of females don't have a job, which of the following statements is TRUE?
    A. Males have approximately 2,600 more jobs than females.
    B. Females have approximately 49,000 more jobs than males.
    C. Females have approximately 26,000 more jobs than males.
    D. None of the above statements are true.

13. How many females between the ages of 15-23 live in Carroll City?
    A. 67,000 B. 24,000 C. 48,000 D. 91,000

14. Assume all males 44-53 living in Carroll City are employed. If two-thirds of males age 44-53 work jobs outside of Carroll City, how many work within city limits?
    A. 31,333
    B. 15,667
    C. 47,000
    D. Cannot answer the question with the information provided

Questions 15-16.

DIRECTIONS: Questions 15 and 16 are labeled as shown. Alphabetize them for filing. Choose the answer that correctly shows the order.

15. (1) AED
    (2) OOS
    (3) FOA
    (4) DOM
    (5) COB

   A. 2-5-4-3-2 B. 1-4-5-2-3 C. 1-5-4-2-3 D. 1-5-4-3-2

15.____

16. Alphabetize the names of the people. Last names are given last.
    (1) Lindsey Jamestown
    (2) Jane Alberta
    (3) Ally Jamestown
    (4) Allison Johnston
    (5) Lyle Moreno

   A. 2-1-3-4-5 B. 3-4-2-1-5 C. 2-3-1-4-5 D. 4-3-2-1-5

16.____

17. Which of the following words is misspelled?
    A. disgust
    B. whisper
    C. locale
    D. none of the above

17.____

Questions 18-21.

DIRECTIONS: Questions 18 through 21 are to be answered on the basis of the following list of employees.

   Robertson, Aaron
   Bacon, Gina
   Jerimiah, Trace
   Gillette, Stanley
   Jacks, Sharon

18. Which employee name would come in third in alphabetized list?
    A. Robertson, Aaron
    B. Jerimiah, Trace
    C. Gillette, Stanley
    D. Jacks, Sharon

18.____

19. Which employee's first name starts with the letter in the alphabet that is five letters after the first letter of their last name?
    A. Jerimiah, Trace
    B. Bacon, Gina
    C. Jacks, Sharon
    D. GIllette, Stanley

19.____

20. How many employees have last names that are exactly five letters long?
    A. 1   B. 2   C. 3   D. 4

20.____

21. How many of the employees have either a first or last name that starts with the letter "G"? 21._____
    A. 1 B. 2 C. 4 D. 5

Questions 22-25.

DIRECTIONS: Questions 22 through 25 are to be answered on the basis of the following chart.

Bicycle Sales (Model #34JA32)							
Country	May	June	July	August	September	October	Total
Germany	34	47	45	54	56	60	296
Britain	40	44	36	47	47	46	260
Ireland	37	32	32	32	34	33	200
Portugal	14	14	14	16	17	14	89
Italy	29	29	28	31	29	31	177
Belgium	22	24	24	26	25	23	144
Total	176	198	179	206	208	207	1166

22. What percentage of the overall total was sold to the German importer? 22._____
    A. 25.3% B. 22% C. 24.1% D. 23%

23. What percentage of the overall total was sold in September? 23._____
    A. 24.1% B. 25.6% C. 17.9% D. 24.6%

24. What is the average number of units per month imported into Belgium over the first four months shown? 24._____
    A. 26 B. 20 C. 24 D. 31

25. If you look at the three smallest importers, what is their total import percentage? 25._____
    A. 35.1% B. 37.1% C. 40% D. 28%

KEY (CORRECT ANSWERS)

1.	A	11.	B
2.	A	12.	C
3.	D	13.	C
4.	D	14.	B
5.	C	15.	D
6.	D	16.	C
7.	A	17.	D
8.	B	18.	D
9.	D	19.	B
10.	C	20.	B

21. B
22. A
23. C
24. C
25. A

TEST 4

DIRECTIONS: Each question or incomplete statement is followed by several suggested answers or completions. Select the one that BEST answers the question or completes the statement. *PRINT THE LETTER OF THE CORRECT ANSWER IN THE SPACE AT THE RIGHT.*

Questions 1-6.

DIRECTIONS: In answering Questions 1 through 6, choose the sentence that represents the BEST example of English grammar.

1. A. Joey and me want to go on a vacation next week.
    B. Gary told Jim he would need to take some time off.
    C. If turning six years old, Jim's uncle would teach Spanish to him.
    D. Fax a copy of your resume to Ms. Perez and me.

2. A. Jerry stood in line for almost two hours.
    B. The reaction to my engagement was less exciting than I thought it would be.
    C. Carlos and me have done great work on this project.
    D. Two parts of the speech needs to be revised before tomorrow.

3. A. Arriving home, the alarm was tripped.
    B. Jonny is regarded as a stand up guy, a responsible parent, and he doesn't give up until a task is finished.
    C. Each employee must submit a drug test each month.
    D. One of the documents was incinerated in the explosion.

4. A. As soon as my parents get home, I told them I finished all of my chores.
    B. I asked my teacher to send me my missing work, check my absences, and how did I do on my test.
    C. Matt attempted to keep it concealed from Jenny and me.
    D. If Mary or him cannot get work done on time, I will have to split them up.

5. A. Driving to work, the traffic report warned him of an accident on Highway 47.
    B. Jimmy has performed well this season.
    C. Since finishing her degree, several job offers have been given to Cam.
    D. Our boss is creating unstable conditions for we employees.

6. A. The thief was described as a tall man with a wiry mustache weighing approximately 150 pounds.
    B. She gave Patrick and I some more time to finish our work.
    C. One of the books that he ordered was damaged in shipping.
    D. While talking on the rotary phone, the car Jim was driving skidded off the road.

Questions 7-9.

DIRECTIONS: Questions 7 through 9 are to be answered on the basis of the following graph.

Ice Lake Frozen Flight (2002-2013)		
Year	Number of Participants	Temperature (Fahrenheit)
2002	22	4°
2003	50	33°
2004	69	18°
2005	104	22°
2006	108	24°
2007	288	33°
2008	173	9°
2009	598	39°
2010	698	26°
2011	696	30°
2012	777	28°
2013	578	32°

7. Which two year span had the LARGEST difference between temperatures?
   A. 2002 and 2003
   B. 2011 and 2012
   C. 2008 and 2009
   D. 2003 and 2004

8. How many total people participated in the years after the temperature reached at least 29°?
   A. 2,295 B. 1,717 C. 2,210 D. 4,543

9. In 2007, the event saw 288 participants, while in 2008 that number dropped to 173. Which of the following reasons BEST explains the drop in participants?
   A. The event had not been going on that long and people didn't know about it.
   B. The lake water wasn't cold enough to have people jump in.
   C. The temperature was too cold for many people who would have normally participated.
   D. None of the above reasons explain the drop in participants.

10. In the following list of numbers, how many times does 4 come just after 2 when 2 comes just after an odd number?
    2365247653898632488572486392424
    A. 2 B. 3 C. 4 D. 5

11. Which choice below lists the letter that is as far after B as S is after N in the alphabet?
    A. G B. H C. I D. J

Questions 12-15.

DIRECTIONS: Questions 12 through 15 are to be answered on the basis of the following directory and list of changes.

Directory		
Name	Emp. Type	Position
Julie Taylor	Warehouse	Packer
James King	Office	Administrative Assistant
John Williams	Office	Salesperson
Ray Moore	Warehouse	Maintenance
Kathleen Byrne	Warehouse	Supervisor
Amy Jones	Office	Salesperson
Paul Jonas	Office	Salesperson
Lisa Wong	Warehouse	Loader
Eugene Lee	Office	Accountant
Bruce Lavine	Office	Manager
Adam Gates	Warehouse	Packer
Will Suter	Warehouse	Packer
Gary Lorper	Office	Accountant
Jon Adams	Office	Salesperson
Susannah Harper	Office	Salesperson

Directory Updates:
- Employee e-mail addresses will adhere to the following guidelines: lastnamefirstname@apexindustries.com (ex. Susannah Harper is harpersusannah@apexindustries.com). Currently, employees in the warehouse share one e-mail, distribution@apexindustries.com.
- The "Loader" position will now be referred to as "Specialist I"
- Adam Gates has accepted a Supervisor position within the Warehouse and is no longer a Packer. All warehouse employees report to the two Supervisors and all office employees report to the Manager.

12. Amy Jones tried to send an e-mail to Adam Gates, but it wouldn't send. Which of the following offers the BEST explanation?
    A. Amy put Adam's first name first and then his last name.
    B. Adam doesn't check his e-mail, so he wouldn't know if he received the e-mail or not.
    C. Adam does not have his own e-mail.
    D. Office employees are not allowed to send e-mails to each other.

13. How many Packers currently work for Apex Industries?
    A. 2   B. 3   C. 4   D. 5

14. What position does Lisa Wong currently hold?
    A. Specialist I   B. Secretary
    C. Administrative Assistant   D. Loader

15. If an employee wanted to contact the office manager, which of the following e-mails should the e-mail be sent to?
    A. officemanager@apexindustries.com
    B. brucelavine@apexindustries.com
    C. lavinebruce@apexindustries.com
    D. distribution@apexindustries.com

15.____

Questions 16-19.

DIRECTIONS: In answering Questions 16 through 19, compare the three names, numbers or addresses.

16. Smiley Yarnell   Smiley Yarnel   Smily Yarnell
    A. All three are exactly alike.
    B. The first and second are exactly alike.
    C. The second and third are exactly alike.
    D. All three are different.

16.____

17. 1583 Theater Drive   1583 Theater Drive   1583 Theatre Drive
    A. All three are exactly alike.
    B. The first and second are exactly alike.
    C. The second and third are exactly alike.
    D. All three are different.

17.____

18. 3341893212   3341893212   3341893212
    A. All three are exactly alike.
    B. The first and second are exactly alike.
    C. The second and third are exactly alike.
    D. All three are different.

18.____

19. Douglass Watkins   Douglas Watkins   Douglass Watkins
    A. All three are exactly alike.
    B. The first and third are exactly alike.
    C. The second and third are exactly alike.
    D. All three are different.

19.____

Questions 20-24.

DIRECTIONS: In answering Questions 20 through 24, you will be presented with a word. Choose the synonym that BEST represents the word in question.

20. Flexible
    A. delicate   B. inflammable   C. strong   D. pliable

20.____

21. Alternative
    A. choice   B. moderate   C. lazy   D. value

21.____

22. Corroborate
    A. examine   B. explain   C. verify   D. explain   22.____

23. Respiration
    A. recovery   B. breathing   C. sweating   D. selfish   23.____

24. Negligent
    A. lazy   B. moderate   C. hopeless   D. lax   24.____

25. Plumber is to Wrench as Painter is to   25.____
    A. pipe   B. shop   C. hammer   D. brush

KEY (CORRECT ANSWERS)

1. D
2. A
3. D
4. C
5. B

6. C
7. C
8. B
9. C
10. C

11. A
12. C
13. A
14. A
15. C

16. D
17. B
18. A
19. B
20. D

21. A
22. C
23. B
24. D
25. D

CODING
EXAMINATION SECTION
COMMENTARY

An ingenious question-type called coding, involving elements of alphabetizing, filing, name and number comparison, and evaluative judgment and application, has currently won wide acceptance in testing circles for measuring clerical aptitude and general ability, particularly on the senior (middle) grades (levels).

While the directions for this question usually vary in detail, the candidate is generally asked to consider groups of names, codes, and numbers, and then, according to a given plan, to arrange codes in alphabetic order; to arrange these in numerical sequence; to re-arrange columns of names and numbers in correct order; to espy errors in coding; to choose the correct coding arrangement in consonance with the given directions and examples, etc.

This question-type appear to have few parameters in respect to form, substance, or degree of difficulty.

Accordingly, acquaintance with, and practice in, the coding question is recommended for the serious candidate.

TEST 1

DIRECTIONS: Questions 1 through 8 are to be answered on the basis of the code table and the instructions given below.

Code Letter for Traffic Problem	B	H	Q	J	F	L	M	I
Code Number for Action Taken	1	2	3	4	5	6	7	8

Assume that each of the capital letters on the above chart is a radio code for a particular traffic problem and that the number immediately below each capital letter is the radio code for the correct action to be taken to deal with the problem. For instance, "1" is the action to be taken to deal with problem "B", "2" is the action to be taken to deal with problem "H", and so forth.

In each question, a series of code letters is given in Column 1. Column 2 gives four different arrangements of code numbers. You are to pick the answer (A, B, C, or D) in Column 2 that gives the code numbers that match the code letters in the same order.

SAMPLE QUESTION

Column 1
BHLFMQ

Column 2
A. 125678
B. 216573
C. 127653
D. 126573

According to the chart, the code numbers that correspond to these code letters are as follows: B – 1, M – 2, L – 6, F – 5, M – 7, Q – 3. Therefore, the right answer is 126573. This answer is D in Column 2.

2 (#1)

	Column 1	Column 2	
1.	BHQLMI	A. 123456 B. 123567 C. 123678 D. 125678	1.____
2.	HBJQLF	A. 214365 B. 213456 C. 213465 D. 214387	2.____
3.	QHMLFJ	A. 321654 B. 345678 C. 327645 D. 327654	3.____
4.	FLQJIM	A. 543287 B. 563487 C. 564378 D. 654378	4.____
5.	FBIHMJ	A. 518274 B. 152874 C. 528164 D. 517842	5.____
6.	MIHFQB	A. 872341 B. 782531 C. 782341 D. 783214	6.____
7.	JLFHQIM	A. 465237 B. 456387 C. 4652387 D. 4562387	7.____
8.	LBJQIFH	A. 614382 B. 6134852 C. 61437852 D. 61431852	8.____

KEY (CORRECT ANSWERS)

1. C
2. A
3. D
4. B
5. A
6. B
7. C
8. A

TEST 2

DIRECTIONS: Each question or incomplete statement is followed by several suggested answers or completions. Select the one that BEST answers the question or completes the statement. *PRINT THE LETTER OF THE CORRECT ANSWER IN THE SPACE AT THE RIGHT.*

Questions 1-5.

DIRECTIONS: Questions 1 through 5 are based on the following list showing the name and number of each of nine inmates.

1. Johnson   4. Thompson   7. Gordon
2. Smith   5. Frank   8. Porter
3. Edwards   6. Murray   9. Lopez

Each question consists of 3 sets of numbers and letters. Each set should consist of the numbers of three inmates and the first letter of each of their names. The letters should be in the same order as the numbers. In at least two of the three choices, there will be an error. On your answer sheet, mark only that choice in which the letters correspond with the numbers and are in the same order. If all three sets are wrong, mark choice D in your answer space.

SAMPLE QUESTION
A. 386 EPM
B. 542 FST
C. 474 LGT

Since 3 corresponds to E for Edwards, 8 corresponds to P for Porter, and 6 corresponds to M for Murray, choice A is correct and should be entered in your answer space. Choice B is wrong because letters T and S have been reversed. Choice C is wrong because the first number, which is 4, does NOT correspond with the first letter of choice C, which is L. It should have been T. If choice A were also wrong, then D would be the correct answer.

1. A. 382 EGS   B. 461 TMJ   C. 875 PLF   1._____

2. A. 549 FLT   B. 692 MJS   C. 758 GSP   2._____

3. A. 936 LEM   B. 253 FSE   C. 147 JTL   3._____

4. A. 569 PML   B. 716 GJP   C. 842 PTS   4._____

5. A. 356 FEM   B. 198 JPL   C. 637 MEG   5._____

Questions 6-10.

DIRECTIONS: Questions 6 through 10 are to be answered on the basis of the following information:

2 (#3)

In order to make sure stock is properly located, incoming units are stored as follows:

STOCK NUMBERS	BIN NUMBERS
00100 – 39999	D30, L44
40000 – 69999	14L, D38
70000 – 99999	41L, 80D
100000 and over	614, 83D

Using the above table, choose the answer A, B, C, or D, which lists the correct Bin Number for the Stock Number given.

6. 17243
    A. 41L   B. 83D   C. 14L   D. D30
6.____

7. 9219
    A. D38   B. L44   C. 614   D. 41L
7.____

8. 90125
    A. 41L   B. 614   C. D38   D. D30
8.____

9. 10001
    A. L44   B. D38   C. 80D   D. 83D
9.____

10. 200100
    A. 41L   B. 14L   C. 83D   D. D30
10.____

KEY (CORRECT ANSWERS)

1.	B	6.	D
2.	D	7.	B
3.	A	8.	A
4.	C	9.	A
5.	C	10.	C

TEST 3

DIRECTIONS: Each question or incomplete statement is followed by several suggested answers or completions. Select the one that BEST answers the question or completes the statement. *PRINT THE LETTER OF THE CORRECT ANSWER IN THE SPACE AT THE RIGHT.*

Questions 1-9.

DIRECTIONS: Assume that the Police Department is planning to conduct a statistical study of individuals who have been convicted of crimes during a certain year. For the purpose of this study, identification numbers are being assigned to individuals in the following manner:

The first two digits indicate the age of the individual.
The third digit indicates the sex of the individual:
    1. Male
    2. Female
The fourth digit indicates the type of crime involved:
    1. criminal homicide
    2. forcible rape
    3. robbery
    4. aggravated assault
    5. burglary
    6. larceny
    7. auto theft
    8. other
The fifth and sixth digits indicate the month in which the conviction occurred:
    01.   January
    02.   February, etc.

Questions 1 through 9 are to be answered SOLELY on the basis of the above information and the following list of individuals and identification numbers.

Abbott, Richard	271304	Morris, Chris	212705
Collins, Terry	352111	Owens, William	231412
Elders, Edward	191207	Parker, Leonard	291807
George, Linda	182809	Robinson, Charles	311102
Hill, Leslie	251702	Sands, Jean	202610
Jones, Jackie	301106	Smith, Michael	42108
Lewis, Edith	402406	Turner, Donald	191601
Mack, Helen	332509	White, Barbara	242803

1. The number of women on the above list is   1.____
    A. 6   B. 7   C. 8   D. 9

2. The two convictions which occurred during February were for the crimes of   2._____
   A. aggravated assault and auto theft
   B. auto theft and criminal homicide
   C. burglary and larceny
   D. forcible rape and robbery

3. The ONLY man convicted of auto theft was   3._____
   A. Richard Abbott   B. Leslie Hill
   C. Chris Morris   D. Leonard Parker

4. The number of people on the list who were 25 years old or older is   4._____
   A. 6   B. 7   C. 8   D. 9

5. The OLDEST person on the list is   5._____
   A. Terry Collins   B. Edith Lewis
   C. Helen Mack   D. Michael Smith

6. The two people on the list who are the same age are   6._____
   A. Richard Abbott and Michael Smith
   B. Edward Elders and Donald Turner
   C. Linda George and Helen Mack
   D. Leslie Hill and Charles Robinson

7. A 28-year-old man who was convicted of aggravated assault in October would have identification number   7._____
   A. 281410   B. 281509   C. 282311   D. 282409

8. A 33-year-old woman convicted in April of criminal homicide would have identification number   8._____
   A. 331140   B. 331204   C. 332014   D. 332104

9. The number of people on the above list who were convicted during the first six months of the year is   9._____
   A. 6   B. 7   C. 8   D. 9

Questions 10-19.

DIRECTIONS: The following is a list of patients who were referred by various clinics to the laboratory for tests. After each name is a patient identification number. Questions 10 through 19 are to be answered on the basis of the information contained in this list and the explanation accompanying it.

The first digit refers to the clinic which made the referral:
1. cardiac
2. Renal
3. Pediatrics
4. Ophthalmology
5. Orthopedics
6. Hematology
7. Gynecology
8. Neurology
9. Gastroenterology

3 (#2)

The second digit refers to the sex of the patient:
1. male
2. female

The third and fourth digits give the age of the patient

The last two digits give the day of the month the laboratory tests were performed

LABORATORY REFERRALS DURING JANUARY

Adams, Jacqueline	320917	Miller, Michael	511806
Black, Leslie	813406	Pratt, William	214411
Cook, Marie	511616	Rogers, Ellen	722428
Fisher, Pat	914625	Saunders, Sally	310229
Jackson, Lee	923212	Wilson, Jan	416715
James, Linda	624621	Wyatt, Mark	321326
Lane, Arthur	115702		

10. According to the list, the number of women referred to the laboratory during January was
    A. 4   B. 5   C. 6   D. 7

11. The clinic from which the MOST patients were referred was
    A. Cardiac
    B. Gynecology
    C. Ophthalmology
    D. Pediatrics

12. The YOUNGEST patient referred from any clinic other than Pediatrics was
    A. Leslie Black
    B. Marie Cook
    C. Arthur Lane
    D. Sally Saunders

13. The number of patients whose laboratory tests were performed on or before January 16 was
    A. 7   B. 8   C. 9   D. 10

14. The number of patients referred for laboratory tests who are under age 45 is
    A. 7   B. 8   C. 9   D. 10

15. The OLDEST patient referred to the clinic during January was
    A. Jacqueline Adams
    B. Linda James
    C. Arthur Lane
    D. Jan Wilson

16. The ONLY patient treated in the Orthopedics clinic was
    A. Marie Cook
    B. Pat Fisher
    C. Ellen Rogers
    D. Jan Wilson

17. A woman, age 37 was referred from the Hematology clinic to the laboratory. Her laboratory tests were performed on January 9.
    Her identification number would be
    A. 610937   B. 623709   C. 613790   D. 623790

18. A man was referred for lab tests from the Orthopedics clinic. He is 30 years old 18.____
and his tests were performed on January 6.
His identification number would be
 A. 413006 B. 510360 C. 513006 D. 513060

19. A 4-year-old boy was referred from the Pediatrics clinic to have laboratory 19.____
tests on January 23.
His identification number was
 A. 310422 B. 310423 C. 310433 D. 320403

KEY (CORRECT ANSWERS)

1.	B	11.	D
2.	B	12.	B
3.	B	13.	A
4.	D	14.	C
5.	D	15.	D
6.	B	16.	A
7.	A	17.	B
8.	D	18.	C
9.	C	19.	B
10.	B		

TEST 4

DIRECTIONS: Each question or incomplete statement is followed by several suggested answers or completions. Select the one that BEST answers the question or completes the statement. *PRINT THE LETTER OF THE CORRECT ANSWER IN THE SPACE AT THE RIGHT.*

Questions 1-10.

DIRECTIONS: Questions 1 through 10 are to be answered on the basis of the information and directions given below.

Assume that you are a Senior Stenographer assigned to the personnel bureau of a city agency. Your supervisor has asked you to classify the employees in your agency into the following five groups:

- A. Employees who are college graduates, who are at least 35 years of age but less than 50, and who have been employed by the City for five years or more;
- B. Employees who have been employed by the City for less than five years, who are not college graduates, and who earn at least $32,500 a year but less than $34,500;
- C. Employees who have been City employees for five years or more, who are at least 21 years of age but less than 35, and who are not college graduates;
- D. Employee who earn at least $34,500 a year but less than $36,000 who are college graduates, and who have been employed by the City for less than five years;
- E. Employees who are not included in any of the foregoing groups.

NOTE: In classifying these employees you are to compute age and period of service as of January 1, 2003. In all cases, it is to be assumed that each employee has been employed continuously in City service. In each question, consider only the information which will assist you in classifying each employee Any information which is of no assistance in classifying an employee would not be considered.

SAMPLE: Mr. Brown, a 29-year-old veteran, was appointed to his present position of Clerk on June 1, 2000. He has completed two years of college. His present salary is $33,050.

The correct answer to this sample is B, since the employee has been employed by the City for less than five years, is not a college graduate, and earn at least $32,500 a year but less than $34,500.

Questions 1 through 10 contain excerpts from the personnel records of 10 employees in the agency. In the correspondingly numbered space at the right print the capital letter preceding the appropriate group into which you would place each employee.

1. Mr. James has been employed by the City since 1993, when he was graduated from a local college. Now 35 years of age, he earns $36,000 a year. 1.____

2. Mr. Worth began working in City service early in 1999. He was awarded his college degree in 1994, at the age of 21. As a result of a recent promotion, he now earns $34,500 a year. 2.____

2 (#4)

3. Miss Thomas has been a City employee since August 1, 1998. Her salary is $34,500 a year. Miss Thomas, who is 25 years old, has had only three years of high school training.

3._____

4. Mr. Williams has had three promotions since entering City service on January 1, 1991. He was graduated from college with honors in 1974, when he was 20 years of age. His present salary is $37,000 a year.

4._____

5. Miss Jones left college after two years of study to take an appointment to a position in the City service paying $33,300 a year. She began work on March 1, 1997 when she was 19 years of age.

5._____

6. Mr. Smith was graduated from an engineering college with honors in January 1998 and became a City employee three months later. His present salary is $35,810. Mr. Smith was born in 1976.

6._____

7. Miss Earnest was born on May 31, 1979. Her education consisted of four years of high school and one year of business school. She was appointed as a typist in a City agency on June 1, 1997. Her annual salary is $33,500.

7._____

8. Mr. Adams, a 24-year-old clerk, began his City service on July 1, 1999, soon after being discharged from the U.S. Army. A college graduate, his present annual salary is $33,200.

8._____

9. Miss Charles attends college in the evenings, hoping to obtain her degree is 2004, when she will be 30 years of age. She has been a City employee since April 1998, and earns $33,350.

9._____

10. Mr. Dolan was just promoted to his present position after six years of City service. He was graduated from high school in 1982, when he was 18 years of age, but did not go on to college. Mr. Dolan's present salary is $33,500.

10._____

KEY (CORRECT ANSWERS)

1. A
2. D
3. E
4. A
5. C
6. D
7. C
8. E
9. B
10. E

TEST 5

DIRECTIONS: Questions 1 through 4 each contain five numbers that should be arranged in numerical order. The number with the lowest numerical value should be first and the number with the highest numerical value should be last. Pick that option which indicates the CORRECT order of the numbers.

Examples: A. 9; 18; 14; 15; 27
B. 9; 14; 15; 18; 27
C. 14; 15; 18; 27; 9
D. 9; 14; 15; 27; 18

The correct answer is B, which contains the proper arrangement of the five numbers.

1. A. 20573; 20753; 20738; 20837; 20098
   B. 20098; 20753; 20573; 20738; 20837
   C. 20098; 20573; 20753; 20837; 20738
   D. 20098; 20573; 20738; 20753; 20837

2. A. 113492; 113429; 111314; 113114; 131413
   B. 111314; 113114; 113429; 113492; 131413
   C. 111314; 113429; 113492; 113114; 131413
   D. 111314; 113114; 131413; 113429; 113492

3. A. 1029763; 1030421; 1035681; 1036928; 1067391
   B. 1030421; 1029763; 1035681; 1067391; 1036928
   C. 1030421; 1035681; 1036928; 1067391; 1029763
   D. 1029763; 1039421; 1035681; 1067391; 1036928

4. A. 1112315; 1112326; 1112337; 1112349; 1112306
   B. 1112306; 1112315; 1112337; 1112326; 1112349
   C. 1112306; 1112315; 1112326; 1112337; 1112349
   D. 1112306; 1112326; 1112315; 1112337; 1112349

KEY (CORRECT ANSWERS)

1. D
2. B
3. A
4. C

TEST 6

DIRECTIONS: The phonetic filing system is a method of filing names in which the alphabet is reduced to key code letters. The six key letters and their equivalents are as follows:

KEY LETTERS	EQUIVALENTS
b	p, f, v
c	s, k, g, j, q, x, z
d	t
l	none
m	n
r	none

A key letter represents itself.
Vowels (a, e, i, o, and u) and the letters w, h, and y are omitted.
For example, the name GILMAN would be represented as follows:
    G is represented by the key letter C.
    I is a vowel and is omitted.
    L is a letter and represents itself.
    M is a key letter and represents itself.
    A is a vowel and is omitted.
    N is represented by the key letter M.

Therefore, the phonetic filing code for the name GILMAN is CLMM.

Answer Questions 1 through 10 based on the information below.

1. The phonetic filing code for the name FITZGERALD would be
   A. BDCCRLD   B. BDCRLD   C. BDZCRLD   D. BTZCRLD

2. The phonetic filing code CLBR may represent any one of the following names EXCEPT
   A. Calprey   B. Flower   C. Glover   D. Silver

3. The phonetic filing code LDM may represent any one of the following names EXCEPT
   A. Halden   B. Hilton   C. Walton   D. Wilson

4. The phonetic filing code for the name RODRIGUEZ would be
   A. RDRC   B. RDRCC   C. RDRCZ   D. RTRCC

5. The phonetic filing code for the name MAXWELL would be
   A. MCLL   B. MCWL   C. MCWLL   D. MXLL

6. The phonetic filing code for the name ANDERSON would be
   A. AMDRCM   B. ENDRSM   C. MDRCM   D. NDERCN

7. The phonetic filing code for the name SAVITSKY would be
   A. CBDCC   B. CBDCY   C. SBDCC   D. SVDCC

2 (#6)

8. The phonetic filing code CMC may represent any one of the following names EXCEPT 8.____
   A. James   B. Jayes   C. Johns   D. Jones

9. The ONLY one of the following names that could be represented by the phonetic filing code CDDDM would be 9.____
   A. Catalano   B. Chesterton   C. Cittadino   D. Cuttlerman

10. The ONLY one of the following names that could be represented by the phonetic filing code LLMCM would be 10.____
    A. Ellington   B. Hallerman   C. Inslerman   D. Willingham

KEY (CORRECT ANSWERS)

1. A   6. C
2. B   7. A
3. D   8. B
4. B   9. C
5. A   10. D

NAME AND NUMBER CHECKING
EXAMINATION SECTION
TEST 1

DIRECTIONS: This test is designed to measure your speed/and accuracy. You are urged to work both quickly and accurately and to do correctly as many lists as you can in the time allowed. The test consists of lists or pairs of names and numbers. Count the number of IDENTICAL pairs in each list. Then, select the correct number, 1, 2, 3, 4, 5, and indicate your choice in the space at the right. Two sample questions are presented for your guidance, together with the correct solutions.

SAMPLE LIST A
Adelphi College	– Adelphia College
Braxton Corp	– Braxeton Corp.
Wassaic State School	– Wassaic State School
Central Islip State Hospital	– Central Isllip State Hospital
Greenwich House	– Greenwich House

NOTE: There are only two correct pairs—Wassaic State School and Greenwich House. Therefore, the CORRECT answer is 2.

SAMPLE LIST B
78453694	– 78453684
784530	– 784530
533	– 534
67845	– 67845
2368745	– 2368755

NOTE: There are only two correct pairs—784530 and 67845. Therefore, the CORRECT answer is 2.

LIST 1   1.____
    98654327   - 98654327
    74932564   - 7492564
    61438652   - 61438652
    01297653   - 01287653
    1865439765   - 1865439765

LIST 2   2.____
    478362   - 478363
    278354792   - 278354772
    9327   - 9327
    297384625   - 27384625
    6428156   - 6428158

2 (#1)

LIST 3
    Abbey House — - Abbey House
    Actor's Fund Home — - Actor's Fund Home
    Adrian Memorial — - Adrian Memorial
    A. Clayton Powell Home — - Clayton Powell House
    Abbot E. Kittredge Club — - Abbott E. Kitteredge Club

3.____

LIST 4
    3682 — - 3692
    21937453829 — - 31927453829
    723 — - 733
    2763920 — - 2763920
    47293 — - 47293

4.____

LIST 5
    Adra House — - Adra House
    Adolescents' Court — - Adolescents' Court
    Cliff Villa — - Cliff Villa
    Clark Neighborhood House — - Clark Neighborhood House
    Alma Mathews House — - Alma Mathews House

5.____

LIST 6
    28734291 — - 28734271
    63810263849 — - 63810263846
    26831027 — - 26831027
    368291 — - 368291
    7238102637 — - 7238102637

6.____

LIST 7
    Albion State T.S. — - Albion State T.C.
    Clara de Hirsch Home — - Clara De Hirsch Home
    Alice Carrington Royce — - Alice Carington Royce
    Alice Chopin Nursery — - Alice Chapin Nursery
    Lighthouse Eye Clinic — - Lighthouse Eye Clinic

7.____

LIST 8
    327 — - 329
    712438291026 — - 712438291026
    2753829142 — - 275382942
    826287 — - 826289
    26435162839 — - 26435162839

8.____

LIST 9
    Letchworth Village — - Letchworth Village
    A.A.A.E. Inc. — - A.A.A.E. Inc.
    Clear Pool Camp — - Clear Pool Camp
    A.M.M.L.A. Inc. — - A.M.M.L.A. Inc.
    J.G. Harbard — - J.G. Harbord

9.____

3 (#1)

LIST 10
    8254   - 8256
    2641526   - 2641526
    4126389012   - 4126389102
    725   - 725
    76253917287   - 76253917287

10._____

LIST 11
    Attica State Prison   - Attica State Prison
    Nellie Murrah   - Nellie Murrah
    Club Marshall   - Club Marshal
    Assissium Casea-Maria   - Assissium Casa-Maria
    The Homestead   - The Homestead

11._____

LIST 12
    2691   - 2691
    623819253627   - 623819253629
    28637   - 28937
    278392736   - 278392736
    52739   - 52739

12._____

LIST 13
    A.I.C.P. Boys Camp   - A.I.C.P. Boy's Camp
    Einar Chrystie   - Einar Christyie
    Astoria Center   - Astoria Center
    G. Frederick Brown   - G. Federick Browne
    Vacation Service   - Vacation Services

13._____

LIST 14
    728352689   - 728352688
    643728   - 643728
    37829176   - 37827196
    8425367   - 8425369
    65382018   - 65382018

14._____

LIST 15
    E.S. Streim   - E.S. Strim
    Charles E. Higgins   - Charles E. Higgins
    Baluvelt, N.Y.   - Blauwelt, N.Y.
    Roberta Magdalen   - Roberto Magdalen
    Ballard School   - Ballard School

15._____

LIST 16
    7382   - 7392
    281374538299   - 291374538299
    623   - 633
    6273730   - 6273730
    63392   - 63392

16._____

LIST 17   17.____
   Orrin Otis — Orrin Otis
   Barat Settlement — Barat Settlemen
   Emmanuel House — Emmanuel House
   William T. McCreery — William T. McCreery
   Seamen's Home — Seaman's Home

LIST 18   18.____
   72824391 — 72834371
   3729106237 — 37291106237
   82620163849 — 82620163846
   37638921 — 37638921
   82631027 — 82631027

LIST 19   19.____
   Commonwealth Fund — Commonwealth Fund
   Anne Johnsen — Anne Johnson
   Bide-A-Wee Home — Bide-a-Wee Home
   Riverdale-on-Hudson — Riverdal-on-Hudson
   Bialystoker Home — Bailystoker Home

LIST 20   20.____
   9271 — 9271
   392918352627 — 392018852629
   72637 — 72637
   927392736 — 927392736
   92739 — 92739

LIST 21   21.____
   Charles M. Stump — Charles M. Stump
   Bourne Workshop — Buorne Workshop
   B'nai Bi'rith — B'nai Brith
   Poppenhuesen Institute — Poppenheusen Institute
   Consular Service — Consular Service

LIST 22   22.____
   927352689 — 927352688
   647382 — 648382
   93729176 — 93727196
   649536718 — 649536718
   5835367 — 5835369

LIST 23   23.____
   L.S. Bestend — L.S. Bestent
   Hirsch Mfg. Co. — Hircsh Mfg. Co.
   F.H. Storrs — F.P. Storrs
   Camp Wassaic — Camp Wassaic
   George Ballingham — George Ballingham

5 (#1)

LIST 24
    372846392048   - 372846392048
    334   - 334
    7283524678   - 7283524678
    7283   - 7283
    7283629372   - 7283629372

24.____

LIST 25
    Dr. Stiles Company   - Dr. Stills Company
    Frances Hunsdon   - Frances Hunsdon
    Northrop Barrert   - Nothrup Barrent
    J.D. Brunjes   - J.D. Brunjes
    Theo. Claudel & Co.   - Theo. Claudel co.

25.____

KEY (CORRECT ANSWERS)

1.	3		11.	3
2.	1		12.	3
3.	2		13.	1
4.	2		14.	2
5.	5		15.	2
6.	3		16.	2
7.	1		17.	3
8.	2		18.	2
9.	4		19.	2
10.	3		20.	4

21.   2
22.   1
23.   2
24.   5
25.   2

TEST 2

DIRECTIONS: This test is designed to measure your speed/and accuracy. You are urged to work both quickly and accurately and to do correctly as many lists as you can in the time allowed. The test consists of lists or pairs of names and numbers. Count the number of IDENTICAL pairs in each list. Then, select the correct number, 1, 2, 3, 4, 5, and indicate your choice in the space at the right.

LIST 1 1.____
    82728 - 82738
    82736292637 - 82736292639
    728 - 738
    83926192527 - 83726192529
    82736272 - 82736272

LIST 2 2.____
    L. Pietri - L. Pietri
    Mathewson, L.F. - Mathewson, L.F.
    Funk & Wagnall - Funk & Wagnalls
    Shimizu, Sojio - Shimizu, Sojio
    Filing Equipment Bureau - Filing Equipment Buraeu

LIST 3 3.____
    63801829374 - 63801839474
    283577657 - 283577657
    65689 - 65689
    3457892026 - 3547893026
    2779 - 2778

LIST 4 4.____
    August Caille - August Caille
    The Well-Fare Service - The Wel-Fare Service
    K.L.M. Process co. - R.L.M. Process Co.
    Merrill Littell - Merrill Littell
    Dodd & Sons - Dodd & Son

LIST 5 5.____
    998745732 - 998745733
    723 - 723
    463849102983 - 463849102983
    8570 - 8570
    279012 - 279012

LIST 6 6.____
    M.A. Wender - M.A. Winder
    Minneapolis Supply Co. - Minneapolis Supply Co.
    Beverly Hills Corp - Beverley Hills Corp.
    Trafalgar Square - Trafalgar Square
    Phifer, D.T. - Phiefer, D.T.

2 (#2)

LIST 7
    7834629   - 7834629
    3549806746   - 3549806746
    97802564   - 97892564
    689246   - 688246
    2578024683   - 2578024683

7.____

LIST 8
    Scadrons'   - Scadrons'
    Gensen & Bro.   - Genson & Bro.
    Firestone Co.   - Firestone Co.
    H.L. Eklund   - H.L. Eklund
    Oleomargarine Co.   - Oleomargarine Co.

8.____

LIST 9
    782039485618   - 782039485618
    53829172639   - 63829172639
    892   - 892
    82937482   - 829374820
    52937456   - 53937456

9.____

LIST 10
    First Nat'l Bank   - First Nat'l Bank
    Sedgwick Machine Works   - Sedgewick Machine Works
    Hectographia Co.   - Hectographia Corp.
    Levet Bros.   - Levet Bros.
    Multistamp Co., Inc.   - Multistamp Co., Inc.

10.____

LIST 11
    7293   - 7293
    6382910293   - 6382910292
    981928374012   - 981928374912
    58293   - 58393
    18203649271   - 283019283745

11.____

LIST 12
    Lowrey Lb'r Co.   - Lowrey Lb'r Co.
    Fidelity Service   - Fidelity Service
    Reumann, J.A.   - Reumann, J.A.
    Duophoto Ltd.   - Duophotos Ltd.
    John Jarratt   - John Jaratt

12.____

LIST 13
    6820384   - 6820384
    383019283745   - 383019283745
    63927102   - 63928102
    91029354829   - 91029354829
    58291728   - 58291728

13.____

LIST 14 14.____
    Standard Press Co.   - Standard Press Co.
    Reliant Mf'g. Co.   - Relant Mf'g Co.
    M.C. Lynn   - M.C. Lynn
    J. Fredericks Company   - G. Fredericks Company
    Wandermann, B.S.   - Wanderman, B.S.

LIST 15 15.____
    4283910293   - 4283010203
    992018273648   - 992018273848
    620   - 629
    752937273   - 752937373
    5392   - 5392

LIST 16 16.____
    Waldorf Hotel   - Waldorf Hotel
    Aaron Machinery Co.   - Aaron Machinery Co.
    Caroline Ann Locke   - Caroline Ane Locke
    McCabe Mfg. Co.   - McCabe Mfg. Co.
    R.L. Landres   - R.L. Landers

LIST 17 17.____
    68391028364   - 68391028394
    68293   - 68293
    739201   - 739201
    72839201   - 72839211
    739917   - 739719

LIST 18 18.____
    Balsam M.M.   - Balsamm, M.M.
    Steinway & Co.   - Stienway & M. Co.
    Eugene Elliott   - Eugene A. Elliott
    Leonard Loan Co.   - Leonard Loan Co.
    Frederick Morgan   - Frederick Morgen

LIST 19 19.____
    8929   - 9820
    392836472829   - 392836572829
    462   - 4622039271
    827   - 2039276837
    53829   - 54829

LIST 20 20.____
    Danielson's Hofbrau   - Danielson's Hafbrau
    Edward A. Truarme   - Edward A. Truame
    Insulite Co.   - Insulite Co.
    Reisler Shoe Corp.   - Rielser Shoe Corp.
    L.L. Thompson   - L.L. Thompson

4 (#2)

LIST 21
    92839102837   - 92839102837
    58891028   - 58891028
    7291728   - 7291928
    272839102839   - 272839102839
    428192   - 428102

21.____

LIST 22
    K.L. Veiller   - K.L. Veiller
    Webster, Roy   - Webster, Ray
    Drasner Spring Co.   - Drasner Spring Co.
    Edward J. Cravenport   - Edward J. Cravanport
    Harold Field   - Harold A. Field

22.____

LIST 23
    2293   - 2293
    4283910293   - 5382910292
    871928374012   - 871928374912
    68293   - 68393
    8120364927   - 81293649271

23.____

LIST 24
    Tappe, Inc   - Tappe, Inc.
    A.M. Wentingworth   - A.M. Wentinworth
    Scott A. Elliott   - Scott A. Elliott
    Echeverria Corp.   - Echeverria Corp.
    Bradford Victor Company - Bradford Victer Company

24.____

LIST 25
    4820384   - 4820384
    393019283745   - 283919283745
    63917102   - 63927102
    91029354829   - 91029354829
    48291728   - 48291728

25.____

KEY (CORRECT ANSWERS)

1.	1		11.	1
2.	3		12.	3
3.	2		13.	4
4.	2		14.	2
5.	4		15.	1
6.	2		16.	3
7.	3		17.	2
8.	4		18.	1
9.	2		19.	1
10.	3		20.	2

21. 3
22. 2
23. 1
24. 2
25. 4

READING COMPREHENSION
UNDERSTANDING AND INTERPRETING WRITTEN MATERIAL
EXAMINATION SECTION
TEST 1

Questions 1-8.

DIRECTIONS: Each question or incomplete statement is followed by several suggested answers or completions. Select the one that BEST answers the question or completes the statement. *PRINT THE LETTER OF THE CORRECT ANSWER IN THE SPACE AT THE RIGHT.*

Questions 1 and 2.

DIRECTIONS: Your answers to Questions 1 and 2 must be based ONLY on the information given in the following paragraph.

Hospitals maintained wholly by public taxation may treat only those compensation cases which are emergencies and may not treat such emergency cases longer than the emergency exists; provided, however, that these restrictions shall not be applicable where there is not available a hospital other than a hospital maintained wholly by taxation.

1. According to the above paragraph, compensation cases

    A. are regarded as emergency cases by hospitals maintained wholly by public taxation
    B. are seldom treated by hospitals maintained wholly by public taxation
    C. are treated mainly by privately endowed hospitals
    D. may be treated by hospitals maintained wholly by public taxation if they are emergencies

2. According to the above paragraph, it is MOST reasonable to conclude that where a privately endowed hospital is available,

    A. a hospital supported wholly by public taxation may treat emergency compensation cases only so long as the emergency exists
    B. a hospital supported wholly by public taxation may treat any compensation cases
    C. a hospital supported wholly by public taxation must refer emergency compensation cases to such a hospital
    D. the restrictions regarding the treatment of compensation cases by a tax-supported hospital are not wholly applicable

Questions 3-7.

DIRECTIONS: Answer Questions 3 through 7 ONLY according to the information given in the following passage.

THE MANUFACTURE OF LAUNDRY SOAP

The manufacture of soap is not a complicated process. Soap is a fat or an oil, plus an alkali, water and salt. The alkali used in making commercial laundry soap is caustic soda. The salt used is the same as common table salt. A fat is generally an animal product that is not a liquid at room temperature. If heated, it becomes a liquid. An oil is generally liquid at room temperature. If the temperature is lowered, the oil becomes a solid just like ordinary fat.

At the soap plant, a huge tank five stories high, called a *kettle,* is first filled part way with fats and then the alkali and water are added. These ingredients are then heated and boiled together. Salt is then poured into the top of the boiling solution; and as the salt slowly sinks down through the mixture, it takes with it the glycerine which comes from the melted fats. The product which finally comes from the kettle is a clear soap which has a moisture content of about 34%. This clear soap is then chilled so that more moisture is driven out. As a result, the manufacturer finally ends up with a commercial laundry soap consisting of 88% clear soap and only 12% moisture.

3. An ingredient used in making laundry soap is

    A. table sugar
    B. potash
    C. glycerine
    D. caustic soda

4. According to the above passage, a difference between fats and oils is that fats

    A. cost more than oils
    B. are solid at room temperature
    C. have less water than oils
    D. are a liquid animal product

5. According to the above passage, the MAIN reason for using salt in the manufacture of soap is to

    A. make the ingredients boil together
    B. keep the fats in the kettle melted
    C. remove the glycerine
    D. prevent the loss of water from the soap

6. According to the passage, the purpose of chilling the clear soap is to

    A. stop the glycerine from melting
    B. separate the alkali from the fats
    C. make the oil become solid
    D. get rid of more moisture

7. According to the passage, the percentage of moisture in commercial laundry soap is

    A. 12%   B. 34%   C. 66%   D. 88%

8. The x-ray has gone into business. Developed primarily to aid in diagnosing human ills, the machine now works in packing plants, in foundries, in service stations, and in a dozen ways to contribute to precision and accuracy in industry.
The above statement means *most nearly* that the x-ray

    A. was first developed to aid business
    B. is of more help to business than it is to medicine
    C. is being used to improve the functioning of business
    D. is more accurate for packing plants than it is for foundries

8.____

Questions 9-25.

DIRECTIONS: Each question consists of a statement. You are to indicate whether the statement is TRUE (T) or FALSE (F). *PRINT THE LETTER OF THE CORRECT ANSWER IN THE SPACE AT THE RIGHT.*

Questions 9-12.

DIRECTIONS: Read the paragraph below about *shock* and then answer Questions 9 through 12 according to the information given in the paragraph.

SHOCK

While not found in all injuries, shock is present in all serious injuries caused by accidents. During shock, the normal activities of the body slow down. This partly explains why one of the signs of shock is a pale, cold skin, since insufficient blood goes to the body parts during shock.

9. If the injury caused by an accident is serious, shock is sure to be present.   9.____

10. In shock, the heart beats faster than normal.   10.____

11. The face of a person suffering from shock is usually red and flushed.   11.____

12. Not enough blood goes to different parts of the body during shock.   12.____

Questions 13-18.

DIRECTIONS: Questions 13 through 18, inclusive, are to be answered SOLELY on the basis of the information contained in the following statement and NOT upon any other information you may have.

Blood transfusions are given to patients at the hospital upon recommendation of the physicians attending such cases. The physician fills out a *Request for Blood Transfusion* form in duplicate and sends both copies to the Medical Director's office, where a list is maintained of persons called *donors* who desire to sell their blood for transfusions. A suitable donor is selected, and the transfusion is given. Donors are, in many instances, medical students and employees of the hospital. Donors receive twenty-five dollars for each transfusion.

13. According to the above paragraph, a blood donor is paid twenty-five dollars for each transfusion.   13.____

14. According to the above paragraph, only medical students and employees of the hospital are selected as blood donors. 14.___

15. According to the above paragraph, the *Request for Blood Transfusion* form is filled out by the patient and sent to the Medical Director's office. 15.___

16. According to the above paragraph, a list of blood donors is maintained in the Medical Director's office. 16.___

17. According to the above paragraph, cases for which the attending physicians recommend blood transfusions are usually emergency cases. 17.___

18. According to the above paragraph, one copy of the *Request for Blood Transfusion* form is kept by the patient and one copy is sent to the Medical Director's office. 18.___

Questions 19-25.

DIRECTIONS: Questions 19 through 25, inclusive, are to be answered SOLELY on the basis of the information contained in the following passage and NOT upon any other information you may have.

Before being admitted to a hospital ward, a patient is first interviewed by the Admitting Clerk, who records the patient's name, age, sex, race, birthplace, and mother's maiden name. This clerk takes all of the money and valuables that the patient has on his person. A list of the valuables is written on the back of the envelope in which the valuables are afterwards placed. Cash is counted and placed in a separate envelope, and the amount of money and the name of the patient are written on the outside of the envelope. Both envelopes are sealed, fastened together, and placed in a compartment of a safe.

An orderly then escorts the patient to a dressing room where the patient's clothes are removed and placed in a bundle. A tag bearing the patient's name is fastened to the bundle. A list of the contents of the bundle is written on property slips, which are made out in triplicate. The information contained on the outside of the envelopes containing the cash and valuables belonging to the patient is also copied on the property slips.

According to the above passage,

19. patients are escorted to the dressing room by the Admitting Clerk. 19.___

20. the patient's cash and valuables are placed together in one envelope. 20.___

21. the number of identical property slips that are made out when a patient is being admitted to a hospital ward is three. 21.___

22. the full names of both parents of a patient are recorded by the Admitting Clerk before a patient is admitted to a hospital ward. 22.___

23. the amount of money that a patient has on his person when admitted to the hospital is entered on the patient's property slips. 23.___

24. an orderly takes all the money and valuables that a patient has on his person. 24.___

25. the patient's name is placed on the tag that is attached to the bundle containing the patient's clothing. 25.___

KEY (CORRECT ANSWERS)

1. D
2. A
3. D
4. B
5. C

6. D
7. A
8. C
9. T
10. F

11. F
12. T
13. T
14. F
15. F

16. T
17. T
18. F
19. F
20. F

21. T
22. F
23. T
24. F
25. T

TEST 2

DIRECTIONS: Each question or incomplete statement is followed by several suggested answers or completions. Select the one that BEST answers the question or completes the statement. *PRINT THE LETTER OF THE CORRECT ANSWER IN THE SPACE AT THE RIGHT.*

Questions 1-4.

DIRECTIONS: Questions 1 through 4 are to be answered in accordance with the following paragraphs.

One fundamental difference between the United States health care system and the health care systems of some European countries is the way that hospital charges for long-term illnesses affect their citizens.

In European countries such as England, Sweden, and Germany, citizens can face, without fear, hospital charges due to prolonged illness, no matter how substantial they may be. Citizens of these nations are required to pay nothing when they are hospitalized, for they have prepaid their treatment as taxpayers when they were well and were earning incomes.

On the other hand, the United States citizen, in spite of the growth of payments by third parties which include private insurance carriers as well as public resources, has still to shoulder 40 percent of hospital care costs, while his private insurance contributes only 25 percent and public resources the remaining 35 percent.

Despite expansion of private health insurance and social legislation in the United States, out-of-pocket payments for hospital care by individuals have steadily increased. Such payments, currently totalling $23 billion, are nearly twice as high as ten years ago.

Reform is inevitable and, when it comes, will have to reconcile sharply conflicting interests. Hospital staffs are demanding higher and higher wages. Hospitals are under pressure by citizens, who as patients demand more and better services but who as taxpayers or as subscribers to hospital insurance plans, are reluctant to pay the higher cost of improved care. An acceptable reconciliation of these interests has so far eluded legislators and health administrators in the United States.

1. According to the above passage, the one of the following which is an ADVANTAGE that citizens of England, Sweden, and Germany have over United States citizens is that, when faced with long-term illness,   1.__

    A. the amount of out-of-pocket payments made by these European citizens is small when compared to out-of-pocket payments made by United States citizens
    B. European citizens have no fear of hospital costs no matter how great they may be
    C. more efficient and reliable hospitals are available to the European citizen than is available to the United States citizens
    D. a greater range of specialized hospital care is available to the European citizens than is available to the United States citizens

2. According to the above passage, reform of the United States system of health care must reconcile all of the following EXCEPT
   A. attempts by health administrators to provide improved hospital care
   B. taxpayers' reluctance to pay for the cost of more and better hospital services
   C. demands by hospital personnel for higher wages
   D. insurance subscribers' reluctance to pay the higher costs of improved hospital care

3. According to the above passage, the out-of-pocket payments for hospital care that individuals made ten years ago was APPROXIMATELY _____ billion.
   A. $32   B. $23   C. $12   D. $3

4. According to the above passage, the GREATEST share of the costs of hospital care in the United States is paid by
   A. United States citizens
   B. private insurance carriers
   C. public resources
   D. third parties

Questions 5-8.

DIRECTIONS: Questions 5 through 8 are to be answered SOLELY on the basis of the information contained in the following passage.

Effective cost controls have been difficult to establish in most hospitals in the United States. Ways must be found to operate hospitals with reasonable efficiency without sacrificing quality and in a manner that will reduce the amount of personal income now being spent on health care and the enormous drain on national resources. We must adopt a new public objective of providing higher quality health care at significantly lower cost. One step that can be taken to achieve this goal is to carefully control capital expenditures for hospital construction and expansion. Perhaps the way to start is to declare a moratorium on all hospital construction and to determine the factors that should be considered in deciding whether a hospital should be built. Such factors might include population growth, distance to the nearest hospital, availability of medical personnel, and hospital bed shortage.

A second step to achieve the new objective is to increase the ratio of out-of-hospital patient to in-hospital patient care. This can be done by using separate health care facilities other than hospitals to attract patients who have increasingly been going to hospital clinics and overcrowding them. Patients should instead identify with a separate health care facility to keep them out of hospitals.

A third step is to require better hospital operating rules and controls. This step might include the review of a doctor's performance by other doctors, outside professional evaluations of medical practice, and required refresher courses and re-examinations for doctors. Other measures might include obtaining mandatory second opinions on the need for surgery in order to avoid unnecessary surgery, and outside review of work rules and procedures to eliminate unnecessary testing of patients.

A fourth step is to halt the construction and public subsidizing of new medical schools and to fill whatever needs exist in professional coverage by emphasizing the medical training of physicians with specialities that are in short supply and by providing a better geographic distribution of physicians and surgeons.

5. According to the above passage, providing higher quality health care at lower cost can be achieved by the

   A. greater use of out-of-hospital facilities
   B. application of more effective cost controls on doctors' fees
   C. expansion of improved in-hospital patient care services at hospital clinics
   D. development of more effective training programs in hospital administration

6. According to the above passage, the one of the following which should be taken into account in determining if a hospital should be constructed is the

   A. number of out-of-hospital health care facilities
   B. availability of public funds to subsidize construction
   C. number of hospitals under construction
   D. availability of medical personnel

7. According to the above passage, it is IMPORTANT to operate hospitals efficiently because

   A. they are currently in serious financial difficulties
   B. of the need to reduce the amount of personal income going to health care
   C. the quality of health care services has deteriorated
   D. of the need to increase productivity goals to take care of the growing population in the United States

8. According to the above passage, which one of the following approaches is MOST LIKELY to result in better operating rules and controls in hospitals?

   A. Allocating doctors to health care facilities on the basis of patient population
   B. Equalizing the workloads of doctors
   C. Establishing a physician review board to evaluate the performance of other physicians
   D. Eliminating unnecessary outside review of patient testing

Questions 9-14.

DIRECTIONS: Questions 9 through 14 are to be answered SOLELY on the basis of the information contained in the following passage.

The United States today is the only major industrial nation in the world without a system of national health insurance or a national health service. Instead, we have placed our prime reliance on private enterprise and private health insurance to meet the need. Yet, in a recent year, of the 180 million Americans under 65 years of age, 34 million had no hospital insurance, 38 million had no surgical insurance, 63 million had no out-patient x-ray and laboratory insurance, 94 million had no insurance for prescription drugs, and 103 million had no insurance for physician office visits or home visits. Some 35 million Americans under the age of 65 had no health insurance whatsoever. Some 64 million additional Americans under age 65 had health insurance coverage that was less than that provided to the aged under Medicare.

Despite more than three decades of enormous growth, the private health insurance industry today pays benefits equal to only one-third of the total cost of private health care, leaving the rest to be borne by the patient—essentially the same ratio which held true a decade ago. Moreover, nearly all private health insurance is limited; it provides partial benefits, not comprehensive benefits; acute care, not preventive care; it siphons off the young and healthy, and ignores the poor and medically indigent. The typical private carrier usually pays only the cost of hospital care, forcing physicians and patients alike to resort to wasteful and inefficient use of hospital facilities, thereby giving further impetus to the already soaring costs of hospital care. Valuable hospital beds are used for routine tests and examinations. Unnecessary hospitalization, unnecessary surgery, and unnecessarily extended hospital stays are encouraged. These problems are exacerbated by the fact that administrative costs of commercial carriers are substantially higher than they are for Blue Shield, Blue Cross, or Medicare.

9. According to the above passage, the PROPORTION of total private health care costs paid by private health insurance companies today as compared to ten years ago has

    A. *increased* by approximately one-third
    B. *remained* practically the same
    C. *increased* by approximately two-thirds
    D. *decreased* by approximately one-third

10. According to the above passage, the one of the following which has contributed MOST to wasteful use of hospital facilities is the

    A. increased emphasis on preventive health care
    B. practice of private carriers of providing comprehensive health care benefits
    C. increased hospitalization of the elderly and the poor
    D. practice of a number of private carriers of paying only for hospital care costs

11. Based on the information in the above passage, which one of the following patients would be LEAST likely to receive benefits from a typical private health insurance plan?
    A

    A. young patient who must undergo an emergency appendectomy
    B. middle-aged patient who needs a costly series of x-ray and laboratory tests for diagnosis of gastrointestinal complaints
    C. young patient who must visit his physician weekly for treatment of a chronic skin disease
    D. middle-aged patient who requires extensive cancer surgery

12. Which one of the following is the MOST accurate inference that can be drawn from the above passage?

    A. Private health insurance has failed to fully meet the health care needs of Americans.
    B. Most Americans under age 65 have health insurance coverage better than that provided to the elderly under Medicare.
    C. Countries with a national health service are likely to provide poorer health care for their citizens than do countries that rely primarily on private health insurance.
    D. Hospital facilities in the United States are inadequate to meet the nation's health care needs.

13. Of the total number of Americans under age 65, what percentage belonged in the combined category of persons with NO health insurance or health insurance less than that provided to the aged under Medicare? 13.___

    A. 19%   B. 36%   C. 55%   D. 65%

14. According to the above passage, the one of the following types of health insurance which covered the SMALLEST number of Americans under age 65 was 14.___

    A. hospital insurance
    B. surgical insurance
    C. insurance for prescription drugs
    D. insurance for physician office or home visits

Questions 15-17.

DIRECTIONS: Questions 15 through 17 are to be answered SOLELY on the basis of the information contained in the following passage.

Statistical studies have demonstrated that disease and mortality rates are higher among the poor than among the more affluent members of our society. Periodic surveys conducted by the United States Public Health Service continue to document a higher prevalence of infectious and chronic diseases within low income families. While the basic life style and living conditions of the poor are to a considerable extent responsible for this less favorable health status, there are indications that the kind of health care received by the poor also plays a significant role. The poor are less likely to be aware of the concepts and practices of scientific medicine and less likely to seek health care when they need it. Moreover, they are discouraged from seeking adequate health care by the depersonalization, disorganization, and inadequate emphasis on preventive care which characterize the health care most often provided for them.

To achieve the objective of better health care for the poor, the following approaches have been suggested: encouraging the poor to seek preventive care as well as care for acute illness and to establish a lasting one-to-one relationship with a single physician who can treat the poor patient as a whole individual; sufficient financial subsidy to put the poor on an equal footing with *paying patients,* thereby giving them the opportunity to choose from among available health services providers; inducements to health services providers to establish public clinics in poverty areas; and legislation to provide for health education, earlier detection of disease, and coordinated health care.

15. According to the above passage, the one of the following which is a function of the United States Public Health Service is 15.___

    A. gathering data on the incidence of infectious diseases
    B. operating public health clinics in poverty areas lacking private physicians
    C. recommending legislation for the improvement of health care in the United States
    D. encouraging the poor to participate in programs aimed at the prevention of illness

16. According to the above passage, the one of the following which is MOST characteristic of the health care currently provided for the poor is that it

    A. aims at establishing clinics in poverty areas
    B. enables the poor to select the health care they want through the use of financial subsidies
    C. places insufficient stress on preventive health care
    D. over-emphasizes the establishment of a one-to-one relationship between physician and patient

17. The above passage IMPLIES that the poor lack the financial resources to

    A. obtain adequate health insurance coverage
    B. select from among existing health services
    C. participate in health education programs
    D. lobby for legislation aimed at improving their health care

Questions 18-20.

DIRECTIONS: Questions 18 through 20 are to be answered SOLELY on the basis of the information contained in the following passage.

The concept of *affiliation,* developed more than ten years ago, grew out of a series of studies which found evidence of faulty care, surgery of *questionable* value and other undesirable conditions in the city's municipal hospitals. The affiliation agreements signed shortly thereafter were designed to correct these deficiencies by assuring high quality medical care. In general, the agreements provided the staff and expertise of a voluntary hospital—sometimes connected with a medical school—to operate various services or, in some cases, all of the professional divisions of a specific municipal hospital. The municipal hospitals have paid for these services, which last year cost the city $200 million, the largest single expenditure of the Health and Hospitals Corporation. In addition, the municipal hospitals have provided to the voluntary hospitals such facilities as free space for laboratories and research. While some experts agree that affiliation has resulted in improvements in some hospital care, they contend that many conditions that affiliation was meant to correct still exist. In addition, accountability procedures between the Corporation and voluntary hospitals are said to be so inadequate that audits of affiliation contracts of the past five years revealed that there may be more than $200 million in charges for services by the voluntary hospitals which have not been fully substantiated. Consequently, the Corporation has proposed that future agreements provide accountability in terms of funds, services supplied, and use of facilities by the voluntary hospitals.

18. According to the above passage, *affiliation* may BEST be defined as an agreement whereby

    A. voluntary hospitals pay for the use of municipal hospital facilities
    B. voluntary and municipal hospitals work to eliminate duplication of services
    C. municipal hospitals pay voluntary hospitals for services performed
    D. voluntary and municipal hospitals transfer patients to take advantage of specialized services

19. According to the above passage, the MAIN purpose for setting up the *affiliation* agreement was to

    A. supplement the revenues of municipal hospitals
    B. improve the quality of medical care in municipal hospitals
    C. reduce operating costs in municipal hospitals
    D. increase the amount of space available to municipal hospitals

19.___

20. According to the above passage, inadequate accountability procedures have resulted in

    A. unsubstantiated charges for services by the voluntary hospitals
    B. emphasis on research rather than on patient care in municipal hospitals
    C. unsubstantiated charges for services by the municipal hospitals
    D. economic losses to voluntary hospitals

20.___

Questions 21-25.

DIRECTIONS: Questions 21 through 25 are to be answered SOLELY on the basis of the information contained in the following passage.

The payment for medical services covered under the Outpatient Medical Insurance Plan (OMI) may be made, by OMI, directly to a physician or to the OMI patient. If the physician and the patient agree that the physician is to receive payment directly from OMI, the payment will be officially assigned to the physician; this is the assignment method. If payment is not assigned, the patient receives payment directly from OMI based on an itemized bill he submits, regardless of whether or not he has already paid his physician.

When a physician accepts assignment of the payment for medical services, he agrees that total charges will not be more than the allowed charge determined by the OMI carrier administering the program. In such cases, the OMI patient pays any unmet part of the $85 annual deductible, plus 10 percent of the remaining charges to the physician. In unassigned claims, the patient is responsible for the total amount charged by the physician. The patient will then be reimbursed by the program 90 percent of the allowed charges in excess of the annual deductible.

The rates of acceptance of assignments provide a measure of how many OMI patients are spared *administrative participation* in the program. Because physicians are free to accept or reject assignments, the rate in which assignments are made provide a general indication of the medical community's satisfaction with the OMI program, especially with the level of amounts paid by the program for specific services and the promptness of payment.

21. According to the above passage, in order for a physician to receive payment directly from OMI for medical services to an OMI patient, the physician would have to accept the assignment of payment, to have the consent of the patient, AND to

    A. submit to OMI a paid itemized bill
    B. collect from the patient 90% of the total bill
    C. collect from the patient the total amount of the charges for his services, a portion of which he will later reimburse the patient
    D. agree that his charges for services to the patient will not exceed the amount allowed by the program

21.___

22. According to the above passage, if a physician accepts assignment of payment, the patient pays 22._____

    A. the total amount charged by the physician and is reimbursed by the program for 90 percent of the allowed charges in excess of the applicable deductible
    B. any unmet part of the $85 annual deductible, plus 90 percent of the remaining charges
    C. the total amount charged by the physician and is reimbursed by the program for 10 percent of the allowed charges in excess of the $85 annual deductible
    D. any unmet part of the $85 annual deductible, plus 10 percent of the remaining charges

23. A physician has accepted the assignment of payment for charges to an OMI patient. The physician's charges, all of which are allowed under OMI, amount to $115. This is the first time the patient has been eligible for OMI benefits and the first time the patient has received services from this physician. 23._____
    According to the above passage, the patient must pay the physician

    A. $27   B. $76.50   C. $88   D. $103.50

24. In an unassigned claim, a physician's charges, all of which are allowed under OMI, amount to $165. The patient paid the physician the full amount of the bill. 24._____
    If this is the FIRST time the patient has been eligible for OMI benefits, he will receive from OMI a reimbursement of

    A. $72   B. $80   C. $85   D. $93

25. According to the above passage, if the rate of acceptance of assignments by physicians is high, it is LEAST appropriate to conclude that the medical community is generally satisfied with the 25._____

    A. supplementary medical insurance program
    B. levels of amounts paid to physicians by the program
    C. number of OMI patients being spared administrative participation in the program
    D. promptness of the program in making payment for services

KEY (CORRECT ANSWERS)

1. B	11. C	21. D
2. A	12. A	22. D
3. C	13. C	23. C
4. D	14. D	24. A
5. A	15. A	25. C
6. D	16. C	
7. B	17. B	
8. C	18. C	
9. B	19. B	
10. D	20. A	

EXAMINATION SECTION
TEST 1

DIRECTIONS: Each question or incomplete statement is followed by several suggested answers or completions. Select the one that BEST answers the question or completes the statement. *PRINT THE LETTER OF THE CORRECT ANSWER IN THE SPACE AT THE RIGHT.*

1. Records of one type or another are kept in every office. The MOST important of the following reasons for the supervisor of a clerical or stenographic unit to keep statistical records of the work done in his unit is generally to

    A. supply basic information needed in planning the work of the unit
    B. obtain statistics for comparison with other units
    C. serve as the basis for unsatisfactory employee evaluation
    D. provide the basis for special research projects on program budgeting

    1.____

2. It is better for an employee to report and be responsible directly to several supervisors than to report and be responsible to only one supervisor.
   This statement directly CONTRADICTS the supervisory principle generally known as

    A. span of control   B. unity of command
    C. delegation of authority   D. accountability

    2.____

3. The one of the following which would MOST likely lead to friction among clerks in a unit is for the unit supervisor to

    A. defend the actions of his clerks when discussing them with his own supervisor
    B. praise each of his clerks "in confidence" as the best clerk in the unit
    C. get his men to work together as a team in completing the work of the unit
    D. consider the point of view of the rank and file clerks when assigning unpleasant tasks

    3.____

4. You become aware that one of the employees you supervise has failed to follow correct procedure and has been permitting various reports to be prepared, typed, and transmitted improperly.
   The BEST action for you to take FIRST in this situation is to

    A. order the employee to review all departmental procedures and reprimand him for having violated them
    B. warn the employee that he must obey regulations because uniformity is essential for effective departmental operation
    C. confer with the employee both about his failure to follow regulations and his reasons for doing so
    D. watch the employee's work very closely in the future but say nothing about this violation

    4.____

5. The supervisory clerk who would be MOST likely to have poor control over his subordinates is the one who

    A. goes to unusually great lengths to try to win their approval
    B. pitches in with the work they are doing during periods of heavy workload when no extra help can be obtained

    5.____

141

C. encourages and helps his subordinates toward advancement
D. considers suggestions from his subordinates before establishing new work procedures involving them

6. Suppose that a clerk who has been transferred to your office from another division in your agency because of difficulties with his supervisor has been placed under your supervision.
The BEST course of action for you to take FIRST is to

   A. instruct the clerk in the duties he will be performing in your office and make him feel "wanted" in his new position
   B. analyze the clerk's past grievance to determine if the transfer was the best solution to the problem
   C. advise him of the difficulties that his former supervisor had with other employees and encourage him not to feel badly about the transfer
   D. warn him that you will not tolerate any nonsense and that he will be under continuous surveillance while assigned to you

7. A certain office supervisor takes the initiative to represent his employees' interests related to working conditions, opportunities for advancement, etc. to his own supervisor and the administrative levels of the agency. This supervisor's actions will MOST probably have the effect of

   A. preventing employees from developing individual initiative in their work goals
   B. encouraging employees to compete openly for the special attention of their supervisor
   C. depriving employees of the opportunity to be represented by persons and/or unions of their own choosing
   D. building employee confidence in their supervisor and a spirit of cooperation in their work

8. Suppose that you have been promoted, assigned as a supervisor of a certain unit and asked to reorganize its functions so that specific routine procedures can be established. Before deciding which routines to establish, the FIRST of the following steps you should take is to

   A. decide who will perform each task in the routine
   B. determine the purpose to be served by each routine procedure
   C. outline the sequence of steps in each routine to be established
   D. calculate if more staff will be needed to carry out the new procedures

9. When routine procedures covering the ordinary work of an office are established, the supervisor of the office tends to be relieved of the need to

   A. make repeated decisions on the handling of recurring similar situations
   B. check the accuracy of the work completed by his subordinates
   C. train his subordinates in new work procedures
   D. plan and schedule the work of his office

10. Of the following, the method which would be LEAST helpful to a supervisor in effectively applying the principles of on-the-job safety to the daily work of his unit is for him to

A. initiate corrections of unsafe layouts of equipment and unsafe work processes
B. take charge of operations that are not routine to make certain that safety precautions are established and observed
C. continue to "talk safety" and promote safety consciousness in his subordinates
D. figure the cost of all accidents which could possibly occur on the job

11. A clerk is assigned to serve as receptionist for a large and busy office. Although many members of the public visit this office, the clerk often experiences periods of time in which he has nothing to do.
In these circumstances, the MOST advisable of the following actions for the supervisor to take is to

   A. assign a number of relatively low priority clerical jobs to the receptionist to do in the slow periods
   B. regularly rotate this assignment so that all the clerks experience this lighter work load
   C. assign the receptionist job as part of the duties of a number of clerks whose desks are nearest the reception room
   D. overlook the situation, since most of the receptionist's time is spent in performing a necessary and meaningful function

12. For a supervisor to require all stenographers in a stenographic pool to produce the same amount of work on a particular day is

   A. *advisable;* since it will prove that the supervisor plays no favorites
   B. *fair;* since all the stenographers are receiving approximately the same salary, their output should be equivalent
   C. *not necessary;* since the fast workers will compensate for the slow workers
   D. *not realistic;* since individual differences in abilities and work assignment must be taken into consideration

13. The establishment of a centralized typing pool to service the various units in an organization is MOST likely to be worthwhile when there is

   A. wide fluctuation from time to time in the needs of the various units for typing service
   B. a large volume of typing work to be done in each of the units
   C. a need by each unit for different kinds of typing service
   D. a training program in operation to develop and maintain typing skills

14. A newly appointed supervisor should learn as much as possible about the backgrounds of his subordinates. This statement is generally CORRECT because

   A. knowing their backgrounds assures they will be treated objectively, equally, and without favor
   B. effective handling of subordinates is based upon knowledge of their individual differences
   C. subordinates perform more efficiently under one supervisor than under another
   D. subordinates have confidence in a supervisor who knows all about them

15. The use of electronic computers in modern businesses has produced many changes in office and information management. Of the following, it would NOT be correct to state that computer utilization

A. broadens the scope of managerial and supervisory authority
B. establishes uniformity in the processing and reporting of information
C. cuts costs by reducing the personnel needed for efficient office operation
D. supplies management rapidly with up-to-date data to facilitate decision-making

16. The CHIEF advantage of having a single, large open office instead of small partitioned ones for a clerical unit or stenographic pool is that the single, large open office

    A. affords privacy without isolation for all office workers not directly dealing with the public
    B. assures the smoother, more continuous inter-office flow of work that is essential for efficient work production
    C. facilitates the office supervisor's visual control over and communication with his subordinates
    D. permits a more decorative and functional arrangement of office furniture and machines

17. When a supervisor provides a new employee with the information necessary for a basic knowledge and a general understanding of practices and procedures of the agency, he is applying the type of training generally known as _____ training.

    A. pre-employment   B. induction
    C. on-the-job   D. supervisory

18. Many government agencies require the approval by a central forms control unit of the design and reproduction of new office forms.
    The one of the following results of this procedure that is a DISADVANTAGE is that requiring prior approval of a central forms control unit USUALLY

    A. limits the distribution of forms to those offices with justifiable reasons for receiving them
    B. permits checking whether existing forms or modifications of them are in line with current agency needs
    C. encourages reliance on only the central office to set up all additional forms when needed
    D. provides for someone with a specialized knowledge of forms design to review and criticize new and revised forms

19. Suppose that a large quantity of information is in the files which are located a good distance from your desk. Almost every worker in your office must use these files constantly. Your duties in particular require that you daily refer to about 25 of the same items. They are short, one-page items distributed throughout the files.
    In this situation, your BEST course would be to

    A. take the items that you use daily from the files and keep them on your desk, inserting "out cards" in their place
    B. go to the files each time you need the information so that the items will be there when other workers need them
    C. make xerox copies of the information you use most frequently and keep them in your desk for ready reference
    D. label the items you use most often with different colored tabs for immediate identification

20. Of the following, the MOST important advantage of preparing manuals of office procedures in loose-leaf form is that this form

    A. permits several employees to use different sections simultaneously
    B. facilitates the addition of new material and the removal of obsolete material
    C. is more readily arranged in alphabetical order
    D. reduces the need for cross-references to locate material carried under several headings

21. Suppose that you establish a new clerical procedure for the unit you supervise.
    Your keeping a close check on the time required by your staff to handle the new procedure is wise MAINLY because such a check will find out

    A. whether your subordinates know how to handle the new procedure
    B. whether a revision of the unit's work schedule will be necessary as a result of the new procedure
    C. what attitude your employees have toward the new procedure
    D. what alterations in job descriptions will be necessitated by the new procedure

22. From the viewpoint of an office supervisor, the BEST of the following reasons for distributing the incoming mail *before* the beginning of the regular work day is that

    A. distribution can be handled quickly and most efficiently at that time
    B. distribution later in the day may be distracting to or interfere with other employees
    C. the employees who distribute the mail can then perform other tasks during the rest of the day
    D. office activities for the day based on the mail may then be started promptly

23. Suppose you are the head of a unit with ten staff members who are located in several different rooms. If you want to inform your staff of a *minor* change in procedure, the BEST and LEAST expensive way of doing so would usually be to

    A. send a mimeographed copy to each staff member
    B. call a special staff meeting and announce the change
    C. circulate a memo, having each staff member initial it
    D. have a clerk tell each member of the staff about the change

24. The numbered statements below relate to the stenographic skill of taking dictation.
    According to authorities on secretarial practices, which of these are GENERALLY recommended guides to development of efficient stenographic skills?
    A stenographer should

    I. date her notebook daily to facilitate locating certain notes at a later time
    II. make corrections of grammatical mistakes while her boss is dictating to her
    III. draw a line through the dictated matter in her notebook after she has transcribed it
    IV. write in longhand unfamiliar names and addresses dictated to her

    The CORRECT answer is:

    A. I, II, III
    B. II, III, IV
    C. I, III, IV
    D. All of the above

25. A bureau of a city agency is about to move to a new location.
    Of the following, the FIRST step that should be taken in order to provide a good layout for the office at the new location is to

A. decide the exact amount of space to be assigned to each unit of the bureau
B. decide whether to lay out a single large open office or one consisting of small partitioned units
C. ask each unit chief in the bureau to examine the new location and submit a request for the amount of space he needs
D. prepare a detailed plan of the dimensions of the floor space to be occupied by the bureau at the new location

KEY (CORRECT ANSWERS)

1. A
2. B
3. B
4. C
5. A

6. A
7. D
8. B
9. A
10. D

11. A
12. D
13. A
14. B
15. A

16. C
17. B
18. C
19. C
20. B

21. B
22. D
23. C
24. C
25. D

TEST 2

DIRECTIONS: Each question or incomplete statement is followed by several suggested answers or completions. Select the one that BEST answers the question or completes the statement. *PRINT THE LETTER OF THE CORRECT ANSWER IN THE SPACE AT THE RIGHT.*

1. Suppose you are the supervisor of the mailroom of a large agency where the mail received daily is opened by machine, sorted by hand for delivery and time-stamped. Letters and any enclosures are removed from envelopes and stapled together before distribution. One of your newest clerks asks you what should be done when a letter makes reference to an enclosure, but no enclosure is in the envelope.
You should tell him that in this situation the BEST procedure is to

   A. make an entry of the sender's name and address in the "missing enclosures" file and forward the letter to its proper destination
   B. return the letter to its sender, attaching a request for the missing enclosure
   C. put the letter aside until a proper investigation may be made concerning the missing enclosure
   D. route the letter to the person for whom it is intended, noting the absence of the enclosure on the letter margin

1.____

2. The term "work flow," when used in connection with office management or the activities in an office, GENERALLY means the

   A. use of charts in the analysis of various office functions
   B. rate of speed at which work flows through a single section of an office
   C. step-by-step physical routing of work through its various procedures
   D. number of individual work units which can be produced by the average employee

2.____

3. Physical conditions can have a definite effect on the efficiency and morale of an office. Which of the following statements about physical conditions in an office is CORRECT?

   A. Hard, non-porous surfaces reflect more noise than linoleum on the top of a desk.
   B. Painting in tints of bright yellow is more appropriate for sunny, well-lit offices than for dark, poorly-lit offices.
   C. Plate glass is better than linoleum for the top of a desk.
   D. The central typing room needs less light than a conference room does.

3.____

4. In a certain filing system, documents are consecutively numbered as they are filed, a register is maintained of such consecutively numbered documents, and a record is kept of the number of each document removed from the files and its destination.
This system will NOT help in

   A. finding the present whereabouts of a particular document
   B. proving the accuracy of the data recorded on a certain document
   C. indicating whether observed existing documents were ever filed
   D. locating a desired document without knowing what its contents are

4.____

5. In deciding the kind and number of records an agency should keep, the administrative staff must recognize that records are of value in office management PRIMARILY as

5.____

147

A. informational bases for agency activities
B. data for evaluating the effectiveness of the agency
C. raw material on which statistical analyses are to be based
D. evidence that the agency is carrying out its duties and responsibilities

6. Complaints are often made by the public about the city government's procedures. Although in most cases such procedures cannot be changed since various laws and regulations require them, it may still be possible to reduce the number of complaints. Which one of the following actions by personnel dealing with applicants for city services is LEAST likely to reduce complaints concerning city procedures?

    A. Treating all citizens alike and explaining to them that no exceptions to required procedures can be made
    B. Explaining briefly to the citizen why he should comply with regulations
    C. Being careful to avoid mistakes which may make additional interviews or correspondence necessary
    D. Keeping the citizen informed of the progress of his correspondence when immediate disposition cannot be made

7. In answering a complaint made by a member of the public that a certain essential procedure required by your agency is difficult to follow, it would be BEST for you to stress MOST

    A. that a change in the rules may be considered if enough complaints are received
    B. why the operation of a large agency sometimes proves a hardship in individual cases
    C. the necessity for the procedure
    D. the origin of the procedure

8. When talking to a citizen, it is BEST for an employee of government to

    A. use ordinary conversational phrases and a natural manner
    B. try to copy the pronunciation and level of education shown by the citizen
    C. try to speak in a very cultured manner and tone
    D. use technical terms to show his familiarity with his own work

9. Employees who service the public should maintain an attitude which is both sympathetic and objective.
An UNSYMPATHETIC and SUBJECTIVE attitude would be shown by a public employee who

    A. says "no" with a smile when a citizen's request must be denied
    B. listens attentively to a long complaint from a citizen about the government's "red tape"
    C. responds with sarcasm when a citizen asks a question which has an obvious answer
    D. suggests a definite solution to a citizen's problems

10. You are a supervisor in a city agency and are holding your first interview with a new employee.
In this interview, you should strive MAINLY to

A. show the new employee that you are an efficient and objective supervisor, with a completely impersonal attitude toward your subordinates
B. complete the entire orientation process including the giving of detailed job-duty instructions
C. make it clear to the employee that all your decisions are based on your many years of experience
D. lay the groundwork for a good employee-supervisor relationship by gaining the new employee's confidence

11. A senior clerk or senior typist may be required to help train a newly-appointed clerk. Which of the following is LEAST important for a newly-appointed clerk to know in order to perform his work efficiently?

    A. Acceptable ways of answering and recording telephone calls
    B. The number of files in the storage files unit
    C. The filing methods used by his unit
    D. Proper techniques for handling visitors

12. In your agency, you have the responsibility of processing clients who have appointments with agency representatives. On a particularly busy day, a client comes to your desk and insists that she must see the person handling her case although she has no appointment.
Under the circumstances, your FIRST action should be to

    A. show her the full appointment schedule
    B. give her an appointment for another day
    C. ask her to explain the urgency
    D. tell her to return later in the day

13. Which of the following practices is BEST for a supervisor to use when assigning work to his staff?

    A. Give workers with seniority the most difficult jobs
    B. Assign all unimportant work to the slower workers
    C. Permit each employee to pick the job he prefers
    D. Make assignments based on the workers' abilities

14. In which of the following instances is a supervisor MOST justified in giving commands to people under his supervision? When

    A. they delay in following instructions which have been given to them clearly
    B. they become relaxed and slow about work, and he wants to speed up their production
    C. he must direct them in an emergency situation
    D. he is instructing them on jobs that are unfamiliar to them

15. Which of the following supervisory actions or attitudes is MOST likely to result in getting subordinates to try to do as much work as possible for a supervisor? He

    A. shows that his most important interest is in schedules and production goals
    B. consistently pressures his staff to get the work out
    C. never fails to let them know he is in charge
    D. considers their abilities and needs while requiring that production goals be met

16. Assume that a senior clerk has been explaining certain regulations to a new clerk under his supervision.
    The MOST efficient way for the senior clerk to make sure that the clerk has understood the explanation is to

    A. give him written materials on the regulations
    B. ask him if he has any further questions about the regulations
    C. ask him specific questions based on what has just been explained to him
    D. watch the way he handles a situation involving these regulations

17. One of your unit clerks has been assigned to work for a Mr. Jones in another office for several days. At the end of the first day, Mr. Jones, saying the clerk was not satisfactory, asks that she not be assigned to him again. This clerk is one of your most dependable workers, and no previous complaints about her work have come to you from any other outside assignments.
    To get to the root of this situation, your FIRST action should be to

    A. ask Mr. Jones to explain in what way her work was unsatisfactory
    B. ask the clerk what she did that Mr. Jones considered unsatisfactory
    C. check with supervisors for whom she previously worked to see if your own rating of her is in error
    D. tell Mr. Jones to pick the clerk he would prefer to have work for him the next time

18. A senior typist, still on probation, is instructed to type, as quickly as possible, one section of a draft of a long, complex report. Her part must be typed and readable before another part of the report can be written. Asked when she can have the report ready, she gives her supervisor an estimate of a day longer than she knows it will actually take. She then finishes the job a day sooner than the date given her supervisor.
    The judgment shown by a senior typist in giving an overestimate of time in a situation like this is, in general,

    A. *good,* because it prevents the supervisor from thinking she works slowly
    B. *good,* because it keeps unrealistic supervisors from expecting too much
    C. *bad,* because she should have used the time left to further check and proofread her work
    D. *bad,* because schedules and plans for other parts of the project may have been based on her false estimate

19. Suppose a new clerk, still on probation, is placed under your supervision and refuses to do a job you ask him to do.
    What is the FIRST thing you should do?

    A. Explain that you are the supervisor, and he must follow your instructions.
    B. Tell him he may be suspended if he refuses.
    C. Ask someone else to do the job, and rate him accordingly.
    D. Ask for his reason for objecting to the request.

20. As a supervisor of a small group of people, you have blamed worker A for something that you later find out was really done by worker B.
The BEST thing for you to do now would be to

   A. say nothing to worker A, but criticize worker B for his mistake while worker A is near so that A will realize that you know who made the mistake
   B. speak to each worker separately, apologize to worker A for your mistake, and discuss worker B's mistake with him
   C. bring both workers together, apologize to worker A for your mistake, and discuss worker B's mistake with him
   D. say nothing new but be careful about mixing up worker A with worker B in the future

21. You have just learned one of your staff is grumbling that she thinks you are not pleased with her work. As far as you are concerned, this is not true at all. In fact, you have paid no particular attention to this worker lately because you have been very busy. You have just finished preparing an important report and "breaking in" a new clerk.
Under the circumstances, the BEST thing to do is

   A. ignore her; after all, it is just a figment of her imagination
   B. discuss the matter with her now to try to find out and eliminate the cause of this problem
   C. tell her not to worry about it; you have not had time to think about her work
   D. make a note to meet with her at a later date in order to straighten out the situation

22. A most important job of a supervisor is to positively motivate employees to increase their work production. Which of the following LEAST indicates that a group of workers has been positively motivated?

   A. Their work output becomes constant and stable.
   B. Their cooperation at work becomes greater.
   C. They begin to show pride in the product of their work.
   D. They show increased interest in their work.

23. Which of the following traits would be LEAST important in considering a person for a merit increase?

   A. Punctuality
   B. Using initiative successfully
   C. High rate of production
   D. Resourcefulness

24. Of the following, the action LEAST likely to gain a supervisor the cooperation of his staff is for him to

   A. give each person consideration as an individual
   B. be as objective as possible when evaluating work performance
   C. rotate the least popular assignments
   D. expect subordinates to be equally competent

25. It has been said that, for the supervisor, nothing can beat the "face-to-face" communication of talking to one subordinate at a time.
This method is, however, LEAST appropriate to use when the

   A. supervisor is explaining a change in general office procedure
   B. subject is of personal importance
   C. supervisor is conducting a yearly performance evaluation of all employees
   D. supervisor must talk to some of his employees concerning their poor attendance and punctuality

KEY (CORRECT ANSWERS)

1. D
2. C
3. A
4. B
5. A

6. A
7. C
8. A
9. C
10. D

11. B
12. C
13. D
14. C
15. D

16. C
17. A
18. D
19. D
20. B

21. B
22. A
23. A
24. D
25. A

TEST 3

DIRECTIONS: Each question or incomplete statement is followed by several suggested answers or completions. Select the one that BEST answers the question or completes the statement. *PRINT THE LETTER OF THE CORRECT ANSWER IN THE SPACE AT THE RIGHT.*

1. While you are on the telephone answering a question about your agency, a visitor comes to your desk and starts to ask you a question. There is no emergency or urgency in either situation, that of the phone call or that of answering the visitor's question.
   In this case, you should

   A. continue to answer the person on the telephone until you are finished and then tell the visitor you are sorry to have kept him waiting
   B. excuse yourself to the person on the telephone and tell the visitor that you will be with him as soon as you have finished on the phone
   C. explain to the person on the telephone that you have a visitor and must shorten the conversation
   D. continue to answer the person on the phone while looking up occasionally at the visitor to let him know that you know he is waiting

2. While speaking on the telephone to someone who called, you are disconnected.
   The FIRST thing you should do is

   A. hang up, but try to keep your line free to receive the call back
   B. immediately get the dial tone and continually dial the person who called you until you reach him
   C. signal the switchboard operator and ask her to re-establish the connection
   D. dial "O" for Operator and explain that you were disconnected

3. The type of speech used by an office worker in telephone conversation greatly affects the communication.
   Of the following, the BEST way to express your ideas when telephoning is with a vocabulary that consists MAINLY of

   A. formal, intellectual sounding words
   B. often used colloquial words
   C. technical, emphatic words
   D. simple, descriptive words

4. Suppose a clerk under your supervision has taken a personal phone call and is at the same time needed to answer a question regarding an assignment being handled by another member of your office. He appears confused as to what he should do. How should you instruct him later as to how to handle a similar situation?
   You should tell him to

   A. tell the caller to hold on while he answers the question
   B. tell the caller to call back a little later
   C. return the call during an assigned break
   D. finish the conversation quickly and answer the question

5. You are asked to place a telephone call by your supervisor. When you place the call, you receive what appears to be a wrong number.
   Of the following, you should FIRST

   A. check the number with your supervisor to see if the number he gave you is correct
   B. ask the person on the other end what his number is and who he is
   C. check with the person on the other end to see if the number you dialed is the number you received
   D. apologize to the person on the other end for disturbing him and hang up

6. When you select someone to serve as supervisor of your unit during your absence on vacation and at other times, it would generally be BEST to choose the employee who is

   A. able to move the work along smoothly, without friction
   B. on staff longest
   C. liked best by the rest of the staff
   D. able to perform the work of each employee to be supervised

7. Successful supervision of handicapped persons employed in a department depends MOST on providing them with a work place and work climate

   A. which is safe and accident-free
   B. that requires close and direct supervision by others
   C. that requires the performance of routine, repetitive tasks under a minimum of pressure
   D. where they will be accepted by the other employees

8. Studies have indicated that when employees feel that their work is aimless and unchallenging, the allocation or payment of more money for this type of work is likely to

   A. contribute little to increased production
   B. bring more status to this work
   C. increase employees' feelings of security
   D. give employees greater motivation

9. An employee's performance has fallen below established minimum standards of quantity and quality.
   The threat of monetary or other disciplinary action as a device for improving this employee's performance would probably be acceptable and MOST effective

   A. only if applied as soon as the performance fell below standard
   B. only after more constructive techniques have failed
   C. at any time provided the employee understands that the punishment will be carried out
   D. at no time

10. A supervisor must, on short notice, ask his staff to work overtime.
    Of the following, a technique that is MOST likely to win their willing cooperation would be to

    A. explain that occasional overtime is part of the job requirement
    B. explain that they will be doing him a personal favor which he will appreciate very much

C. explain why the overtime is necessary
D. promise them that they can take the extra time off in the near future

11. On checking a completed work assignment of an employee, the supervisor finds that the work was not done correctly because the employee had not understood his instructions. Of the following, the BEST way to prevent repetition of this situation next time is for the supervisor to

   A. ask the employee whether he fully understood the instructions and tell him to ask questions in the future whenever anything is unclear
   B. ask the employee to repeat the instructions given and test his understanding with several key questions
   C. give the instructions a second time, emphasizing the more complicated aspects of the job
   D. give work instructions in writing

11._____

12. If, as a supervisor, you find yourself pressured for time to handle all of your job responsibilities, the one of the following tasks which it would be MOST appropriate for you to delegate to a subordinate is

   A. attending a staff conference of unit supervisors to discuss the implementation of a new departmental policy
   B. making staff work assignments
   C. interviewing a new employee
   D. checking work of certain employees for accuracy

12._____

13. Suppose you are unavoidably late for work one morning. When you arrive at 10 o'clock, you find there are several matters demanding your attention.
Which one of the following matters should you handle LAST?

   A. A visitor who had a 9:30 appointment with you has been waiting to see you since 9 o'clock.
   B. An employee on an assignment which should have been completed that morning is absent, and the work will have to be reassigned.
   C. Several letters which you dictated at the end of the previous day have been typed and are on your desk for signature and mailing.
   D. Your superior called asking you to get certain information for him when you come in and to call him back.

13._____

14. Suppose that you have assigned a typist to type a report containing considerable statistical and tabular material and have given her specific instructions as to how this material is to be laid out on each page. When she returns the completed report, you find that it was not prepared according to your instructions, but you may possibly be able to use it the way it was typed. When you question her, she states that she thought her layout was better but you were unavailable for consultation when she began the work.
Of the following, the BEST action for you to take is to

   A. criticize her for not doing the work according to your instructions
   B. have her retype the report
   C. praise her for her work but tell her she should have waited until she could consult you
   D. praise her for using initiative

14._____

15. Of the following, the MOST effective way for a supervisor to correct poor work habits of an employee which result in low and poor quality output is to give the employee

    A. additional training
    B. less demanding assignments until his work improves
    C. continuous supervision
    D. more severe criticism

16. Of the following, the BEST way for a supervisor to teach an employee how to do a new and somewhat complicated job is to

    A. assign him to observe another employee who is already skilled in this work and instruct him to consult this employee if he has any questions
    B. explain to him how to do it, then demonstrate how it is done, then observe and correct the employee as he does it, then follow up
    C. give him a written, detailed, step-by-step explanation of how to do the job and instruct him to ask questions if anything is unclear when he does the work
    D. teach him the easiest part of the job first, then the other parts one at a time, in order of their difficulty, as the employee masters the easier parts

17. After an employee has completed telling his supervisor about a grievance against a co-worker, the supervisor tells the employee that he will take action to remove the cause of the grievance.
    The action of the supervisor was

    A. *good*, because ill feeling between subordinates interferes with proper performance
    B. *poor*, because the supervisor should give both employees time to "cool off"
    C. *good*, because grievances that appear petty to the supervisor are important to subordinates
    D. *poor*, because the supervisor should tell the employee that he will investigate the matter before he comes to any conclusion

18. During work on an important project, one employee in a secretarial pool turns in several pages of typed copy, one page of which contains several errors.
    Of these four comments which her supervisor might possibly make, which one would be MOST constructive?

    A. "You did such a poor job on this; I will have to have it done over."
    B. "You will have to do better, more consistently than this, if you want to be in charge of a secretarial pool yourself someday."
    C. "How come you made so many mistakes here? Your other pages were all right."
    D. "If my boss saw this, he would be very displeased with you."

19. A supervisor has general supervision over a large, complex project with many employees. The work is subdivided among small units of employees, each with a senior clerk or senior stenographer in charge. At a staff meeting, after all work assignments have been made, the supervisor tells all the employees that they are to take orders only from their immediate supervisor and instructs them to let him know if anyone else tries to give them orders.
    This instruction by the supervising clerk is

A. *good,* because it may prevent the issuance of orders by unauthorized persons, which would interfere with the accomplishment of the assignment
B. *poor,* because employees should be instructed to take up such problems with their immediate supervisor
C. *good,* because orders issued by immediate supervisors would be precise and directly related to the tasks of the assignments while those issued by others would not be
D. *poor,* because it places upon all employees a responsibility which should not normally be theirs

20. A supervisor who is to direct a team of senior clerks and clerks in a complex project, calls them together beforehand to inform them of the tasks each employee will perform on this job.
Of the following, the CHIEF value of this action by the supervisor is that each member of this team will be able to

    A. work independently in the absence of the supervisor
    B. understand what he will do and how this will fit into the total picture
    C. share in the process of decision-making as an equal participant
    D. judge how well the plans for this assignment have been made

21. A supervisor who has both younger and older employees under his supervision may sometimes find that employee absenteeism seriously interferes with accomplishment of goals.
Studies of such employee absenteeism have shown that the absences of employees

    A. under 35 years of age are usually unexpected and the absences of employees over 45 years of age are usually unnecessary
    B. of all age groups show the same characteristics as to length of absence
    C. under 35 years of age are for frequent, short periods while the absences of employees over 45 years of age are less frequent but of longer duration
    D. under 35 years of age are for periods of long duration and the absences of employees over 45 years of age are for periods of short duration

22. Suppose you have a long-standing procedure for getting a certain job done by your subordinates that is apparently a good one. Changes in some steps of the procedure are made from time to time to handle special problems that come up.
For you to review this procedure periodically is desirable MAINLY because

    A. the system is working well
    B. checking routines periodically is a supervisor's chief responsibility
    C. subordinates may be confused as to how the procedure operates as a result of the changes made
    D. it is necessary to determine whether the procedure has become outdated or is in need of improvement

23. Suppose that a stranger enters the office you are in charge of and asks for the address and telephone number of one of your employees.
Of the following, it would be BEST for you to

    A. find out why he needs the information and release it if his reason is a good one
    B. explain that you are not permitted to release such information to unauthorized persons

C. give him the information but tell him it must be kept confidential
D. ask him to leave the office immediately

24. A member of the public approaches an employee who is at work at his desk. The employee cannot interrupt his work in order to take care of this person.
Of the following, the BEST and MOST courteous way of handling this situation is for the employee to

    A. avoid looking up from his work until he is finished with what he is doing
    B. tell this person that he will not be able to take care of him for quite a while
    C. refer the individual to another employee who can take care of him right away
    D. chat with the individual while he continues with his work

25. You answer a phone call from a citizen who urgently needs certain information you do not have, but you think you know who may have it. He is angry because he has already been switched to two different offices.
Of the following, it would be BEST for you to

    A. give him the phone number of the person you think may have the information he wants, but explain you are not sure
    B. tell him you regret you cannot help him because you are not sure who can give him the information
    C. advise him that the best way he can be sure of getting the information he wants is to write a letter to the agency
    D. get the phone number where he can be reached and tell him you will try to get the information he wants and will call him back later

KEY (CORRECT ANSWERS)

1. B
2. A
3. D
4. C
5. C

6. A
7. D
8. A
9. B
10. C

11. B
12. D
13. C
14. A
15. A

16. B
17. D
18. C
19. B
20. B

21. C
22. D
23. B
24. C
25. D

EXAMINATION SECTION
TEST 1

DIRECTIONS: Each question or incomplete statement is followed by several suggested answers or completions. Select the one that BEST answers the question or completes the statement. *PRINT THE LETTER OF THE CORRECT ANSWER IN THE SPACE AT THE RIGHT.*

1. Ms. Palmer is a manager who has the reputation of being tough, but fair-minded. She has just been promoted into a different part of the agency, and now heads a unit of thirty employees. She has observed that there are several employees who stick together. They seem to really enjoy working together, and she has observed them discussing how to solve work problems even on their lunch breaks. While she realizes they are effective and good at what they do, she does not like the idea of this informal work group staying together and possibly becoming more powerful and a threat to her authority. She decides to take steps to weaken its effectiveness.
The proposed action of Ms. Palmer is a

    A. *good* idea, since supervisors need complete control of their units
    B. *bad* idea, since the employees are having a good time and not causing trouble
    C. *good* idea, since the informal work group is most likely seen as a clique and resented by other employees
    D. *bad* idea, since the informal work group is functioning effectively, and she is most likely reacting in a defensive manner

1.____

2. The middle manager is both *player* and *coach* and needs to combine different skills and actions. A middle manager must see the *big picture,* be detached, and have a more long-range perspective. But he or she also needs to have detailed knowledge of the job, abundant job experience, and the ability to become deeply involved in the work.
It is sometimes difficult for a middle manager to know if he or she is employing the correct blend of these roles. Is he or she too involved in being a player—doing too many things that should be done by others? Or is he or she being too much of a coach—delegating too much and not being involved enough? How much one needs to be player or coach is unique to every situation and very much influenced, not only by the actual job to be done, but also by the needs and demands of bosses, co-workers, and employees.
With which of the following choices would the author MOST likely agree?

    A. When in doubt, a middle manager is likely to be better off delegating an assignment.
    B. If a middle manager has very competent employees, he or she is likely to be better off being a *player* than a *coach.*
    C. If a middle manager has a very demanding boss, he or she is likely to be better off being a *player.*
    D. If a situation calls for technical information that only the middle manager has, he or she is likely to be better off being a *player.*

2.____

3. Bob supervises fifteen employees in Unit 2, a position he has held for nine months. Before being promoted, he had worked in the same unit for four years and was well liked by all of his co-workers. He was an excellent employee and worked very hard. Bob has had a number of problems since receiving his promotion, however. A new employee in his unit seems to have an aversion to work. He frequently comes in late and makes many personal phone calls during the day. Bob has noticed this behavior, but is reluctant to do anything about it. Because he is not sure if the work he assigns the employee will get done, he gives much less work to him than to the others. Since the unit has a higher workload than ever, the work is piling up, and everyone in the unit is concerned.
One day, one of the personnel managers approaches Bob, tells him that the employees in the unit are upset about the situation, and urges him to take action. The next day, Bob calls a meeting of the staff and announces that *some people in the unit are coming in late, spending too much time on the phone, and not getting any work done.* He also says that this has to stop. That afternoon, Bob sends everyone in his unit a memo which emphasizes these points and bans any future personal calls in the office. Bob's way of handling this situation was

    A. *wise,* since this should have the effect of *shaping up* the other workers in the unit as well
    B. *unwise,* since it will lower productivity
    C. *unwise,* since it is too indirect and punitive a response
    D. *wise,* since he would have hurt the new employee's feelings if he had confronted him alone

4. You supervise a large unit of thirty employees. Diane, an employee in the unit, comes to you and says she can't work for Alan, her supervisor, anymore because he checks on her work all the time and is very critical of her.
She says she has tried to talk to him about the situation, but he won't listen to her.
Of the following, it would be BEST if you responded by saying

    A. "I'm sure Alan is treating you no differently than he treats everyone else"
    B. "Do you feel Alan is too critical of you?"
    C. "I don't think you should have gone over Alan's head by coming to me with this minor problem."
    D. "You wouldn't want Alan to accept poor quality work, would you?"

5. Which of the following statements is MOST accurate?

    A. It is much better for supervisors to focus on an employee's behavior rather than on his or her personality.
    B. It is not common for supervisors to procrastinate, hoping a problem will go away.
    C. Problems in working habits are always more difficult for supervisors to deal with than performance problems.
    D. When discussing an employee's behavior, it is wise for a supervisor to attribute motives to the behavior.

6. All of the following are likely to be true of a new supervisory situation EXCEPT: 6._____
   A. New supervisors are often on the spot during their first few weeks on the job
   B. Some new supervisors swell with responsibility instead of growing with it
   C. It is best if a new supervisor begins by making a lot of changes
   D. Former cronies of the new supervisor may expect special treatment and become resentful if it is not given

7. You have been the supervisor of a small unit for four months. One of the employees you supervise has consistently performed very poorly. You have talked with her on many occasions and evaluated her performance and set goals regularly. None of this has helped, although she does have the necessary skills to do the job. It seems that she just does not like to work very hard. She has been employed by the organization for thirty years, and other long-time employees have told you she has always performed poorly, but her other supervisors always overlooked her poor performance because they knew she would make a lot of trouble if she were formally disciplined. Your unit's workload has increased significantly in the past three months, and now the other employees must do a great deal of the work she is unwilling to do. 7._____
   Of the following, which would be the BEST action for you to take?

   A. Discuss the situation with the employee and tell her you will have to begin formal discipline procedures if her performance does not improve.
   B. Ask the employee to resign.
   C. Ask one of the long-time employees to discuss the situation with her, encouraging her to resign.
   D. Ask your supervisor to fire her.

8. An employee you supervise is extremely competitive and very abrasive. The other employees in your unit are very resentful of this employee, who often *shows them up* with the very high quality of his work. 8._____
   Of the following, it would be BEST if you

   A. let him know that, while you appreciate his concern and attempts to produce high quality work, the ability to get along with others and work as a team is just as important as technical ability
   B. ignore the situation, since his work is of such high quality
   C. let him know that, although you appreciate the high quality of his work, you can't help but get irritated by some of his behavior
   D. try to understand why he is acting the way he is

9. You have the responsibility of making a big decision, and you would like to get some group input. 9._____
   Of the following, it is MOST important that you

   A. make sure everyone in the group has a chance to speak
   B. make it clear whether you will abide by their suggestions, or whether you just want to hear these suggestions to help you arrive at a possible solution
   C. wait until everyone has spoken before silently deciding whether to consider their ideas
   D. use good problem-solving techniques during the meeting

10. Which of the following statements is LEAST accurate?

    A. Most workers want to satisfy physical, social, and personal needs.
    B. A supervisor can have a significant impact upon an employee's personal life.
    C. Supervisors who emphasize getting to know the needs of their employees are not using their time wisely.
    D. Most workers want responsibilities they can handle, results they can demonstrate, and recognition for what they accomplish.

11. You are the supervisor of a unit of twenty employees. Janet, one of the employees, comes to you and says that Mark, her supervisor, is not supervising. She says he does not take the time to give her direction or feedback on her work. Janet also says that she often has had to do assignments that should have been handled by Mark. Janet understands that Mark has a large workload, but says that she does too. She has tried to talk to Mark several times about the situation, but says he won't acknowledge that there is a problem. Both Janet and Mark have performed well in the past.
    How would you handle this situation?

    A. Inform Janet that she should not have ignored the chain of command by going over Mark's head.
    B. Ask Janet to be more understanding of the pressures faced by Mark.
    C. Thank Janet for coming to you, but explain that there is nothing you can do.
    D. Discuss the situation with Mark.

12. It is now widely recognized that salaries, benefits, and working conditions have more of an impact on job satisfaction than on motivation. If they are not satisfactory, work performance and morale will suffer. But even when they are very good, employees will not necessarily be motivated to work well. For example, The Wall Street Journal recently reported that as many as 40% or 50% of newly hired Wall Street lawyers (whose salaries start at upwards of $90,000) quit within the first three years, citing long hours, pressures, and monotony as the prime offenders. It seems there is just not enough of an intellectual challenge in their jobs. An up-and-coming money-market executive concluded:
    Whether it was $1 million or $100 million, the procedure was the same. Except for the tension, a baboon could have done my job. When money and benefits are adequate, the most important additional determinants of job satisfaction are more responsibility, a sense of achievement, recognition, and a chance to advance. And all of these have a more significant influence on employee motivation and performance.
    If you were a supervisor who agreed with the above passage, which of the following would you MOST likely do?

    A. Press hard for large monetary bonuses for well-paid executives that you supervise
    B. Encourage employee involvement in establishing employee assistance programs
    C. Encourage employee participation in job design and decision-making
    D. Encourage *Employee of the Year* awards

13. A supervisor feels very comfortable with two of the employees she supervises because they have work styles very similar to her own.
    Of the following, the supervisor should

    A. feel confident that the employees are doing a very good job
    B. try to view their work as subjectively as possible
    C. try to view their work as objectively as possible
    D. carefully reevaluate their past work performance

14. Nelson is a perfectionist who often becomes overwhelmed because he is trying to do too much too well. He has extremely high expectations and seems to be showing signs of *burnout*. Nelson just cannot say no—he will take on anything, even if someone else could or should do it. And nothing leaves his desk unless it is done perfectly. You know he is taking a lot of work home with him in order to keep up.
    Assume that you are Nelson's supervisor.
    Which of the following do you feel would be the BEST way to handle the above situation?

    A. Enroll Nelson in a course on assertiveness.
    B. Discuss with Nelson the issues of working too hard and trying to be perfect and the consequences of these.
    C. Sit down with Nelson and let him know it is all right to make mistakes.
    D. Enroll Nelson in a course on establishing priorities.

15. Which of the following statements is LEAST accurate?

    A. In order to be highly productive, it usually does not matter whether a work group feels the general organizational climate is a fair and friendly one.
    B. Work groups are likely to contain an informal alignment based on status and authority.
    C. Supervisors should accept the subgroups that often form within work units.
    D. It is not desirable for a supervisor to be seen as an outsider imposing controls on members of the work group.

16. When conducting a corrective interview, a supervisor should do all of the following EXCEPT

    A. state the purpose of the interview
    B. change the employee's point of view
    C. state the problem, review expectations, and review the employee's current performance
    D. give time frames

17. Derogatory criticism of a person's work can be very harmful. A supervisor should be able to correct an employee without destroying his or her self-worth. A very minor example is a typist's mistake or typographical error that is sent back along with a 3x5 sheet of paper on which the typist's name is written, underlined, and deliberately misspelled. To me and the other typists in my department, it is a little degrading and implies a certain amount of ignorance and a lack of respect. Little things add up to a lot.
    Which of the following statements is BEST supported by the above passage?

A. Respect and dignity on the job are important to employees.
B. Supervisors should only criticize an employee's work when they absolutely have to.
C. A supervisor's ability to take criticism well is important in order to set an example for the supervisor's employees.
D. Give employees an inch and they'll take a mile.

18. You have just received a promotion to a different unit. Until he failed the oral exam for the title, Murray, a long-time and well-liked employee, had briefly held this position provisionally. You have been in the job for two weeks and have noticed that Murray is very bitter about the situation and is subtly undermining your authority. Of the following, it would be BEST if you

    A. had Murray transferred as soon as possible
    B. spoke with Murray about the situation
    C. spoke with your supervisor about the situation and asked him or her to talk with the employee
    D. ignored the situation for two more weeks to give Murray more time to adjust to it

19. *I believe that many of the problems I encountered were problems of fit with the informal organization. My peers and supervisors were unable to perceive me as being able to perform the job that the company hired me for. Their reaction to me was disbelief. I was out of the "place" normally filled by black people in the company; and since no black person had preceded me successfully, it was easy for my antagonists to believe I was inadequate, and to act as if I were.*
    – A black manager on his experience in the early 1960's

    Which of the following statements is BEST supported by the above passage?

    A. The informal organization is often beyond a supervisor's best efforts to control it.
    B. Expectations can significantly affect behavior and perceptions.
    C. Informal organizations wield little power.
    D. Informal organizations are very powerful.

20. You supervise a unit of twenty employees. Sometimes you must ask your employees to work overtime. You are careful to allocate the overtime fairly. Most of the employees are cooperative, but Andy always resists. Tonight he said that you deliberately pick him to work on Monday nights because you are afraid to ask anyone else to miss the football game on TV.
    Of the following, it would be BEST if you responded by saying:

    A. "It's your own fault for always resisting overtime."
    B. "If you think you aren't getting a fair deal on over time, we can discuss it, but I do need you to work overtime tonight."
    C. "It's only a game. Besides, I've been fairly allocating overtime on Monday nights to every employee on a regular schedule."
    D. "I really don't think I've been singling you out."

21. When supervising, it is BEST for supervisors to 21.____

    A. focus primarily on appearances
    B. refine their hidden expectations
    C. focus on an employee's attitude toward the job as a basis for performance evaluation
    D. know the job standards and be sure employees know them too

22. You are the manager of a large unit of fifty employees. Jane, a typist in the unit, comes to 22.____
    you with a complaint about her supervisor, Marie. Marie is a program analyst who transferred to your unit last year. Jane, a very good and reliable worker, tells you that Marie has been taking up a lot of the secretaries' and other workers' time by talking with them a great deal about projects she is working on. Jane says she realizes that Marie is insecure about her work and needs a lot of support, but her behavior is causing some disruption. Because you are Marie's supervisor, she asks you to intervene.
    Of the following choices, it would be BEST if you

    A. went over Marie's personnel records for clues of poor performance and then discuss the situation with her
    B. told Jane she should have gone directly to Marie to discuss the problem, instead of coming to you
    C. asked Jane for more proof
    D. called Marie in to ask her how she is doing, and asked if you could do anything to make her feel more comfortable on the job

23. Of the following statements, which would MOST likely be appropriate for a supervisor to 23.____
    say to someone he or she supervises?

    A. "I'm concerned about the impact your long coffee breaks are having on the other employees. I'd like you to shorten them."
    B. "Time off next week? You must be kidding!"
    C. "You must be pretty thirsty to take all those long coffee breaks."
    D. "I get annoyed every time I see you coming in late."

24. When Napoleon was asked why he reinstituted the symbolic and practically worthless 24.____
    Legion of Honor Medal, he replied, *you lead men by baubles, not words.*
    Another way to say that would be that a supervisor

    A. gives all of the employees she supervises *outstanding* evaluations
    B. never overly praises those he supervises
    C. passes out trophies annually to outstanding employees
    D. praises those she supervises only when they deserve it

25. All of the following are common problems faced by new supervisors EXCEPT 25.____

    A. difficulty in making decisions because of the fear of making a mistake
    B. spending too much time procrastinating or collecting data before making a decision
    C. success in delegating work
    D. succumbing to waves of inertia because of fear

KEY (CORRECT ANSWERS)

1.	D	11.	D
2.	D	12.	C
3.	C	13.	C
4.	B	14.	B
5.	A	15.	A
6.	C	16.	B
7.	A	17.	A
8.	A	18.	B
9.	B	19.	B
10.	C	20.	B

21. D
22. A
23. A
24. C
25. C

TEST 2

DIRECTIONS: Each question or incomplete statement is followed by several suggested answers or completions. Select the one that BEST answers the question or completes the statement. *PRINT THE LETTER OF THE CORRECT ANSWER IN THE SPACE AT THE RIGHT.*

1. Which of the following is NOT true about planning and organizing work? 1.____

    A. Good planning skills are not as important as good people skills.
    B. Well-written operating manuals and other guides can allow a supervisor to primarily manage by exception.
    C. Every operation needs planning, even when it looks routine.
    D. A good supervisor should have alternatives readily available for potential problems that are predictable.

2. Two weeks ago, you asked one of your employees to be sure to keep a copy of all mail-in requests that come in to your office requesting information about an important project. You have just found out he has not been doing it. He explains that he thought you said it would be *nice* if he kept copies. You are quite upset about this. Of the following, it would be BEST if you 2.____

    A. tried to find out how the possible misunderstanding occurred and ask him to follow your instructions
    B. tried to find out how the possible misunderstanding occurred and then ask him if he is willing to keep the copies
    C. assigned the task to someone else
    D. told him that when you say *it would be nice if,* you mean he should do something

3. You have just been appointed supervisor of a large unit of thirty employees. You immediately notice there is a sort of *caste system* in the office, which runs along salary-grade lines. Although it is in their job descriptions, certain employees are not allowed to answer the phone when it rings. They must wait for a higher-grade employee to answer it. The slightly higher-grade employees have a number of privileges and also get to decide things like when the blinds should be open. There is a great deal of divisiveness in the unit. 3.____
Of the following, it would be BEST if you

    A. waited at least a month before taking any sort of action in order to acquire more information
    B. held a staff meeting as soon as possible to discuss the situation
    C. asked the former supervisor why things had gotten to this stage
    D. slowly, but firmly, began changing policies

4. Seymour seems allergic to detail. He thinks of himself as a man of action who gets right to the heart of the issue—and very often he does. He hands in his work early, but occasionally it needs to be redone because a key detail has been overlooked. Seymour is a very valuable, intelligent employee, who has a lot of enthusiasm. You have noticed, however, that this enthusiasm for undertaking new projects sometimes gets in the way of his follow-through. 4.____
If you were Seymour's supervisor, which of the following do you feel would be the BEST way to handle the above situation?

A. Whenever possible, assign a co-worker who is good at handling details to work on projects with Seymour.
B. Discuss the matter honestly with Seymour and order him to change his work habits.
C. Anonymously send Seymour an article on the importance of attention to detail and of follow-through.
D. Discuss the matter honestly with Seymour and ask him to establish work goals.

5. You supervise a small unit of five employees. The day before you are about to leave for a much needed and well-deserved two-week vacation abroad, the most competent worker asks to speak privately with you. The employee tells you that she has just been offered a better paying job with another organization. She is the employee who has been in the unit the longest and knows a great deal of valuable information about procedures and tasks that the other employees do not know. There has been talk for a while of upgrading her position.
Of the following, it would be BEST if you

   A. sincerely stated that you do not want to stand in her way, congratulate her, and let her know that you will miss her very much
   B. changed procedures so that never again would so much expertise be left to just one employee
   C. discussed the matter fully with the employee, and if she wished to stay with your unit, assured her that you would instruct your replacement supervisor to immediately begin the process of upgrading her
   D. discussed the matter with the employee, letting her know how valuable she is, and then asked her to stay long enough to train someone fully before she leaves

6. You have assigned a new project to one of the employees you supervise. Soon after the assignment, she comes into your office and asks that you give the project to another worker. She feels she is not qualified to complete it correctly and that she will do a poor job.
Of the following, it would be BEST if you

   A. urged her to complete the project because this is a golden opportunity for her to shine
   B. allowed her to express her doubts, and then provided support in helping her organize and master the project
   C. reassigned the project to someone who would like to do it
   D. asked her why she is so insecure about doing the project

7. All of the following are true EXCEPT:
   A. Support on the job can reduce stress
   B. An employee's self-esteem is rarely a critical determinant of performance
   C. Employees who are allowed to participate in making decisions about how a task is to be performed are more enthusiastic about the task and are more likely to do the task well
   D. A supervisor's behavior has a greater effect on his or her employees than most supervisors recognize

8. Our control systems are designed under the apparent assumption that ninety percent of the people are lazy ne'er-do-wells, just waiting to lie, cheat, steal.... We demoralize the ninety-five percent of the workforce who do act like adults by designing systems to cover our tails against the five percent who are bad actors.
   A supervisor who believed the above statement would MOST likely

   A. give employees more discretion in performing tasks
   B. supervise employees very closely
   C. supervise problem employees more loosely than other supervisors would
   D. give employees less discretion in performing tasks

9. All of the following are common problems found in new supervisors EXCEPT

   A. an over- or underestimation of what they can accomplish
   B. an unwillingness to accept positive feedback from those they supervise
   C. overly flattering behavior towards their supervisors
   D. a tendency to become overly concerned with appearance rather than substance

10. Phyllis is a typist who works in a small typing pool. She has worked there for a year and a half, and has received excellent evaluations. Phyllis is a 24-year-old white female. Her supervisor is Patricia, a 45-year-old white female. They have always gotten along well, and morale in the unit is good. There are five white females and one Hispanic female in the unit.
    One night, Phyllis and her husband, who is black, ran into Patricia and her husband as they were leaving the movie theater. Phyllis noticed that Patricia seemed uncomfortable, but didn't think much more about it. The following Monday, Patricia asked Phyllis how she enjoyed the movie. She also asked if that was Phyllis' husband with her. When Phyllis replied that it was, Patricia gave her a weak smile, talked a little more, and left. Since that time, Patricia has been quite cold to Phyllis. For the last month, Phyllis has noticed that she has been getting all of the assignments for typing tabular material and other difficult typing that no one else wants. Previously, this work had been evenly distributed among all of the typists.
    The above passage is an example of

    A. comparable worth
    B. subtle discrimination
    C. sexual harassment
    D. equal pay for equal work

11. At a staff meeting, another supervisor made a comment that you felt was very critical of your department. You are about to meet with him in his office.
    Of the following, it would be BEST if you said,

    A. "I really didn't appreciate that comment you made about my department during the staff meeting."
    B. "That sure was an interesting staff meeting. I learned a lot. How about you?"
    C. "I was concerned about your comments on my department this morning. Do you have any suggestions on how I might improve things?"
    D. "I was interested in what you had to say today in the staff meeting. I feel some of your remarks were critical of my department, and I'd like to talk with you about them."

12. Donna's style has no doubt increased her supervisor's risk of heart attack significantly. She is a procrastinator and a last minute operator. She seems to thrive on the challenge of these self-imposed tight deadlines. Her supervisor has even tried lying and pushing the deadline of a project up a week before it was really due, but somehow she always finds out the truth. The quality of her work is excellent, but her supervisor never can be sure a project will be finished on time. Her supervisor feels he could not constantly work under that sort of stress and cannot imagine that Donna is not going to succumb to the pressure one of these days and miss a deadline. Besides, he feels all that stress is not good for her health.
The BEST way to handle the above situation is for Donna's superior to

   A. do nothing
   B. call her in to his office and lecture her about the importance of not procrastinating
   C. anonymously send her a book on planning and time management
   D. threaten her with severe formal disciplinary action unless she stops procrastinating

13. Barbara is an employee who has a reputation for being a troublemaker. She comes to her supervisor, Jack Burns, and says she is being sexually harassed. Barbara accuses Jack's superior, David London, who has been a close friend of Jack's for many years.
Jack should

   A. take Barbara's complaint seriously
   B. refer Barbara to counseling or to an employee assistance program
   C. listen to Barbara sympathetically, advise her to go to the affirmative action office to file a complaint, but also warn David that a complaint is going to be filed against him
   D. ask Barbara if she has any documentation to support her allegations

14. Which of the following statements about supervision is LEAST accurate?

   A. Once an employee performs well, he or she will continue to perform at that level.
   B. It is important for supervisors to encourage the employees they supervise to employ good delegation skills.
   C. Hidden expectations a supervisor may have, like assuming an employee does not mind taking work home, can be harmful.
   D. Supervisors should always be trying to improve their supervisory skills.

15. Which of the following would NOT be considered an example of subtle discrimination against an employee who is a protected class member?
A superior

   A. protects a protected class member by never giving negative feedback and by giving easy assignments
   B. asks a highly respected protected class member in the unit to talk with a Hispanic employee about a performance problem
   C. treats black male employees with more respect than she treats white male employees
   D. shares important information much more with male employees than with female employees

16. You supervise eight employees. In order to protect all of them from eyestrain, one particular assignment that requires close eyework is rotated and shared by everyone. One of the employees has just complained to you that he receives more of this work than the others, and he wants to be excused from doing the work today. You are not completely sure that he is incorrect.
Of the following, it would be BEST if you responded by saying:

   A. "Let me review my records to see if I have assigned the work fairly, and I will get right back to you."
   B. "I have given a lot of thought to how assignments are allocated, and it is fair for everyone. Please go back to work."
   C. "Last week you complained about needing a new electric stapler. The week before, you said you lost money in the vending machine. Isn't there anything you like around here?"
   D. "I am really sorry things have worked out this way, but I have to ask you to do the work anyway."

17. Morgan works very, very hard but is not as productive as he could be, considering how hard he works. He seems to have a hard time setting priorities and determining what is really important. There have been a number of occasions when you have found him hard at work on projects that were of much lower priority than others that were sitting on his desk. He also loves to collect information and thinks tons of information (some relevant, some not) will help him make the *perfect decision.*
If you were Morgan's supervisor, which of the following do you feel would be the BEST way to handle the above situation?

   A. Sit down with him and assist him in improving his decision–making skills.
   B. Meet with him to discuss your observations and then review his projects, establish priorities, and set realistic goals together
   C. Have him attend a training course on improving self–esteem
   D. Have him attend a training program on improving decision–making skills

18. *A few years back, I had the occasion to work at an agency where a new manager came in. We soon found out that the happy atmosphere we had all enjoyed for the past few years was slowly eroding. We started receiving memos for everything and anything; such as no more placing sweaters on chairs, absolutely clear desk tops, personal chattering is forbidden at all times, compulsory signing in and out at lunch time, and so on. This soon brought a big change in our health. We got nervous stomachs, headaches, high blood pressure, and so on. He also stated that women were taking men's jobs away and should be at home. Many of us spoke to the higher-ups, but nothing was done. So now I had to make a big decision. I loved my job but not the atmosphere I was working in. I was fortunate in having a friend who helped me to get into another agency where I still work. This atmosphere caused quite a few more people to leave, and it was a big shame because we all were good, productive workers. In fact, in many cases the agency had to hire two workers to do the job one of us had been able to do so well.*
What could the administrators have done to avoid the above situation?

A. Conducted exit interviews of the employees who left to determine their reasons for leaving
B. Instituted the above changes more slowly
C. Realized the changes were hurting employee morale and withdrawn them
D. Used the carrot-and-stick approach to management

19. John is a 25-year-old black training specialist trainee in Agency X. He has been with the agency for eight months. John works with Ed, a 28-year-old white training specialist who has been in his position for four years. Their supervisor is Daniel, a 30-year-old white male who has been supervisor for six years. Daniel and Ed are good friends. John has become upset because he and Ed are treated so differently. Ed is allowed to come in late and leave early. On days when Ed drives his car to the office, he is allowed to leave every 90 minutes to change his parking place so that he won't get a parking ticket. Ed never has to let Daniel know where he is going or what meetings he is attending. John is not allowed any leave violations, however minor. The second time he was a few minutes late to work, Daniel called him in to his office and reprimanded him. There is a training conference in Washington, D.C. that Ed and Daniel are going to. John has asked permission to go, but has been told he cannot go because he would not benefit as much as Ed and Daniel would.
Of the following statements, which BEST applies to the above paragraph?

19.___

A. Bad supervision can look a lot like discrimination.
B. Friends should never work together.
C. Agencies should provide parking for their employees in order to improve productivity and reduce friction.
D. Supervisors should be careful in choosing when to reprimand employees.

20. All of the following are common problems faced by new supervisors EXCEPT:

20.___

A. One's former peers are now people one has to supervise, and this can lead to confusion, conflict, or resentment
B. The supervisor may have been *top dog* in the previous title and now has to start at the *bottom* in the new position; this can lead to arrogant or defensive behavior
C. New supervisors usually experience low levels of stress
D. The new supervisor is often selected because he or she was a very competent employee, not because he or she demonstrated leadership or supervisory skills, and the lack of these skills can lead to serious problems with those he or she supervises

KEY (CORRECT ANSWERS)

1. A
2. A
3. D
4. A
5. C

6. B
7. B
8. A
9. B
10. B

11. D
12. A
13. A
14. A
15. C

16. A
17. B
18. C
19. A
20. C

EXAMINATION SECTION
TEST 1

DIRECTIONS: Each question or incomplete statement is followed by several suggested answers or completions. Select the one that BEST answers the question or completes the statement. *PRINT THE LETTER OF THE CORRECT ANSWER IN THE SPACE AT THE RIGHT.*

1. Discharge planning is dependent upon the

    A. degree of illness
    B. expected outcome of care
    C. duration and/or length of care
    D. all of the above

2. Advantages of a preadmission planning program include all of the following EXCEPT

    A. familiarizing patients and their families with the available community resources
    B. helping decrease the length of the stay
    C. estimating the cost of treatment
    D. preventing unnecessary admissions

3. A discharge planning nurse should do all of the following EXCEPT

    A. screen and study preadmission records
    B. interview, on admission, only Medicaid patients
    C. assess patients' home situations relative to discharge planning
    D. assess patients' needs, encourage self-expression, self-evaluation, and self-determination

4. A nurse should counsel and involve the patient and/or family with regard to

    A. discharge planning
    B. acceptance of illness, disability, and needed treatment
    C. coping with illness complicated by social and emotional problems
    D. all of the above

5. A nurse should recommend and assist in the placement of a patient in a nursing home but would NOT be expected to

    A. take care of any problems while in the nursing home after discharge
    B. arrange transportation if necessary
    C. inform and interpret Medicare, Medicaid, welfare, and community resources
    D. use community resources to supplement and reinforce discharge planning activities of the hospital

6. While arranging discharge planning, a nurse should make referrals to all of the following EXCEPT

    A. community health agencies
    B. the public health department
    C. the Social Security department
    D. psychiatric social workers

7. A discharge planning nurse functions as a liaison between the

   A. hospital and community
   B. social service department and other community agencies
   C. doctors and patients and families
   D. all of the above

8. A discharge planning nurse functions as a resource for all of the following EXCEPT

   A. patient education, incorporating available facilities such as a public health nurse
   B. available community facilities
   C. financial availability for patient's family
   D. discharge planning for physician and hospital staff

9. Of the following patients, only _____ will probably NOT need discharge planning.

   A. those who are dependent for activities of daily life
   B. teenagers post-pneumonia
   C. patients with special teaching needs
   D. terminal or preterminal patients

10. Patients with _____ usually need discharge planning on an acute medical unit.

    A. arthritis
    B. bronchiolitis
    C. cancer
    D. congestive heart failure

11. Steps for determining a unit's need for nursing information include

    A. understanding department objectives
    B. identifying information required to measure performance
    C. determining the information requirements for each decision
    D. all of the above

12. Computer applications for nursing administration include use in

    A. scheduling
    B. communication
    C. education
    D. all of the above

13. Nurses hope that computers will eventually provide all of the following EXCEPT

    A. intelligent scheduling systems for staff and patient operative procedure
    B. treatment
    C. automated statistical reporting capabilities
    D. automated policy and with manual procedure

14. The key feature of successful future medical information systems will be the broadly based integration of all of the following components EXCEPT

    A. therapeutic
    B. clinical
    C. administrative
    D. financial data

15. The one of the following characteristics that is NOT essential for an effective automated patient classification system is that it be

    A. objective
    B. quick to compute for the user
    C. inflexible
    D. simple

16. A computerized patient classification system can be used to perform all of the following tasks EXCEPT

    A. determining changes in patient mix in a given unit
    B. automating the procedures for patient care
    C. automating the procedure for determining nursing care hours
    D. determining staff mix ratio based on intensity

17. The MAJOR categories of clinical applications of a computerized information system include

    A. charting functions related to the patient's medical record
    B. selected medical and nursing requirements for the evaluation of the quality and appropriateness of patient care
    C. clinical information screens
    D. all of the above

18. All of the following are true regarding managerial reporting EXCEPT:

    A. It should focus on activities rather than achievements
    B. Quantifiable data should be used whenever possible
    C. Reports should be concise
    D. A consistent report format should be selected and used

19. Patients are generally NOT assigned to nurses

    A. geographically
    B. racially
    C. individually
    D. promotionally

20. All of the following are disadvantages of the geographic method of assigning patients EXCEPT

    A. no guarantee of fair caseload
    B. well organized
    C. nurse loses patient when transferred to another district
    D. unclear who is accountable when off duty for long stretches

21. Which of the following is NOT among the advantages of the geographic method of assigning patients?

    A. Stable; easy to keep track of patients
    B. Easier to have consistent secondary coverage
    C. Easier for health team to learn who has what patient
    D. No guarantee of fair caseload

22. All of the following are advantages of the individual method of assigning patients EXCEPT

    A. fair caseload
    B. much time spent in making original and daily assignments
    C. variety of cases
    D. can be maintained when readmitted

23. The individual method of assigning patients is controlled by the   23.____

   A. head nurse
   B. team leader
   C. primary nurse
   D. nursing supervisor

24. Advantages of the promotional method of assigning patients include all of the following EXCEPT   24.____

   A. screening process; only for best professionals
   B. viewed as higher status
   C. large caseload
   D. increased role clarity

25. Disadvantages of the promotional method of assigning patients include   25.____
   I. much delegation of direct patient care
   II. cost of positions
   III. stimulates staff to show competence
   IV. holds back advancement if more nurses are ready to be promoted than positions available

   The CORRECT answer is:

   A. I, III
   B. I, II, III
   C. I, II, IV
   D. II, IV

KEY (CORRECT ANSWERS)

1.	D	11.	D
2.	C	12.	D
3.	B	13.	B
4.	D	14.	A
5.	A	15.	C
6.	C	16.	B
7.	D	17.	D
8.	C	18.	A
9.	B	19.	B
10.	B	20.	B

21.	D
22.	B
23.	A
24.	C
25.	C

TEST 2

DIRECTIONS: Each question or incomplete statement is followed by several suggested answers or completions. Select the one that BEST answers the question or completes the statement. *PRINT THE LETTER OF THE CORRECT ANSWER IN THE SPACE AT THE RIGHT.*

1. All of the following are true regarding decentralization in staffing EXCEPT that it   1.____

    A. maximizes utilization of float pool
    B. maximizes unit staffing
    C. gives head nurse accountability for the entire staffing budget
    D. assigns selection of all unit staff members to head nurse

2. It is NOT true that centralization in staffing   2.____

    A. manages staffing of nursing departments as a whole
    B. maximizes utilization of float pool
    C. gives the head nurse responsibility for 24 hour staffing and scheduling
    D. centralizes updated record of skills required

3. Centralization in staffing   3.____

    A. puts decision-making in the central office
    B. eliminates a centralized float pool
    C. provides that the head nurse keeps updated record of current staff skills
    D. commits staff to making method successful

4. Decentralization in staffing   4.____

    A. gives the head nurse responsibility for 24 hour patient care
    B. assigns core unit staff selection to the head nurse
    C. promotes relationships among sister units
    D. depends more on central office management for success

5. A nursing service administrator is advised to employ _____ for establishing a staffing   5.____
program.

    A. organization of a committee of the nursing staff for purposes of becoming informed about staffing
    B. appointment of an individual to assume responsibility of the program
    C. collection of data about patients
    D. all of the above

6. The coordinator of the staffing study committee carries out all of the following activities   6.____
EXCEPT

    A. educating the members only
    B. instructing and supervising the study team
    C. preparing study materials and data collection forms
    D. preparing the study report

7. The activities of head nurse selected for a study committee include all of the following   7.____
EXCEPT

A. classifying patients according to indicator and guidelines for nursing care requirements
B. preparing the study report
C. assisting the study coordinator in checking observer reports
D. orienting patients to the study

8. The policies and procedures for which the staffing study committee would be responsible include a

   A. written statement of the purpose, philosophy, and objectives of the nursing program of care
   B. written statement of the purpose, philosophy, and objectives of staffing
   C. set of performance standards for the nursing staff
   D. all of the above

9. The difficulty of staffing lies in the range of variable factors that affect selecting a staffing system, such as

   A. organizational system
   B. patient unit arrangement
   C. employment policies
   D. all of the above

10. The CENTRAL document in the staff utilization control system for staffing is the

    A. nursing staff table
    B. weekly nursing utilization report
    C. monthly nursing utilization report
    D. staffing requirement report

11. Components of patient classification systems include all of the following EXCEPT

    A. utilization by nursing personnel
    B. rigidity
    C. ability to be tracked to provide staffing and acuity patterns
    D. compatibility with nursing philosophy and productivity goals

12. The _____ method is NOT a type of patient classification methods.

    A. checklist of nursing tasks
    B. patient needs
    C. hospital needs
    D. descriptive

13. Which of the following patient classification methods is probably the OLDEST? The _____ method.

    A. patient needs
    B. descriptive
    C. checklist of nursing tasks
    D. none of the above

14. In the descriptive patient classification system, the patients who require MINIMAL care are those who

   A. are recovering from the immediate effects of a serious illness
   B. are convalescing and no longer require intensive, moderate, and maximum care
   C. need close attention throughout the shift
   D. are acutely ill

15. In the descriptive patient classification system, the patients classified as requiring MODERATE care are those who

   A. are convalescing
   B. are recovering from the immediate effects of a serious illness
   C. are in the intensive eare unit
   D. need close attention 24 hours a day

16. In the descriptive patient classification system, the patients requiring INTENSIVE care are those who

   A. are convalescing
   B. are recovering from a disease
   C. need close attention 24 hours a day
   D. have a high level of nurse dependency

17. Patients who require only a MINIMAL amount of nursing care, according to the patient needs classification system, include all of the following EXCEPT those

   A. who are mildly ill
   B. whose extreme symptoms have subsided or not yet appeared
   C. who require little treatment and/or observation and/or instruction
   D. without intravenous therapy or many medications

18. According to the patient needs classification system, a patient who requires an AVERAGE amount of nursing care is one who

   A. required periodic treatments and/or observations and/or instructions
   B. is mildly ill
   C. requires little treatment and/or observations and/or instructions
   D. is without intravenous therapy

19. According to the patient needs classification system, patients who require ABOVE AVERAGE nursing care would include all of the following EXCEPT the patient who

   A. is moderately ill
   B. requires treatment as frequently as every two to four hours
   C. is mildly ill
   D. is on complete bed rest

20. Patients who require MAXIMUM care, according to the patient needs classification system, would include all of the following EXCEPT the patient

   A. who is acutely ill
   B. whose activity must be rigidly controlled
   C. who is on complete bed rest
   D. with significant changes in doctor's orders more than six times a day

Questions 21-25.

DIRECTIONS: In Questions 21 through 25, match the numbered definition with the lettered term, listed in the column below, that it BEST describes.

   A. Planning variance
   B. Attrition
   C. Unit supervisor
   D. Layoff
   E. Efficiency variance

21. Difference between the required staffing and the actual staffing 21.____

22. Measures the effectiveness of the utilization forecast procedure in reporting the system of controlling the effectiveness of the staffing system 22.____

23. Over a reasonable time period, only essential vacancies are filled 23.____

24. Termination of job after all other attempts at trimming personnel have been exhausted 24.____

25. Coordinates and supervises administrative management functions for one unit 25.____

KEY (CORRECT ANSWERS)

1.	A	11.	B
2.	C	12.	C
3.	A	13.	B
4.	C	14.	B
5.	D	15.	B
6.	A	16.	D
7.	B	17.	B
8.	D	18.	A
9.	D	19.	C
10.	B	20.	C

21. E
22. A
23. B
24. D
25. C

PHILOSOPHY, PRINCIPLES, PRACTICES, AND TECHNICS OF SUPERVISION, ADMINISTRATION, MANAGEMENT, AND ORGANIZATION

TABLE OF CONTENTS

	Page
MEANING OF SUPERVISION	1
THE OLD AND THE NEW SUPERVISION	1
THE EIGHT (8) BASIC PRINCIPLES OF THE NEW SUPERVISION	1
I. Principle of Responsibility	1
II. Principle of Authority	2
III. Principle of Self-Growth	2
IV. Principle of Individual Worth	2
V. Principle of Creative Leadership	2
VI. Principle of Success and Failure	2
VII. Principle of Science	3
VIII. Principle of Cooperation	3
WHAT IS ADMINISTRATION?	3
I. Practices Commonly Classed as "Supervisory"	3
II. Practices Commonly Classed as "Administrative"	3
III. Practices Commonly Classed as Both "Supervisory" and "Administrative"	4
RESPONSIBILITIES OF THE SUPERVISOR	4
COMPETENCIES OF THE SUPERVISOR	4
THE PROFESSIONAL SUPERVISOR-EMPLOYEE RELATIONSHIP	4
MINI-TEXT IN SUPERVISION, ADMINISTRATION, MANAGEMENT, AND ORGANIZATION	5
I. Brief Highlights	5
A. Levels of Management	6
B. What the Supervisor Must Learn	6
C. A Definition of Supervision	6
D. Elements of the Team Concept	6
E. Principles of Organization	6
F. The Four Important Parts of Every Job	7
G. Principles of Delegation	7
H. Principles of Effective Communications	7
I. Principles of Work Improvement	7
J. Areas of Job Improvement	7
K. Seven Key Points in Making Improvements	8

	L.	Corrective Techniques for Job Improvement	8
	M.	A Planning Checklist	8
	N.	Five Characteristics of Good Directions	9
	O.	Types of Directions	9
	P.	Controls	9
	Q.	Orienting the New Employee	9
	R.	Checklist for Orienting New Employees	9
	S.	Principles of Learning	10
	T.	Causes of Poor Performance	10
	U.	Four Major Steps in On-the-Job Instructions	10
	V.	Employees Want Five Things	10
	W.	Some Don'ts in Regard to Praise	11
	X.	How to Gain Your Workers' Confidence	11
	Y.	Sources of Employee Problems	11
	Z.	The Supervisor's Key to Discipline	11
	AA.	Five Important Processes of Management	12
	BB.	When the Supervisor Fails to Plan	12
	CC.	Fourteen General Principles of Management	12
	DD.	Change	12
II.	Brief Topical Summaries		13
	A.	Who/What is the Supervisor?	13
	B.	The Sociology of Work	13
	C.	Principles and Practices of Supervision	14
	D.	Dynamic Leadership	14
	E.	Processes for Solving Problems	15
	F.	Training for Results	15
	G.	Health, Safety, and Accident Prevention	16
	H.	Equal Employment Opportunity	16
	I.	Improving Communications	16
	J.	Self-Development	17
	K.	Teaching and Training	17
		1. The Teaching Process	17
		a. Preparation	17
		b. Presentation	18
		c. Summary	18
		d. Application	18
		e. Evaluation	18
		2. Teaching Methods	18
		a. Lecture	18
		b. Discussion	18
		c. Demonstration	19
		d. Performance	19
		e. Which Method to Use	19

PHILOSOPHY, PRINCIPLES, PRACTICES, AND TECHNICS OF SUPERVISION, ADMINISTRATION, MANAGEMENT, AND ORGANIZATION

MEANING OF SUPERVISION

The extension of the democratic philosophy has been accompanied by an extension in the scope of supervision. Modern leaders and supervisors no longer think of supervision in the narrow sense of being confined chiefly to visiting employees, supplying materials, or rating the staff. They regard supervision as being intimately related to all the concerned agencies of society, they speak of the supervisor's function in terms of "growth," rather than the "improvement" of employees.

This modern concept of supervision may be defined as follows: Supervision is leadership and the development of leadership within groups which are cooperatively engaged in inspection, research, training, guidance, and evaluation.

THE OLD AND THE NEW SUPERVISION

TRADITIONAL
1. Inspection
2. Focused on the employee
3. Visitation
4. Random and haphazard
5. Imposed and authoritarian
6. One person usually

MODERN
1. Study and analysis
2. Focused on aims, materials, methods, supervisors, employees, environment
3. Demonstrations, intervisitation, workshops, directed reading, bulletins, etc.
4. Definitely organized and planned (scientific)
5. Cooperative and democratic
6. Many persons involved (creative)

THE EIGHT (8) BASIC PRINCIPLES OF THE NEW SUPERVISION

I. Principle of Responsibility
Authority to act and responsibility for acting must be joined.
   A. If you give responsibility, give authority.
   B. Define employee duties clearly.
   C. Protect employees from criticism by others.
   D. Recognize the rights as well as obligations of employees.
   E. Achieve the aims of a democratic society insofar as it is possible within the area of your work.
   F. Establish a situation favorable to training and learning.
   G. Accept ultimate responsibility for everything done in your section, unit, office, division, department.
   H. Good administration and good supervision are inseparable.

II. Principle of Authority
   The success of the supervisor is measured by the extent to which the power of authority is not used.
   A. Exercise simplicity and informality in supervision
   B. Use the simplest machinery of supervision
   C. If it is good for the organization as a whole, it is probably justified.
   D. Seldom be arbitrary or authoritative.
   E. Do not base your work on the power of position or of personality.
   F. Permit and encourage the free expression of opinions.

III. Principle of Self-Growth
   The success of the supervisor is measured by the extent to which, and the speed with which, he is no longer needed.
   A. Base criticism on principles, not on specifics.
   B. Point out higher activities to employees.
   C. Train for self-thinking by employees to meet new situations.
   D. Stimulate initiative, self-reliance, and individual responsibility
   E. Concentrate on stimulating the growth of employees rather than on removing defects.

IV. Principle of Individual Worth
   Respect for the individual is a paramount consideration in supervision.
   A. Be human and sympathetic in dealing with employees.
   B. Don't nag about things to be done.
   C. Recognize the individual differences among employees and seek opportunities to permit best expression of each personality.

V. Principle of Creative Leadership
   The best supervision is that which is not apparent to the employee.
   A. Stimulate, don't drive employees to creative action.
   B. Emphasize doing good things.
   C. Encourage employees to do what they do best.
   D. Do not be too greatly concerned with details of subject or method.
   E. Do not be concerned exclusively with immediate problems and activities.
   F. Reveal higher activities and make them both desired and maximally possible.
   G. Determine procedures in the light of each situation but see that these are derived from a sound basic philosophy.
   H. Aid, inspire, and lead so as to liberate the creative spirit latent in all good employees.

VI. Principle of Success and Failure
   There are no unsuccessful employees, only unsuccessful supervisors who have failed to give proper leadership.
   A. Adapt suggestions to the capacities, attitudes, and prejudices of employees.
   B. Be gradual, be progressive, be persistent.
   C. Help the employee find the general principle; have the employee apply his own problem to the general principle.
   D. Give adequate appreciation for good work and honest effort.
   E. Anticipate employee difficulties and help to prevent them.
   F. Encourage employees to do the desirable things they will do anyway.
   G. Judge your supervision by the results it secures.

VII. Principle of Science
Successful supervision is scientific, objective, and experimental. It is based on facts, not on prejudices.
   A. Be cumulative in results.
   B. Never divorce your suggestions from the goals of training.
   C. Don't be impatient of results.
   D. Keep all matters on a professional, not a personal, level.
   E. Do not be concerned exclusively with immediate problems and activities.
   F. Use objective means of determining achievement and rating where possible.

VIII. Principle of Cooperation
Supervision is a cooperative enterprise between supervisor and employee.
   A. Begin with conditions as they are.
   B. Ask opinions of all involved when formulating policies.
   C. Organization is as good as its weakest link.
   D. Let employees help to determine policies and department programs.
   E. Be approachable and accessible—physically and mentally.
   F. Develop pleasant social relationships.

WHAT IS ADMINISTRATION

Administration is concerned with providing the environment, the material facilities, and the operational procedures that will promote the maximum growth and development of supervisors and employees. (Organization is an aspect and a concomitant of administration.)

There is no sharp line of demarcation between supervision and administration; these functions are intimately interrelated and, often, overlapping. They are complementary activities.

I. Practices Commonly Classed as "Supervisory"
   A. Conducting employees' conferences
   B. Visiting sections, units, offices, divisions, departments
   C. Arranging for demonstrations
   D. Examining plans
   E. Suggesting professional reading
   F. Interpreting bulletins
   G. Recommending in-service training courses
   H. Encouraging experimentation
   I. Appraising employee morale
   J. Providing for intervisitation

II. Practices Commonly Classified as "Administrative"
   A. Management of the office
   B. Arrangement of schedules for extra duties
   C. Assignment of rooms or areas
   D. Distribution of supplies
   E. Keeping records and reports
   F. Care of audio-visual materials
   G. Keeping inventory records
   H. Checking record cards and books

    I.   Programming special activities
    J.   Checking on the attendance and punctuality of employees

III. Practices Commonly Classified as Both "Supervisory" and "Administrative"
    A. Program construction
    B. Testing or evaluating outcomes
    C. Personnel accounting
    D. Ordering instructional materials

RESPONSIBILITIES OF THE SUPERVISOR

A person employed in a supervisory capacity must constantly be able to improve his own efficiency and ability. He represent the employer to the employees and only continuous self-examination can make him a capable supervisor.

Leadership and training are the supervisor's responsibility. An efficient working unit is one in which the employees work with the supervisor. It is his job to bring out the best in his employees. He must always be relaxed, courteous, and calm in his association with his employees. Their feelings are important, and a harsh attitude does not develop the most efficient employees.

COMPETENCES OF THE SUPERVISOR

    I.   Complete knowledge of the duties and responsibilities of his position.
    II.   To be able to organize a job, plan ahead, and carry through.
    III.   To have self-confidence and initiative.
    IV.   To be able to handle the unexpected situation and make quick decisions.
    V.   To be able to properly train subordinates in the positions they are best suited for.
    VI.   To be able to keep good human relations among his subordinates.
    VII. To be able to keep good human relations between his subordinates and himself and to earn their respect and trust.

THE PROFESSIONAL SUPERVISOR-EMPLOYEE RELATIONSHIP

There are two kinds of efficiency: one kind is only apparent and is produced in organizations through the exercise of mere discipline; this is but a simulation of the second, or true, efficiency which springs from spontaneous cooperation. If you are a manager, no matter how great or small your responsibility, it is your job, in the final analysis, to create and develop this involuntary cooperation among the people whom you supervise. For, no matter how powerful a combination of money, machines, and materials a company may have, this is a dead and sterile thing without a team of willing, thinking, and articulate people to guide it.

The following 21 points are presented as indicative of the exemplary basic relationship that should exist between supervisor and employee:

1. Each person wants to be liked and respected by his fellow employee and wants to be treated with consideration and respect by his superior.
2. The most competent employee will make an error. However, in a unit where good relations exist between the supervisor and his employees, tenseness and fear do not exist. Thus, errors are not hidden or covered up, and the efficiency of a unit is not impaired.

3. Subordinates resent rules, regulations, or orders that are unreasonable or unexplained.
4. Subordinates are quick to resent unfairness, harshness, injustices, and favoritism.
5. An employee will accept responsibility if he knows that he will be complimented for a job well done, and not too harshly chastised for failure; that his supervisor will check the cause of the failure, and, if it was the supervisor's fault, he will assume the blame therefore. If it was the employee's fault, his supervisor will explain the correct method or means of handling the responsibility.
6. An employee wants to receive credit for a suggestion he has made, that is used. If a suggestion cannot be used, the employee is entitled to an explanation. The supervisor should not say "no" and close the subject.
7. Fear and worry slow up a worker's ability. Poor working environment can impair his physical and mental health. A good supervisor avoids forceful methods, threats, and arguments to get a job done.
8. A forceful supervisor is able to train his employees individually and as a team, and is able to motivate them in the proper channels.
9. A mature supervisor is able to properly evaluate his subordinates and to keep them happy and satisfied.
10. A sensitive supervisor will never patronize his subordinates.
11. A worthy supervisor will respect his employees' confidences.
12. Definite and clear-cut responsibilities should be assigned to each executive.
13. Responsibility should always be coupled with corresponding authority.
14. No change should be made in the scope or responsibilities of a position without a definite understanding to that effect on the part of all persons concerned.
15. No executive or employee, occupying a single position in the organization, should be subject to definite orders from more than one source.
16. Orders should never be given to subordinates over the head of a responsible executive. Rather than do this, the officer in question should be supplanted.
17. Criticisms of subordinates should, whoever possible, be made privately, and in no case should a subordinate be criticized in the presence of executives or employees of equal or lower rank.
18. No dispute or difference between executives or employees as to authority or responsibilities should be considered too trivial for prompt and careful adjudication.
19. Promotions, wage changes, and disciplinary action should always be approved by the executive immediately superior to the one directly responsible.
20. No executive or employee should ever be required, or expected, to be at the same time an assistant to, and critic of, another.
21. Any executive whose work is subject to regular inspection should, wherever practicable, be given the assistance and facilities necessary to enable him to maintain an independent check of the quality of his work.

MINI-TEXT IN SUPERVISION, ADMINISTRATION, MANAGEMENT, AND ORGANIZATION

I. Brief Highlights

Listed concisely and sequentially are major headings and important data in the field for quick recall and review.

A. Levels of Management
Any organization of some size has several levels of management. In terms of a ladder, the levels are:

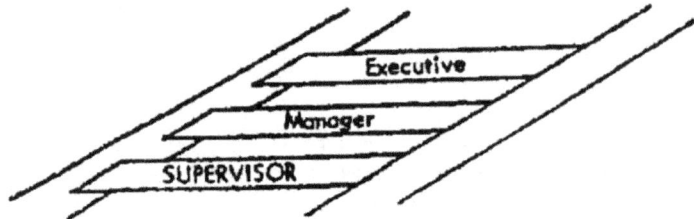

The first level is very important because it is the beginning point of management leadership.

B. What the Supervisor Must Learn
A supervisor must learn to:
1. Deal with people and their differences
2. Get the job done through people
3. Recognize the problems when they exist
4. Overcome obstacles to good performance
5. Evaluate the performance of people
6. Check his own performance in terms of accomplishment

C. A Definition of Supervisor
The term supervisor means any individual having authority, in the interests of the employer, to hire, transfer, suspend, lay-off, recall, promote, discharge, assign, reward, or discipline other employees or responsibility to direct them, or to adjust their grievances, or effectively to recommend such action, if, in connection with the foregoing, exercise of such authority is not of a merely routine or clerical nature but requires the use of independent judgment.

D. Elements of the Team Concept
What is involved in teamwork? The component parts are:
1. Members
2. A leader
3. Goals
4. Plans
5. Cooperation
6. Spirit

E. Principles of Organization
1. A team member must know what his job is.
2. Be sure that the nature and scope of a job are understood.
3. Authority and responsibility should be carefully spelled out.
4. A supervisor should be permitted to make the maximum number of decisions affecting his employees.
5. Employees should report to only one supervisor.
6. A supervisor should direct only as many employees as he can handle effectively.
7. An organization plan should be flexible.

8. Inspection and performance of work should be separate.
9. Organizational problems should receive immediate attention.
10. Assign work in line with ability and experience.

F. The Four Important Parts of Every Job
1. Inherent in every job is the *accountability* for results.
2. A second set of factors in every job is *responsibilities*.
3. Along with duties and responsibilities one must have the *authority* to act within certain limits without obtaining permission to proceed.
4. No job exists in a vacuum. The supervisor is surrounded by key *relationships*.

G. Principles of Delegation
Where work is delegated for the first time, the supervisor should think in terms of these questions:
1. Who is best qualified to do this?
2. Can an employee improve his abilities by doing this?
3. How long should an employee spend on this?
4. Are there any special problems for which he will need guidance?
5. How broad a delegation can I make?

H. Principles of Effective Communications
1. Determine the media.
2. To whom directed?
3. Identification and source authority.
4. Is communication understood?

I. Principles of Work Improvement
1. Most people usually do only the work which is assigned to them.
2. Workers are likely to fit assigned work into the time available to perform it.
3. A good workload usually stimulates output.
4. People usually do their best work when they know that results will be reviewed or inspected.
5. Employees usually feel that someone else is responsible for conditions of work, workplace layout, job methods, type of tools/equipment, and other such factors.
6. Employees are usually defensive about their job security.
7. Employees have natural resistance to change.
8. Employees can support or destroy a supervisor.
9. A supervisor usually earns the respect of his people through his personal example of diligence and efficiency.

J. Areas of Job Improvement
The areas of job improvement are quite numerous, but the most common ones which a supervisor can identify and utilize are:
1. Departmental layout
2. Flow of work
3. Workplace layout
4. Utilization of manpower
5. Work methods
6. Materials handling

7. Utilization
8. Motion economy

K. Seven Key Points in Making Improvements
1. Select the job to be improved
2. Study how it is being done now
3. Question the present method
4. Determine actions to be taken
5. Chart proposed method
6. Get approval and apply
7. Solicit worker participation

l. Corrective Techniques of Job Improvement
Specific Problems
1. Size of workload
2. Inability to meet schedules
3. Strain and fatigue
4. Improper use of men and skills
5. Waste, poor quality, unsafe conditions
6. Bottleneck conditions that hinder output
7. Poor utilization of equipment and machine
8. Efficiency and productivity of labor

General Improvement
1. Departmental layout
2. Flow of work
3. Work plan layout
4. Utilization of manpower
5. Work methods
6. Materials handling
7. Utilization of equipment
8. Motion economy

Corrective Techniques
1. Study with scale model
2. Flow chart study
3. Motion analysis
4. Comparison of units produced to standard allowance
5. Methods analysis
6. Flow chart and equipment study
7. Down time vs. running time
8. Motion analysis

M. A Planning Checklist
1. Objectives
2. Controls
3. Delegations
4. Communications
5. Resources
6. Manpower

7. Equipment
8. Supplies and materials
9. Utilization of time
10. Safety
11. Money
12. Work
13. Timing of improvements

N. Five Characteristics of Good Directions
In order to get results, directions must be:
1. Possible of accomplishment
2. Agreeable with worker interests
3. Related to mission
4. Planned and complete
5. Unmistakably clear

O. Types of Directions
1. Demands or direct orders
2. Requests
3. Suggestion or implication
4. volunteering

P. Controls
A typical listing of the overall areas in which the supervisor should establish controls might be:
1. Manpower
2. Materials
3. Quality of work
4. Quantity of work
5. Time
6. Space
7. Money
8. Methods

Q. Orienting the New Employee
1. Prepare for him
2. Welcome the new employee
3. Orientation for the job
4. Follow-up

R. Checklist for Orienting New Employees   Yes   No
1. Do you appreciate the feelings of new employees
   when they first report for work?   ___   ___
2. Are you aware of the fact that the new employee must
   make a big adjustment to his job?   ___   ___
3. Have you given him good reasons for liking the job and
   the organization?   ___   ___
4. Have you prepared for his first day on the job?   ___   ___
5. Did you welcome him cordially and make him feel needed?   ___   ___

	Yes	No
6. Did you establish rapport with him so that he feels free to talk and discuss matters with you?	___	___
7. Did you explain his job to him and his relationship to you?	___	___
8. Does he know that his work will be evaluated periodically on a basis that is fair and objective?	___	___
9. Did you introduce him to his fellow workers in such a way that they are likely to accept him?	___	___
10. Does he know what employee benefits he will receive?	___	___
11. Does he understand the importance of being on the job and what to do if he must leave his duty station?	___	___
12. Has he been impressed with the importance of accident prevention and safe practice?	___	___
13. Does he generally know his way around the department?	___	___
14. Is he under the guidance of a sponsor who will teach the right way of doing things?	___	___
15. Do you plan to follow-up so that he will continue to adjust successfully to his job?	___	___

S. Principles of Learning
   1. Motivation
   2. Demonstration or explanation
   3. Practice

T. Causes of Poor Performance
   1. Improper training for job
   2. Wrong tools
   3. Inadequate directions
   4. Lack of supervisory follow-up
   5. Poor communications
   6. Lack of standards of performance
   7. Wrong work habits
   8. Low morale
   9. Other

U. Four Major Steps in On-The-Job Instruction
   1. Prepare the worker
   2. Present the operation
   3. Tryout performance
   4. Follow-up

V. Employees Want Five Things
   1. Security
   2. Opportunity
   3. Recognition
   4. Inclusion
   5. Expression

W. Some Don'ts in Regard to Praise
1. Don't praise a person for something he hasn't done.
2. Don't praise a person unless you can be sincere.
3. Don't be sparing in praise just because your superior withholds it from you.
4. Don't let too much time elapse between good performance and recognition of it

X. How to Gain Your Workers' Confidence
Methods of developing confidence include such things as:
1. Knowing the interests, habits, hobbies of employees
2. Admitting your own inadequacies
3. Sharing and telling of confidence in others
4. Supporting people when they are in trouble
5. Delegating matters that can be well handled
6. Being frank and straightforward about problems and working conditions
7. Encouraging others to bring their problems to you
8. Taking action on problems which impede worker progress

Y. Sources of Employee Problems
On-the-job causes might be such things as:
1. A feeling that favoritism is exercised in assignments
2. Assignment of overtime
3. An undue amount of supervision
4. Changing methods or systems
5. Stealing of ideas or trade secrets
6. Lack of interest in job
7. Threat of reduction in force
8. Ignorance or lack of communications
9. Poor equipment
10. Lack of knowing how supervisor feels toward employee
11. Shift assignments

Off-the-job problems might have to do with:
1. Health
2. Finances
3. Housing
4. Family

Z. The Supervisor's Key to Discipline
There are several key points about discipline which the supervisor should keep in mind:
1. Job discipline is one of the disciplines of life and is directed by the supervisor.
2. It is more important to correct an employee fault than to fix blame for it.
3. Employee performance is affected by problems both on the job and off.
4. Sudden or abrupt changes in behavior can be indications of important employee problems.
5. Problems should be dealt with as soon as possible after they are identified.
6. The attitude of the supervisor may have more to do with solving problems than the techniques of problem solving.
7. Correction of employee behavior should be resorted to only after the supervisor is sure that training or counseling will not be helpful.

12

       8.   Be sure to document your disciplinary actions.
       9.   Make sure that you are disciplining on the basis of facts rather than personal feelings.
      10.   Take each disciplinary step in order, being careful not to make snap judgments, or decisions based on impatience.

AA. Five Important Processes of Management
1. Planning
2. Organizing
3. Scheduling
4. Controlling
5. Motivating

BB. When the Supervisor Fails to Plan
1. Supervisor creates impression of not knowing his job
2. May lead to excessive overtime
3. Job runs itself—supervisor lacks control
4. Deadlines and appointments missed
5. Parts of the work go undone
6. Work interrupted by emergencies
7. Sets a bad example
8. Uneven workload creates peaks and valleys
9. Too much time on minor details at expense of more important tasks

CC. Fourteen General Principles of Management
1. Division of work
2. Authority and responsibility
3. Discipline
4. Unity of command
5. Unity of direction
6. Subordination of individual interest to general interest
7. Remuneration of personnel
8. Centralization
9. Scalar chain
10. Order
11. Equity
12. Stability of tenure of personnel
13. Initiative
14. Esprit de corps

DD. Change

Bringing about change is perhaps attempted more often, and yet less well understood, than anything else the supervisor does. How do people generally react to change? (People tend to resist change that is imposed upon them by other individuals or circumstances.

Change is characteristic of every situation. It is a part of every real endeavor where the efforts of people are concerned.

1. Why do people resist change?
   People may resist change because of:
   a. Fear of the unknown
   b. Implied criticism
   c. Unpleasant experiences in the past
   d. Fear of loss of status
   e. Threat to the ego
   f. Fear of loss of economic stability

2. How can we best overcome the resistance to change?
   In initiating change, take these steps:
   a. Get ready to sell
   b. Identify sources of help
   c. Anticipate objections
   d. Sell benefits
   e. Listen in depth
   f. Follow up

II. Brief Topical Summaries

   A. Who/What is the Supervisor?
      1. The supervisor is often called the "highest level employee and the lowest level manager."
      2. A supervisor is a member of both management and the work group. He acts as a bridge between the two.
      3. Most problems in supervision are in the area of human relations, or people problems.
      4. Employees expect: Respect, opportunity to learn and to advance, and a sense of belonging, and so forth.
      5. Supervisors are responsible for directing people and organizing work. Planning is of paramount importance.
      6. A position description is a set of duties and responsibilities inherent to a given position.
      7. It is important to keep the position description up-to-date and to provide each employee with his own copy.

   B. The Sociology of Work
      1. People are alike in many ways; however, each individual is unique.
      2. The supervisor is challenged in getting to know employee differences. Acquiring skills in evaluating individuals is an asset.
      3. Maintaining meaningful working relationships in the organization is of great importance.
      4. The supervisor has an obligation to help individuals to develop to their fullest potential.
      5. Job rotation on a planned basis helps to build versatility and to maintain interest and enthusiasm in work groups.
      6. Cross training (job rotation) provides backup skills.

7. The supervisor can help reduce tension by maintaining a sense of humor, providing guidance to employees, and by making reasonable and timely decisions. Employees respond favorably to working under reasonably predictable circumstances.
8. Change is characteristic of all managerial behavior. The supervisor must adjust to changes in procedures, new methods, technological changes, and to a number of new and sometimes challenging situations.
9. To overcome the natural tendency for people to resist change, the supervisor should become more skillful in initiating change.

C. Principles and Practices of Supervision
1. Employees should be required to answer to only one superior.
2. A supervisor can effectively direct only a limited number of employees, depending upon the complexity, variety, and proximity of the jobs involved.
3. The organizational chart presents the organization in graphic form. It reflects lines of authority and responsibility as well as interrelationships of units within the organization.
4. Distribution of work can be improved through an analysis using the "Work Distribution Chart."
5. The "Work Distribution Chart" reflects the division of work within a unit in understandable form.
6. When related tasks are given to an employee, he has a better chance of increasing his skills through training.
7. The individual who is given the responsibility for tasks must also be given the appropriate authority to insure adequate results.
8. The supervisor should delegate repetitive, routine work. Preparation of recurring reports, maintaining leave and attendance records are some examples.
9. Good discipline is essential to good task performance. Discipline is reflected in the actions of employees on the job in the absence of supervision.
10. Disciplinary action may have to be taken when the positive aspects of discipline have failed. Reprimand, warning, and suspension are examples of disciplinary action.
11. If a situation calls for a reprimand, be sure it is deserved and remember it is to be done in private.

D. Dynamic Leadership
1. A style is a personal method or manner of exerting influence.
2. Authoritarian leaders often see themselves as the source of power and authority.
3. The democratic leader often perceives the group as the source of authority and power.
4. Supervisors tend to do better when using the pattern of leadership that is most natural for them.
5. Social scientists suggest that the effective supervisor use the leadership style that best fits the problem or circumstances involved.
6. All four styles—telling, selling, consulting, joining—have their place. Using one does not preclude using the other at another time.

7. The theory X point of view assumes that the average person dislikes work, will avoid it whenever possible, and must be coerced to achieve organizational objectives.
8. The theory Y point of view assumes that the average person considers work to be a natural as play, and, when the individual is committed, he requires little supervision or direction to accomplish desired objectives.
9. The leader's basic assumptions concerning human behavior and human nature affect his actions, decisions, and other managerial practices.
10. Dissatisfaction among employees is often present, but difficult to isolate. The supervisor should seek to weaken dissatisfaction by keeping promises, being sincere and considerate, keeping employees informed, and so forth.
11. Constructive suggestions should be encouraged during the natural progress of the work.

E. Processes for Solving Problems
1. People find their daily tasks more meaningful and satisfying when they can improve them.
2. The causes of problems, or the key factors, are often hidden in the background. Ability to solve problems often involves the ability to isolate them from their backgrounds. There is some substance to the cliché that some persons "can't see the forest for the trees."
3. New procedures are often developed from old ones. Problems should be broken down into manageable parts. New ideas can be adapted from old one.
4. People think differently in problem-solving situations. Using a logical, patterned approach is often useful. One approach found to be useful includes these steps:
   a. Define the problem
   b. Establish objectives
   c. Get the facts
   d. Weigh and decide
   e. Take action
   f. Evaluate action

F. Training for Results
1. Participants respond best when they feel training is important to them.
2. The supervisor has responsibility for the training and development of those who report to him.
3. When training is delegated to others, great care must be exercised to insure the trainer has knowledge, aptitude, and interest for his work as a trainer.
4. Training (learning) of some type goes on continually. The most successful supervisor makes certain the learning contributes in a productive manner to operational goals.
5. New employees are particularly susceptible to training. Older employees facing new job situations require specific training, as well as having need for development and growth opportunities.
6. Training needs require continuous monitoring.
7. The training officer of an agency is a professional with a responsibility to assist supervisors in solving training problems.

8. Many of the self-development steps important to the supervisor's own growth are equally important to the development of peers and subordinates. Knowledge of these is important when the supervisor consults with others on development and growth opportunities.

G. Health, Safety, and Accident Prevention
1. Management-minded supervisors take appropriate measures to assist employees in maintaining health and in assuring safe practices in the work environment.
2. Effective safety training and practices help to avoid injury and accidents.
3. Safety should be a management goal. All infractions of safety which are observed should be corrected without exception.
4. Employees' safety attitude, training and instruction, provision of safe tools and equipment, supervision, and leadership are considered highly important factors which contribute to safety and which can be influenced directly by supervisors.
5. When accidents do occur, they should be investigated promptly for very important reasons, including the fact that information which is gained can be used to prevent accidents in the future.

H. Equal Employment Opportunity
1. The supervisor should endeavor to treat all employees fairly, without regard to religion, race, sex, or national origin.
2. Groups tend to reflect the attitude of the leader. Prejudice can be detected even in very subtle form. Supervisors must strive to create a feeling of mutual respect and confidence in every employee.
3. Complete utilization of all human resources is a national goal. Equitable consideration should be accorded women in the work force, minority-group members, the physically and mentally handicapped, and the older employee. The important question is: "Who can do the job?"
4. Training opportunities, recognition for performance, overtime assignments, promotional opportunities, and all other personnel actions are to be handled on an equitable basis.

I. Improving Communications
1. Communications is achieving understanding between the sender and the receiver of a message. It also means sharing information—the creation of understanding.
2. Communication is basic to all human activity. Words are means of conveying meanings; however, real meanings are in people.
3. There are very practical differences in the effectiveness of one-way, impersonal, and two-way communications. Words spoken face-to-face are better understood. Telephone conversations are effective, but lack the rapport of person-to-person exchanges. The whole person communicates.
4. Cooperation and communication in an organization go hand in hand. When there is a mutual respect between people, spelling out rules and procedures for communicating is unnecessary.
5. There are several barriers to effective communications. These include failure to listen with respect and understanding, lack of skill in feedback, and misinterpreting the meanings of words used by the speaker. It is also common

practice to listen to what we want to hear, and tune out things we do not want to hear.
6. Communication is management's chief problem. The supervisor should accept the challenge to communicate more effectively and to improve interagency and intra-agency communications.
7. The supervisor may often plan for and conduct meetings. The planning phase is critical and may determine the success or the failure of a meeting.
8. Speaking before groups usually requires extra effort. Stage fright may never disappear completely, but it can be controlled.

J. Self-Development
1. Every employee is responsible for his own self-development.
2. Toastmaster and toastmistress clubs offer opportunities to improve skills in oral communications.
3. Planning for one's own self-development is of vital importance. Supervisors know their own strengths and limitations better than anyone else.
4. Many opportunities are open to aid the supervisor in his developmental efforts, including job assignments; training opportunities, both governmental and non-governmental—to include universities and professional conferences and seminars.
5. Programmed instruction offers a means of studying at one's own rate.
6. Where difficulties may arise from a supervisor's being away from his work for training, he may participate in televised home study or correspondence courses to meet his self-development needs.

K. Teaching and Training
1. The Teaching Process
Teaching is encouraging and guiding the learning activities of students toward established goals. In most cases this process consists of five steps: preparation, presentation, summarization, evaluation, and application.

    a. Preparation
    Preparation is two-fold in nature; that of the supervisor and the employee. Preparation by the supervisor is absolutely essential to success. He must know what, when, where, how, and whom he will teach. Some of the factors that should be considered are:
    1) The objectives
    2) The materials needed
    3) The methods to be used
    4) Employee participation
    5) Employee interest
    6) Training aids
    7) Evaluation
    8) Summarization

    Employee preparation consists in preparing the employee to receive the material. Probably the most important single factor in the preparation of the employee is arousing and maintaining his interest. He must know the objectives of the training, why he is there, how the material can be used, and its importance to him.

b. Presentation
In presentation, have a carefully designed plan and follow it. The plan should be accurate and complete, yet flexible enough to meet situations as they arise. The method of presentation will be determined by the particular situation and objectives.

c. Summary
A summary should be made at the end of every training unit and program. In addition, there may be internal summaries depending on the nature of the material being taught. The important thing is that the trainee must always be able to understand how each part of the new material relates to the whole.

d. Application
The supervisor must arrange work so the employee will be given a chance to apply new knowledge or skills while the material is still clear in his mind and interest is high. The trainee does not really know whether he has learned the material until he has been given a chance to apply it. If the material is not applied, it loses most of its value.

e. Evaluation
The purpose of all training is to promote learning. To determine whether the training has been a success or failure, the supervisor must evaluate this learning.
In the broadest sense, evaluation includes all the devices, methods, skills, and techniques used by the supervisor to keep himself and the employees informed as to their progress toward the objectives they are pursuing. The extent to which the employee has mastered the knowledge, skills, and abilities, or changed his attitudes, as determined by the program objectives, is the extent to which instruction has succeeded or failed.
Evaluation should not be confined to the end of the lesson, day, or program but should be used continuously. We shall note later the way this relates to the rest of the teaching process.

2. Teaching Methods
A teaching method is a pattern of identifiable student and instructor activity used in presenting training material.
All supervisors are faced with the problem of deciding which method should be used at a given time.

a. Lecture
The lecture is direct oral presentation of material by the supervisor. The present trend is to place less emphasis on the trainer's activity and more on that of the trainee.

b. Discussion
Teaching by discussion or conference involves using questions and other techniques to arouse interest and focus attention upon certain areas, and by doing so creating a learning situation. This can be one of the most

valuable methods because it gives the employees an opportunity to express their ideas and pool their knowledge.

    c. Demonstration
The demonstration is used to teach how something works or how to do something. It can be used to show a principle or what the results of a series of actions will be. A well-staged demonstration is particularly effective because it shows proper methods of performance in a realistic manner.

    d. Performance
Performance is one of the most fundamental of all learning techniques or teaching methods. The trainee may be able to tell how a specific operation should be performed but he cannot be sure he knows how to perform the operation until he has done so.
As with all methods, there are certain advantages and disadvantages to each method.

    e. Which Method to Use
Moreover, there are other methods and techniques of teaching. It is difficult to use any method without other methods entering into it. In any learning situation, a combination of methods is usually more effective than any one method alone.

Finally, evaluation must be integrated into the other aspects of the teaching-learning process.

It must be used in the motivation of the trainees; it must be used to assist in developing understanding during the training; and it must be related to employee application of the results of training.

This is distinctly the role of the supervisor.

GLOSSARY OF MEDICAL TERMS

CONTENTS

		Page
Abduction	Arteriosclerosis	1
Artery	Biceps Muscle	2
Bifida	Causalgia	3
Cullulitis	Colon	4
Comminuted	Dermaphytosis	5
Desiccation	Dysuria	6
Ecchymosis	Epigastric	7
Epilepsy, Jacksonian	Fascia	8
Felon	Genito-Urinary	9
Genu	Herniotomy	10
Humerus	Intertrochanteric	11
Intervertebral	Leucocytosis	12
Leucopenia	Metabolism	13
Metacarpus	Neuroma	14
Neuropsychiatric	Orthopnea	15
Os	Paraplegia	16
Paravertebral	Periosteum	17
Periphery	Pneumonia	18
Pneumonoconiosis	Pyelogram	19
Pyogenic	Scaphoid	20
Scapula	Supinate	21
Suture	Tibia	22
Tinnitus	Ununited	23
Ureter	Zygoma	24

GLOSSARY OF MEDICAL TERMS

A

Abduction
Movement of limb away from middle line of the body.
Abrasion
A scraping away of a portion of the skin.
Abscess
Localized collection of pus or matter.
Acetabulum
Cup-shaped depression on external surface of the pelvic bone (innominate) into which the head of femur, or thighbone, fits.
Achilles Reflex
Movement of foot downward when the tendon immediately above the heel bone is struck.
Acromion
Process of bone constituting tip of shoulder.
Adduction
Movement of limb toward middle line of body.
Adhesion
The matting together of two surfaces by inflammation.
Alae Nash
Outer flaring walls of the nostrils.
Allergic
Reaction of tissues of the body to a protein substance to which the body is especially sensitive.
Anemia
A condition in which the red blood cells and/or hemoglobin are reduced.
Aneurysm
Sac, filled with blood, formed by the local dilation of walls of artery.
Angina Pectoris
Pain in chest associated with heart disease.
Ankyloses
Complete absence of motion at a joint.
Anterior
The anatomical "front" of the body.
Aorta
Main trunk of the systemic arterial system, arising from base of left ventricle.
Apex
Extremity of conical or pyramidal structure, such as heart or lung.
Aphasia
Loss of power of speech by damage to speech center.
Apoplexy
Another word for stroke.
Arrhythmia
Loss of normal rhythm of the heart.
Arteriosclerosis
Hardening of the arteries.

Artery
    Blood vessel conveying blood away from the heart to different parts of the body.
Arthritis
    Inflammation of a joint.
Arthrodesis
    Stiffening of a joint.
Articulation
    Joint.
Asbestosis
    Dust disease of asbestos workers.
Aseptic
    Free of germs.
Aspiration
    Withdrawal, by suction, of air or fluid from any cavity.
Asthma
    Disease marked by recurrent attacks of shortness, of breath, due to temporary change in bronchial tubes, making person uncomfortable.
Astigmatism
    An abnormality in the curve of the 'anterior visual surface of the eyeball.
Astragalus
    One of the ankle bones.
Ataxia
    Disturbance of coordination of muscular movements.
Atelectasis
    Collapse of lung tissue due to failure of entrance of air into air-cells.
Atrophy
    Wasting or diminution in size of a structure.
Audiogram
    Graphic record made by an audiometer, an electrical instrument for recording acuity of hearing.
Auricular fibrillation
    Irregular beat as to time and force beginning in auricle of the heart.
Auscultation
    The act of listening to sounds within the body.
Axillary
    Relating to armpit.

B

Baker's Cyst
    Enlargement of synovial sac in the back of the knee joint.
Basal Metabolism
    The energy expended for the absolute minimum requirements of the body at complete rest.
Bell's Palsy
    A form of facial paralysis.
Benign
    Not malignant.
Biceps Muscle
    A muscle over front of arm.

Bifida
   Split or cleft.
Bilateral
   Relating to or having two sides.
Blood Pressure
   Pressure or tension of the blood within the arteries.
Brachial
   Pertaining to the arm.
Bradycardia
   Abnormal slowness of the heartbeat.
Brain
   Mass of nerve tissue which is contained within the skull.
Bronchiectasis
   Dilation of the narrowest portions of the breathing tubes of the lung.
Bronchitis
   Inflammation of mucus membrane of bronchial tubes.
Buerger's Disease
   Thromboangiitis obliterans; obliteration and inflammation of the larger arteries and veins of a limb by clotting and inflammation, involving nerve trunks.
Bursa
   A lubricating sac usually found at pressure points or around joints.
Bursitis
   Inflammation of the bursa.

C

Calcaneum
   The os calcis, or heel bone.
Calcification
   X-ray opaque substance found in serious tissues of the body.
Canthus
   Either extremity of the slit between the eyelids.
Capitellum
   Portion of bone found at the end of the arm bone.
Capsule
   Fibrous membrane which envelopes an organ, joint or a foreign body.
Carbuncle
   Group of boils resulting in localized gangrene or death of affected tissues.
Cardiac
   Pertaining to the heart.
Cardiologist
   Heart specialist.
Catheter
   Hollow cylinder of silver, India rubber or other material, designed to be passed into a hollow area for drainage purposes.
Cartilage
   White substance which covers ends of bones.
Causalgia
   A painful condition.

Cellulitis
Diffuse inflammation of cellular tissue, i.e., especially loose cellular tissue just underneath skin.
Cephalalgia
Headache.
Cerebellum
Back part of the brain, concerned in coordination of movements.
Cerebrum
Front part of the brain, concerned with the conscious processes of the mind.
Cervix
Neck or neck-like part.
Charcot's joint
Painless joint destruction.
Cholecystectomy
Surgical removal of the gall-bladder.
Cholecystis
Inflammation of gall-bladder.
Cholelithiasis
Gallstone.
Chorio-Retinal
Relating to the visual tissue of eye and its supporting structure.
Chondral
Pertaining to cartilage.
Cicatrix
Scar.
Cirrhosis
Fibrosis or sclerosis of any organ; hardening.
Clavicle
Collar bone.
Clonus
Muscular spasm in which contraction and relaxation of muscle follow one another in rapid succession.
Coccydynia
Pain in the coccyx.
Coccygectomy
Removal of the coccyx.
Coccygeal
Relating to the coccyx.
Coccyx
Small bone at the end of the spinal column in man.
Congenital
Existing at birth.
Congestion
Engorgement of blood vessels of a part.
Conjunctiva
Delicate membrane which lines the inner surface of the eyelids and covers the eyeball in front.
Colles Fracture
Fracture of lower end of radius
Colon
The last part of the intestinal tract.

Comminuted
  Broken into more than two fragments.
Concussion
  Injury of a soft structure, as the brain, resulting from a blow or violent shaking.
Coronary Artery
  The artery providing nutrition to the heart muscle.
Cornea
  Transparent structure forming the anterior part of the external layer of eyeball.
Cortex
  Outer portion of an organ, such as the kidney, as distinguished from inner or medullary portion; external layer of gray matter covering hemispheres of cerebrum and cerebellum.
Costal
  Pertaining to the ribs.
Coxa
  Hip joint.
Cranium
  Skull.
Crepitus
  Abnormal sounds heard in the case of fractured bones and diseased tissues when rubbing together.
Curettage
  Scraping the interior of a cavity for the removal of tissue.
Cutaneous
  Relating to the skin.
Cyanosis
  Blueish discoloration of external tissue, e.g. lips, nails, skin.
Cyst
  Abnormal sac which contains a liquid or semi-solid.
Cystoscopy
  Inspection of the interior of the bladder with a cystoscope.
Cystostomy
  Formation of a more or less permanent opening into the urinary bladder.

D

Dactyl
  Digit: Finger or toe.
Decompensation
  Failure to maintain normal function as in heart failure.
Deltoid
  Triangular-shaped muscle of the shoulder.
Dementia
  Form of insanity.
Dermatitis
  Inflammation of the skin.
Dermatologist
  Skin specialist.
Dermaphytosis
  Skin disease due to presence of a vegetable microparasite.

Desiccation
　　The removal of tissue by chemical, physical, electrical, freezing, or x-ray.
Diabetes (Melitus)
　　A disease having symptoms of excessive urine and sugar excretion.
Diaphragm
　　Muscular partition between thorax and abdomen.
Diarrhea
　　Abnormally frequent discharge of fluid fecal matter from the bowel.
Diastasis
　　Simple separation of normally joined parts.
Diastole
　　Period of rest during which heart is filling up for next beat.
Diathermy
　　Local elevation of temperature in tissues, produced by special form of high-frequency current.
Diathesis
　　Predisposition to a disease.
Digit
　　Finger or toe.
Dilatation
　　Enlargement, due to stretching or thinning out of tissues.
Diplopia
　　Double-vision.
Disc
　　A round flat surface variously found in eye and spinal column conditions.
Dislocation
　　Most frequently used in orthopedics to describe a disturbance of normal relationship of bones which enter into formation of a joint.
Distal
　　Farthest from the point of origin; the term is usually used in connection with the extremities.
Diverticulum
　　Pouch or sac opening out from a tubular organ.
Dorsal
　　Relating to the back; posterior.
Dorsum
　　The back; upper or posterior surface or back of any part.
Duct
　　Tube or passage with well-defined walls for passing excretions or secretions.
Duodenum
　　Upper portion of intestinal tube connecting with stomach.
Dupuytren's Contraction
　　Contraction of the palmar fascia causing permanent flexion of one or more fingers.
Dura Mater
　　Outermost and toughest of three membranes covering brain and spinal cord.
Dysphagia
　　Difficulty in swallowing.
Dyspnoea
　　Difficulty in breathing.
Dysuria
　　Difficulty or pain in urination.

E

Ecchymosis
Black and blue spot on the skin.
Ectropion
A rolling outward of the margin of an eyelid.
Eczema
A form of dermatitis.
Edema
Swelling due to watery effusion in the intercellular spaces.
Electrocardiogram
Graph of electric currents in the heart.
Electrocardiograph
Instrument for producing electrocardiogram.
Embolus
Clot or plug brought by blood-current from distant part.
Embolism
The plugging up of a blood vessel by a floating mass.
Eminence
Circumscribed area raised above general area of surrounding surface.
Emphysema
Abnormal distention with loss of elasticity of the air sacs of the lung.
Empyema
Accumulation of pus or matter in normally closed cavity on the surface of the lung.
Encephalitis
Inflammation of the brain substance.
Encephalogram
Roentgenogram of contents of the skull.
Encephalopathy
Conditions of disease of the brain.
Endocrine Gland
A gland which furnishes internal secretion.
Endogenous
Originating or produced within organism or one of its parts.
Enophthalmos
Recession of the eyeball within the orbit.
Epicardium
Cover of the heart.
Epicondyle
Projection from long bone near articular extremity above or upon condyle.
Epidermis
Outermost layer of the skin.
Epididymis
Oblong or boat-shaped body located on back of testicle.
Epidural
Upon the outer envelope of the brain.
Epigastric
Depression at pit of abdominal wall at tip of sword-shaped cartilage of sternum.

Epilepsy, Jacksonian
  Convulsive contractions affecting localized groups of muscles without disturbance of mentality.
Epiphysis
  Ends of long bones.
Epistaxis
  Bloody nose.
Epithelium
  Covering of skin and mucus membrane consisting of epithelial cells.
Epithelioma
  Cancer of the skin or mucus membrane.
Erector spinae
  Muscle keeping the spine erects.
Eruption
  A breaking out; redness, spotting or other visible phenomena on the skin or mucus membrane.
Erythema
  Abnormal redness of the skin.
Esophagus
  Gullet. Tube connecting mouth to stomach.
Etiology
  Cause.
Eversion
  A turning outward, as of the eyelid or foot.
Exacerbation
  Increase in severity of disease or symptoms.
Excision
  Operative removal of a portion of an organ.
Excrescence
  Outgrowth from the surface, especially a pathological growth.
Exogenous
  Originating or produced outside.
Exophthalmus
  Protrusion or prominence of the eyeball.
Exostosis
  Bony tumor springing from surface of a bone, most commonly seen at muscular attachments.
Extensor
  A muscle the contraction of which tends to straighten a limb.
Extrasystole
  Premature contraction of one or more heart chambers.
Exudate
  A fluid, often coagulable, extravasated into tissue or cavity.

F

Facies
  Face, countenance, expression; surface.
Fascia
  Sheet or band of fibrous tissue.

Felon
    Abscess in terminal phalanx of a finger.
Femoral
    Relating to the femur or thigh.
Femur
    Thigh bone.
Fibrillation
    Totally irregular beat.
Fibroma
    Fibroid tumor.
Fibrosis
    Pathological formation of fibrous tissue.
Fibula
    Smaller calf bone.
Fistula
    Abnormal passageway leading to surface of body.
Flexion
    Bending of a joint.
Flexor
    A muscle the action of which is to flex a joint.
Follicle
    Very small excretory or secretory sac or gland.
Foramen
    Aperture through a bone or membranous structure.
Fracture, Comminuted
    Bone broken into more than two pieces.
Fracture, Ununited
    One in which union fails to occur.
Frontal
    Relating to the front of body.
Fundus
    Base of a hollow organ.
Fusiform
    Spindle-shaped, tapering at both ends.

G

Ganglion
    Usually used to describe a cystic tumor occurring on a tendon sheath or in connection with a joint.
Gangrene
    Death or masse of any part of the body.
Gastric
    Pertaining to the stomach.
Gastrocnemius
    One of the calf muscles.
Genitalia
    Organs of reproduction.
Genito-Urinary
    Relation to reproduction and urination, noting organs concerned.

Genu
    Knee
Genu-Valgum
    Knock-knee.
Gladiolus
    Middle and largest division of sternum (chest bone).
Gland
    Secreting organ.
Glaucoma
    Increased pressure in the eyeball.
Gluteal
    Pertaining to the buttocks.
Greenstick Fracture
    Incomplete fracture.
Gynecologist
    Specialist in the treatment of diseases peculiar to women.

H

Hallux
    Great toe.
Hallux valgus
    Deviation of great toe toward inner or lateral side of the foot (bunion).
Haematemesis
    Vomiting of blood.
Haemoglobin
    Coloring matter of blood in red blood corpuscles.
Haemoptysis
    Discharge of blood from the lungs by coughing.
Hemarthrosis
    Effusion of blood into cavity of a joint.
Hematoma
    Swelling formed by effused blood.
Hematuria
    Passage of blood in the urine.
Hemianopsia
    Loss of vision for one-half of visual field.
Hemorrhage
    Bleeding, especially if profuse.
Hemorrhoids
    Piles, a varicose condition causing painful swellings of the anus.
Hepatic
    Pertaining to the liver.
Herania
    Protrusion of organ outside of its normal confines.
Hernioplasty
    Operation for hernia.
Herniotomy
    Operation for relief of hernia.

Humerus
    Bone of the upper arm.
Hydrarthrosis
    Effusion of a serous fluid into a joint cavity.
Hydrocele
    Circumscribed collection of fluid around the testicle.
Hydrone Phrosis
    Dilatation inside kidney due to obstruction of flow of urine.
Hyperaesthesia
    Excessive sensitiveness of the skin to touch or hypersensitiveness of any special sense.
Hyperglycaemia
    Abnormally large proportion of sugar in blood.
Hypertension
    High blood pressure often associated with arteriosclerosis.
Hyperthrophy
    Enlargement, general increase in bulk of a part or organ, not due to tumor formation.
Hypogastrium
    Lower middle region of the abdomen.
Hypoplasia
    Under-development of structure.
Hypothenar
    Fleshy mass at the inner (little finger) side of the palm.
Hysteria
    A functional nervous condition characterized by lack of emotional control and sudden temporary attacks of mental, emotional or physical aberration.

I

Ileum
    Portion of the small intestine.
Ilium
    One of the bones of the pelvis.
Impacted
    Driven in firmly.
Incontinence
    Inability to retain a natural discharge.
Induration
    Hardening; spot or area of hardened tissue
Infarct
    Death of tissue due to lack of blood supply
Inguinal
    Relating to the groin.
In situ
    In position.
Intercostal
    Between the ribs
Interstitial
    Relating to spaces within any structure.
Intertrochanteric
    Between the two trochanters of the femur or thigh bone

Intervertebral
    Between two vertebrae.
Iris
    Circular colored portion of the eye which surrounds pupil
Ischaemia
    Local and temporary deficiency of blood.
Ischium
    One of the pelvic bones.

J

Jaundice
    Yellowness of tissues due to absorption of bile.
Jejunum
    Portion of small intestine about 8 feet long, between duodenum and ileum.

K

Kienboeck Disease
    Increased porosity and softness of certain carpal bones.
Keloid
    Peculiar overgrowth of hyaline connective tissues in the skin of predisposed individuals after injury or scarring.
Keratitis
    Inflammation of the cornea.
Kyphosis
    Curvature of the spine, hump-back, hunch-back.

L

Laceration
    Separation of tissue (cut).
Lacriminal
    Relating to the tears apparatus.
Laminae
    Flattened portions of the sides of a vertebral arch.
Laminectomy
    Removal of one or more laminae from the vertebrae.
Larynx
    Organ of voice production.
Lesion
    Any hurt, wound or degeneration.
Leucocytosis
    Temporary increase in relative number of white blood cells in the blood.

Leucopenia
    Abnormal decrease in number of white blood corpuscles.
Ligament
    Tough fibrous band which connects one bone with another.
Lipoma
    Tumor composed of fatty tissue.
Lordosis
    Anteroposterior curvature of the spine (opposite to kyphosis).
Lue tic
    Syphilitic.
Lumbar
    Lower back.
Lumbar Vertebrae
    The five vertebrae between the thoracic vertebrae and the sacrum.
Luxation
    Dislocation.
Lymphangitis
    Inflammation of the lymphatic vessels.

M

Malar
    Relating to the cheek-bone.
Malignant
    Resistant to treatment; occurring in severe form; tending to grow worse and (in the case of a tumor) to recur after removal. Usually indicates poor end result.
Malleoli
    Rounded bony prominences on both sides of the ankle joint.
Mandible
    Lower jaw.
Manubrium
    Upper portion of the sternum.
Mastectomy
    Amputation of the breast.
Maxilla
    Upper jaw.
Meatus
    Passage or opening.
Meninges
    Membranes, specifically the envelope of brain and spinal cord.
Meningitis
    Inflammation of the meninges.
Meniscus
    Intraarticular fibrocartilage of crescentic or discoid shape found in certain joints.
Mesentery
    Web or membrane connecting bowel tube to posterior abdominal wall (a portion of the peritoneum).
Metabolism
    The total operation of building up and breaking down tissues.

Metacarpus
Part of hand between wrist and fingers; palm; five metacarpal bones collectively which form skeleton of this part.
Metastasis
Transfer of disease, usually malignant, to remote part of the body.
Metatarsalgia
Pain in the region of the metatarsus (or ball of foot).
Metatarsus
Anterior portion of foot between instep and toes, having as its skeleton five long bones articulating anteriorly with the phalanges.
Mottling
Spotting with patches of varying shades of colors.
Mucocutaneous
Relating to mucus membrane and skin, noting the line of junction of the two at the nasal, oral, vaginal and anal orifices.
Musculature
Arrangement of muscles in a part or in the body as a whole.
Myalgia
Muscular pain.
Myelitis
Inflammation of the substance of the spinal cord.
Myelograph
X-ray picture of spinal cord using radio-opaque substance.
Myocardium
Heart Muscle.
Myocarditis
Inflammation of the muscular walls of the heart.
Myositis
Inflammation of a muscle.

N

Navicular
Boat-shaped, noting a bone in the wrist and one in the ankle.
Nausea
Sickness at the stomach; inclination to vomit.
Nephritis
Inflammation of the kidney.
Necrosis
Death en masse of a portion of tissue.
Nephrosis
Non-inflammatory disease of the kidney.
Neuralgia
Pain radiating along a nerve.
Neuritis
Inflammation of a nerve.
Neurologist
Nerve specialist.
Neuroma
Tumor made up largely of nerve tissue.

Neuropsychiatric
   Relating to disease of both mind and nervous system.
Neurosis
   Functional derangement of the nervous system.
Nocturia
   Bed-wetting.
Node
   Knob; circumscribed swelling; circumscribed mass of differentiated tissue; knuckle.
Nucleus Pulposus
   Gelatinous center of an intervertebral disc.
Nystagmus
   Continuous movement of the eyeballs in the horizontal or vertical plains.

O

Occipital
   Relating to the back of the head.
Occlude
   To close up or fit together.
Occular
   Relating to the eye; visual.
Occult
   Hidden; concealed, noting a concealed hemorrhage, the blood being so changed as not to be readily recognized.
Olecranon
   Tip of the elbow.
Omentum
   Web or apron-like membranous structure lying in front of the intestines.
Opacities
   Areas lacking in transparency.
Opthalmia
   Disease of the eye.
Opthalmologist
   Specialist in eye diseases and refractive errors of the eye.
Optic
   Relating to the eye or to vision.
Optometrist
   Person without medical training who fits glasses to correct visual defects.
Orbit
   Eye- socket.
Orchitis
   Inflammation of the testicle.
Orchidectomy
   Castration; removal of one or both testicles.
Orthopedics
   Branch of surgery which has to do with treatment of diseases of joints and spine and correction of deformities.
Orthopnea
   Ability to breathe with comfort only when sitting erect or standing.

Os
    Bone
Oscalcis
    Heel-bone.
Ossification
    Formation of bone; change into bone.
Osteoma
    Bone tumor.
Osteomyelitis
    Inflammation of bone and bone marrow.
Osteoporosis
    Disease of bone marked by increased porosity and softness ("thinning" of bone).
Osteotomy
    Cutting a bone, usually by saw or chisel, for removal of a piece of dead bone, correction of knock-knee or other deformity, or for any purpose whatsoever.
Otologist
    Specialist in diseases of the ear.

P

Paget's Disease
    Usually refers to a bone disease.
Pancreas
    Abdominal digestive gland, extending from duodenum to spleen, containing insulin forming cells.
Palate
    Roof of the mouth.
Palliative
    Mitigating; reducing in severity, noting a method of treating a disease or its symptoms.
Palmar
    Referring to the palm of the hand.
Palpate
    To examine by feeling and pressing with the palms and fingers.
Palpebral
    Relating to an, eyelid or the eyelids.
Papule
    Pimple.
Palsy
    Paralysis.
Paraesthesia
    Abnormal spontaneous sensation, such as a burning, pricking, numbness.
Paralysis
    Loss of power of motion.
Paralysis Agitans
    Shaking paralysis, Parkinson's Disease.
Paraplegia
    Paralysis of legs and lower parts of the body.

Paravertebral
Alongside a vertebra or the spinal column.
Parenchymal
Relating to the specific tissue of a gland or organ.
Paresis
Incomplete paralysis.
Parietal
Pertaining to the walls.
Parkinson's Syndrome
Aggregate symptoms, including raised eyebrows and expressionless face, of paralysis agitans.
Paronychia
Inflammation of structures surrounding the nail or the bone itself of finger or toe.
Paralysis Agitans
Shaking paralysis, Parkinson's Disease.
Paraplegia
Paralysis of legs and lower parts of the body.
Paravertebral
Alongside a vertebra or the spinal column.
Parenchymal
Relating to the specific tissue of a gland or organ.
Paresis
Incomplete paralysis.
Parietal
Pertaining to the walls.
Parkinson's Syndrome
Aggregate symptoms, including raised eyebrows and expressionless face, of paralysis agitans.
Paronychia
Inflammation of structures surrounding the nail or the bone itself of finger or toe.
Passive
Not active.
Past-Pointing
Test of integrity of vestibular apparatus of the ear by rotating person in revolving chair.
Patella
Knee-cap.
Pathology
Branch of medicine which treats of the abnormal tissues in disease.
Pectoral
Relating to the chest.
Pedicle
Stalk or stem forming the attachment of a tumor which is non-sessile, i.e., which does not have a broad base of attachment.
Pellegrini, Stieda's Disease
Bony growth over the internal condyle of the femur, a sequel of stieda's fracture.
Pendulous
Hanging freely or loosely.
Pericardium
Sac enveloping the heart.
Periosteum
Thick, fibrous membrane covering the entire surface of a bone.

Periphery
   Outer part or surface.
Peristalsis
   Worm-like movement of the gastro-intestinal tract.
Peritoneum
   Serous membrane which covers abdominal organs and inner aspect of abdominal walls.
Peritonitis
   Inflammation of the peritoneum.
Peroneal
   Pertaining to the outer aspects of the leg.
Pes
   Foot; foot-like or basal structure or part.
Pes Cavus
   Exaggeration of the normal arch of the foot; hollowfoot.
Pes Equinus
   Permanent extension of the foot so that only the ball rests on the ground.
Petechial
   Relating to minute hemorrhagic spots, of pinpoint to pinhead size, in the skin.
Phalanx
   Bone of a finger or toe.
Phlebitis
   Inflammation of the veins.
Physiology
   Science which treats of functions of different parts of the body.
Physiotherapy
   Use of natural forces in the treatment of disease, as in electro-hydro, and aero-therapy, massage, and therapeutic exercises, and use of mechanical devices in mechanotherapy.
Pill-RollingTremor
   Tremor in paralysis agitans in the form of circular movement of opposed tips of thumb and index finger.
Pilonidal Cyst
   Cyst at the lower end of the spine.
Pisiform
   Pea-shaped or pea-sized.
Plantar
   Relating to the sole of the foot.
Pleura
   Serous membrane which invests lungs and covers inner part of the chest walls (similar to peritoneum in abdominal cavity.)
Pleurisy
   Inflammation of the pleura.
Plexus
   Network or tangle of nerves.
Plumbism
   Lead poisoning.
Pneumoconiosis
   Dust disease of the lungs.
Pneumonia
   Inflammation of lung substance.

Pneumonoconiosis
　　Fibrous hardening of the lungs due to irritation caused by inhalation of dust incident to various occupations.
Pneumothorax
　　Presence of air or gas in the pleural cavity.

Poliomyelitis
　　Inflammation of the anterior portion of the spinal cord.
Polyp
　　Pedunculated swelling or outgrowth from a mucus membrane.
Polyuria
　　Excessive excretion of urine.
Popliteal
　　Relating to the posterior surface of the knee.
Precordium
　　Anterior surface of lower part of the thorax.
Pretibial
　　Relating to anterior portion of the leg.
Proliferative
　　Excess growth.
Pronate
　　To rotate the forearm in such a way that the palm of the hand looks backward when the arm is in the anatomical position, or downward when the arm is extended at a right angle with the body.
Prostate
　　Gland surrounding neck of the male bladder.
Prostatectomy
　　Removal of all or part of the prostate.
Protuberance
　　Outgrowth: swelling; knob.
Proximal
　　Nearest the trunk or point of origin, said of part of an extremity, artery or nerve so situated.
Psychiatrist
　　Alienist; one who specializes in diseases of the mind.
Psychogenic
　　Of mental origin or causation.
Ptosis
　　Drooping down of an eyelid or an organ.
Pubic
　　One of the bones of the pelvis.
Pulmonic
　　Relating to the lungs.
Puritis
　　Itching irritation.
Purulent
　　Having the appearance of pus or matter.
Pyelitis
　　Inflammation of a portion of the kidney.
Pyelogram
　　Roentgenogram of the area of the kidneys and ureter, by use of opaque substances.

Pyogenic
   Pus-forming.

R

Radiologist
   One skilled in the diagnostic and therapeutic use of x-rays.
Radius
   Outer and shorter of the two bones of forearm.
Rales
   Sounds of varied character heard on auscultation of the chest in cases of disease of the lungs or bronchi.
Rectum
   Terminal portion of the digestive tube.
Reflex
   Involuntary or reflected action or movement.
Renal
   Pertaining to the kidney.
Resection
   Removal of articular ends of one or both bones forming a joint, or of a segment of any part, such as the intestine.
Respiration
   Function common to all living plants or animals, consisting in taking in of oxygen and throwing off products of oxidation in the tissues, mainly carbon dioxide and water.
Retina
   Inner, nervous tunic of the eyeball, consisting of an outer pigment layer and an inner layer formed by expansion of the optic nerve.
Retrosternal
   Behind the sternum.
Rib
   One of twenty-four elongated curved bones forming the main portion of bony wall of the chest.
Rhinitis
   Inflammation of the nasal mucus membrane.
Roentgenologist
   One skilled in the diagnostic and therapeutic use of x-rays.

S

Sacroiliac
   Relating to sacrum and ilium, noting articulation between the two bones and associated ligaments.
Sacrum
   Triangular bone at the base of the spine.
Sarcoma
   Malignant tumor of fibrous tissue or its derivatives.
Scaphoid
   Boat-shaped; hollowed.

Scapula
　　Shoulder-blade.
Sciatica
　　Painful affection of the sciatic nerve.
Sclerosis
　　Hardness
Scoliosis
　　Lateral curvature of the spine.
Scrotum
　　Sac containing testes.
Semilunar Cartilages
　　Two intraarticular fibrocartilages of the knee-joint.
Senile
　　Relating to or characteristic of old age.
Septicemia
　　Morbid condition due to presence of septic microbes and their poisons in the blood.
Sequela
　　Morbid condition following as a consequence of another disease.
Sesamoid.
　　Resembling in size or shape a grain of sesame.
Sequestrum
　　Piece of dead bone separated from living bone.
Shock
　　Sudden vital depression due to injury or emotion which makes an untoward depression.
Siderosis
　　Form of dust disease due to presence of iron dust.
Silicosis
　　Form of dust disease due to inhalation of stone dust.
Sinusitis
　　Inflammation of the lining membrane of any sinus, especially of one of the accessory sinuses of the nose.
Spasm
　　Sudden violent involuntary rigid contraction, due to muscular action.
Sphincter
　　Orbicular muscle which, when in state of normal contraction, closes one of the orifices of the body.
Spina Bifida
　　Limited defect in the spinal column consisting in absence of vertebral arches, through which defect spinal membranes protrude.
Spondylolisthesis
　　Forward subluxation of body of vertebra on vertebra below it or on sacrum.
Sprain
　　Wrenching of a joint.
Stenosis
　　Narrowing of an orifice.
Sternoclavicular
　　Relating to sternum and clavicle, noting an articulation and occasional muscle.
Stricture
　　Abnormal narrowing of a channel.
Supinate
　　To turn forearm and hand volar side uppermost.

Suture
Stitch.
Symphysis
Union between two bones by means of fibrocartilage.
Syncope
Fainting.
Syndrome
Complex of symptoms which occur together.
Synovitis
Inflammation of synovial membrane, especially of a joint.
Systole
Period of the heart-beat during which the heart is contracting.

T

Tachycardia
Abnormal increase in rate of the hearts beat, not subsiding on rest, sudden in onset and offset.
Tarsus
Root of the foot or instep.
Temporamandibular
Relating to the temporal bone (bone of the temple) and lower jaw, noting the articulation of the lower jaw.
Tendon
Inelastic fibrous cord or band in which muscle fibers ends and by which muscle is attached to bone or other structure.
Tendosynovitis
Inflammation of the sheath of a tendon.
Tetanus
Lockjaw.
Thorax
Chest, upper part of the trunk between neck and abdomen; it is formed by the twelve dorsal vertebrae, the twelve pairs of ribs, sternum, and muscles and fascias attached to these; it is separated from the abdomen by the diaphragm; it contains chief organs of circulatory and respiratory systems.
Thrombo Angitis Obliterans
Buerger's disease; obliteration of the larger arteries and veins of a limb by thrombi, with subsequent gangrene. See Buerger's Disease.
Thrombophlebitis
Thrombosis with inflammation of the veins.
Thrombosis
Formation of a clot of blood within a blood vessel.
Thyroid
Gland and cartilage of the larynx.
Thyroidectomy
Removal of the thyroid gland.
Tibia
Shin-bone; inner and larger of two bones of the leg.

Tinnitus
    Subjective noises (ringing, whistling, booming, etc.) in the ears.
Tonsillitis
    Inflammation of a tonsil.
Torticollis
    Wry-neck; stiff-neck; spasmodic contraction of muscles of the neck; the head is drawn to one side and usually rotated so that the chin points the other side.
Torsion
    Twisting or rotation of a part upon its axis; twisting the cut end of an artery to arrest hemmorhage.
Toxemia
    Blood-poisoning.
Toxin
    Poison.
Trachea
    Windpipe.
Transillumination
    Shining light through a translucent part to see if fluid is present.
Trapezius
    Muscle extending from back of the head to shoulderblade; it moves head and shoulder.
Trauma
    Wound; injury inflicted usually more or less suddenly by physical agent.
Tremor
    Trembling, shaking, loss of equilibrium.
Trephine
    Cylindrical or crown saw used for removal of a disc of bone, especially from the skull, or of other firm tissue as that of the cornea.
Triceps
    Three-headed muscle extending the forearm. (Covers posterior of upper arm).
Trochanter
    One of two bony prominences developed from independent osseous centers near the upper extremity of the thigh bone.
Tubercle
    Circumscribed, rounded, solid elevation on the skin, mucus membrane, or surface of an organ; lesion of tuberculosis consisting of a small isolated nodule or aggregation of nodules.
Tuberosity
    Broad eminence of bone.

U

Ulcer
    Open sore other than a wound.
Ulna
    Inner and larger of the two bones of the forearm.
Umbilicus
    Navel.
Ununited
    Not united or knit, noting an unhealed fracture.

Ureter
    Musculomembranous tube leading from kidney to bladder.
Urethra
    Membranous tube leading from bladder to external exit.
Urination
    The passing of urine.
Urogram
    Roentgenogram of any part (kidneys, ureters, bladder) of the urinary tract, with the use of opaque substances.
Urologist
    One versed in the branch of medical science which has to do with urine and its modifications in disease.
Urtcaria
    Hives.
Uterus
    Womb.

V

Varicocele
    Varicose veins of the spermatic cord.
Varicose
    Dilated, as used in reference to veins.
Varix
    Enlarged and tortuous vein, artery, or lymphatic vessel.
Vas
    Vessel.
Vasomotor
    Regulating mechanism controlling expansion and contraction of blood vessels.
Ventral
    Relating to anterior portion.
Ventricular
    Relating to a ventricle.
Vertebra
    One of thirty-three bones of the spinal column.
Vertex
    Crown of the head; topmost point of the vault of the skull.
Vertigo
    Dizziness.
Vitiligo
    Appearance on the skin of white patches of greater or lesser extent, due to simple loss of pigment without other trophic changes.
Volar
    Referring to the palm of the hand.

Z

Zygoma
    Strong bar of bone bridging over the depression of the temple; cheek-bone.

GLOSSARY OF ANATOMIC SCIENCES

CONTENTS

	Page
Achilles Tendon …………… Concha	1
Costal…………………………..Iliacus	2
Iliocostal……………………….. Pubis	3
Radius……………………… Zygoma	4

GLOSSARY OF ANATOMIC SCIENCES

ACHILLES TENDON
The tendon which attaches to the heel and originates from the muscles in the calf (gastrocnemius and soleus muscles).
ANCONEUS
This muscle extends from humerus in upper forearm to ulna in forearm. Its function is to straighten the elbow joint.
ARYEPIGLOTTIC
From the arytenoid cartilage to the epiglottis (the structure which closes the windpipe when swallowing). Its function is to close entrance to larynx.
ARYTENOID
From one arytenoid cartilage to other, its function is to close the larynx.
ASTRAGALUS
Located just below tibia and fibula (leg bones) in ankle. It connects with the heel bone.
ATLAS
First vertebra lying just beneath the skull.
AXIS
Second vertebra in neck, just below Atlas.

B

BRACHIALIS
Extends from upper and lower jaw bones too muscles about the mouth. Its function is to pull back angles of the mouth and tighten the cheeks.
BULBO-CAVERNOSUS
Extends from perineum (a point below the genitals) to penis. Its function is to compress urethra.

C

CALCANEUS
Heel bone.
CALVARIUM
Bones which form top of skull.
CAPITATE
Largest bone in wrist, located toward center of wrist joint.
CARPAL
Eight small bones of wrist greater multangular, lesser multangular, lunate, capitate, hamate, navicular, triquetrum, and pisiform bones.
CILIARY
Extends from membrane around iris to ciliary process of iris in the eye. Its function is to open and close the pupil of the eye.
CLAVICLE
Collarbone extending from sternum (breastbone) to shoulder tip.
COCCYX
Tailbone, the last vertebrae at base of spine.
CONCHA
Shell-shaped small bone located along the outer side of the nasal cavity.

COSTAL
  Ribs; 12 bones on each side, arising from the spinal column.
COXAE
  Hipbone; joins with sacrum and other hipbone to form the bon pelvis. The Coxae is composed of 3 fused bones: ilium, ischium, and pubis.
CRICOARYTENOID
  From cricoid cartilages to arytenoid cartilages in the neck. It function is to open and close the vocal chords.
CUROID
  Cube-shaped small bone of foot.

D

DELTOID
  Extends from the collarbone and the scapula, over the shoulder, to the humerus in the upper arm. Its function is to lift the upper arm away from the body.

E

ETHMOID
  Small bone located in front of base of skull, forming part of orbit and nose. Within it are spaces, making up the ethmoid sinuses.
EXTENSOR CARPI RADIALIS
  From humerus to bones of wrist. Its function is to straighten the wrist.

F

FEMUR
  The thighbone, extending from hip to knee.
FIBULA
  Outer bone of leg, extending from knee to ankle
FLEXOR CARPI RADIALIS
  Extends from humerus to bones in front of the wrist. Its function is to bend the wrist.
FRONTAL
  Bones of forehead, parts of orbit and nose.

G

GASTROCNEMIUS
  Extends down leg from femur to heel bone. Its function is to bend ankle in downward direction and to help flex knee.

H

HAMSTRING
  Three large muscles extending down back of the thigh from ischium to tibia below the knee. Its function is to flex the knee joint.
HUMERUS
  Arm bone, extending from shoulder to elbow.
HYOID
  Thin U-shaped bone beneath the chin and above the larynx.

ILIACUS
  Extends from pelvis bones to femur in the thigh. Its function is to flex hip joint.

ILIOCOSTAL
   From ribs to vertebral column. Its function is to straighten spinal column and bend trunk sideways.
ILLIUM
   Part of hipbone, into which the femur fits.
INCUS
   The anvil. One of 3 small bones of middle ear, adjacent to eardrum.
ISCHIUM
   Part of hipbone

L

LONGISSIMUS
   Extends up back near spine. Its function is to straighten spine. LONGUS CAPITIS Extends from vertebrae in neck to base of the skull. Its function is to flex the head.

M

MALAR
   Cheekbone; the zygoma.
MALLEUS
   The hammer. One of 3 small bones of middle ear; adjacent to eardrum.
MANDIBLE
   Jawbone. Attached to the skull at the temperanandibular joint in front of the ear.
MASSETER
   Extends from cheekbone to the lower jawbone. Its function is to close the mouth.
MAXILLA
   Upper jawbone. Makes up part of the face, orbit, nose, etc.
METACARPAL
   The 5 bones of the hand to which the finger bones are attached.
METATARSAL
   The 5 bones of the foot to which the toe bones are attached.

N

NASALIS
   Maxillary bone of face to bridge. Alters expression of face.
NAVICULAR
   Small bones of the hands and feet; shaped like a boat.

O

OBTURATOR
   Extends from bones of pubis to femur (thighbone). Rotates thigh outward.
OCCIPITAL
   The back and part of base of the skull.

P

PALMARIS
   Extends down front of forearm to palm of the hand. Helps to flex the wrist and make "hollow of the hand."
PARIETAL
   This bone makes up part of the side and top of the skull.
PATELLA
   The kneecap.
PELVIS
   The bony pelvis is made up of the hipbones, sacrum, and coccyx.
PHALANGES
   The bones of the fingers and toes.
PUBIS
   The bone in front of the pelvis.

R

RADIUS
Long bone on outer side of the forearm, extending from elbow to wrist.

S

SACRUM
Five fused vertebrae in lower back which make up the back part of the bony pelvis.

SCALENE
Extends from vertebra in the neck to the first and second ribs. Bends the head and neck sideways.

SCAPULA
The shoulder blade (wing bone).

SPHENOID
Irregularly shaped bone making up front portion of the base of the skull and parts of the orbit and nose.

SPLENIUS
Extends from the vertebrae in the chest and the neck to back of the head. Straightens the head and spine.

STAPES
The stirrup. One of 3 small bones of middle ear adjacent to the eardrum.

STERNUM
The breastbone.

T

TALUS
The same as the astragalus.

TARSAL
The same as the foot bones.

TEMPORAL
The bone forming front portion of the side of the skull and part of the base. Extends from temple to lower jaw. Closes the mouth.

TIBIA
The large inner bone of the leg, extending from knee to the ankle (It is responsible for weight bearing.)

TURBINATE
Three bones located on the outer side of the nasal cavity.

U

ULNA
The long bone on the inner side of the forearm, extending from the elbow to the wrist.

V

VASTUS
It extends down the entire front of the thigh to the kneecap and tibia in the leg its function is to straighten the knee.

VOMER
This bone forms the back segment of the nasal septum which separates the two side of the nose

Z

ZYGOMA
The cheekbone; the malar bone.

www.ingramcontent.com/pod-product-compliance
Lightning Source LLC
Chambersburg PA
CBHW081805300426
44116CB00014B/2243